Praise for *Death by L...*

"If you're overwhelmed by debt, Ayres's account assures you that you're not alone, and just might crack you up in the meantime."
—*New York Daily News*

"Ayres is a master craftsman. . . . The turbo-charged, air-conditioned ride is enlightening and frequently hilarious." —*Daily Express*

"Distressingly funny." —*The Times* (London)

"Delicious . . . Although we know that the inevitable crash is looming, we can't help but wish for a shot at such glorious self-destruction ourselves." —*The Herald*

"On the surface, *Death by Leisure* is a wry slice of L.A. ladlit, but beneath the catalogue of bumbling mishaps is a searing analysis of a nation at the mercy of greed, consumption, and nature." —*Daily Record*

"A very funny book . . . Any man who asks 'How in the name of Christ did I manage to screw up a date that cost $5,000?' (there's a clue: it involved Michael Jackson) is, like L.A. itself, too silly to resist." —*The Guardian*

Praise for *War Reporting for Cowards*

"Hilarious . . . Imagine George Costanza from *Seinfeld* being sent off to cover the Iraq War . . . Reads as though Larry David had rewritten *M*A*S*H* and Evelyn Waugh's *Scoop* as a comic television episode, even as it provides the reader with a visceral picture of the horrors of combat and the peculiar experience of being an embedded reporter."
—Michiko Kakutani, *The New York Times*

"Ayres's book is heartbreakingly funny and often tender and always insightful." —Anthony Swofford, author of *Jarhead*

"*War Reporting for Cowards* reminded me of the granddaddy of the genre, Evelyn Waugh's novel *Scoop*, and that Ayres's book can be mentioned in the same sentence is a tribute. . . . Chronicles many of the absurdities, horrors, and discomforts of life during wartime . . . and the honor and steadfastness of the men and women who have to endure them." —Gary Shteyngart, *The New York Times Book Review*

DEATH
by
LEISURE

Also by the author

War Reporting for Cowards

DEATH
by
LEISURE

A Cautionary Tale

chris ayres

Grove Press
New York

Published simultaneously in Canada
Printed in the United States of America

ISBN-13: 978-0-8021-4365-5

Grove Press
an imprint of Grove/Atlantic. Inc.
841 Broadway
New York, NY 10003

Distributed by Publishers Group West

www.groveatlantic.com

10 11 12 13   10 9 8 7 6 5 4 3 2 1

For Milos

Contents

"The sky is darkening like a stain;
Something is going to fall like rain,
And it won't be flowers."

—from "The Witnesses" (1935)
W. H. Auden

Preface

The first thing I should tell you is that the money is gone. All of it—every last borrowed penny. In the end the bubble did what all bubbles do. I should have known. Of course I should have known.

As for the weather—the weather is a problem, I agree. With every season now it's a new apocalypse. When it's not the drought, it's the floods. When it's not the fires, it's the hurricanes.

I'm sorry about the weather. We're all very sorry about the weather.

For now at least I'm safe—we're safe—here in this white room, in this mopped and bleached holding facility, as the women go about their work in their face masks and their uniforms.

As you can see, I wrote everything down—for future reference. I didn't have many notes to work from (this was life, not work) so forgive the remembered dialogue, the dramatic editing, and the occasional embellishments. Reassure yourself that it all happened pretty much as it appears on the page, even though some names and personal details had to be changed.

Thumbing through these chapters now, I'm reminded of that cautionary tale for children "Jim, Who Ran Away from His Nurse, and Was Eaten by a Lion." Who wrote that again? Ah, yes, Hilaire Belloc. Like Jim, I didn't listen to the warnings. Like Jim, I didn't think they were real. Out there in Los Angeles, I too let go of my nurse's hand—and by the time I heard the rustle and snarl from the undergrowth it was too late.

Then again, we've all been living cautionary tales lately, haven't we? None of us listened to the warnings. And now we must all wait as the plot unfolds according to the rules of the genre: the horrible surprise, the implausible violence, the gruesome conclusion . . .

If Belloc were still around today, I suspect he would find it all immensely satisfying. He might even want to give this book a more literal title. Something like, "Chris, Who Kept Buying Stuff with Other People's Money, and Froze to Death in an Ice Age."

DEATH
by
LEISURE

1

Poolside at the Leisureplex

The girl next to me kept looking over.

I knew this because I was holding up my sunglasses to clean them with the cuff of my sweater. And there she was, in the dull, curved reflection: white bikini, straw hat, gold necklace. Had we met before? I surely would have remembered. Yes, this was the kind of girl you would *remember*.

I watched. I waited.

There, she did it again.

And again.

Jesus, what was her *problem*?

I shifted uncomfortably on my recliner. It was unusually hot, out there by the pool of the Park Wellington apartment complex, and there was a dry wind that kept blowing grit into my left contact lens. I couldn't decide what was more uncomfortable: the heat, the dust, or the girl's scrutiny. There was another discomfort, of course: that of being so close to a strange woman, an attractive woman, an *American* woman, who was approximately fifteen square inches of sculpted fabric away from being completely naked. In an attempt to distract myself I looked up at the rioting mansions of the Hollywood Hills. I saw Tuscan villas, Normandy castles, adobe mud huts, mid-century pleasurepods, French medieval spires, and Saudi compounds, all of them doing their very worst to the mountain. You've got to wonder what it would take to send these glued and bolted palaces tobogganing down the face of the decomposing granite to the traffic lights at Sunset and La Cienega Boulevard. Not much, I would bet. A light breeze, perhaps; an afternoon's drizzle.

"Are you *going* somewhere?" asked the girl, finally.

The accent was soft, southern, and infused with sleep: sleep of the warmest, of the most luxurious kind.

"Me?" I said, looking around.

"Who else?"

"Am I *going* somewhere?"

"That's what I was wondering, yes."

I couldn't work out what was stranger: the question itself or the fact that a girl in a white bikini was trying to make conversation with me. No one apart from Steve, the Park Wellington guard (nice bloke, quiet, a little sad in the eyes), ever tries to make conversation with me. Then again, it's unusual to have any company at all in this place. If it wasn't for the woman in apartment 53B, the one who fakes an orgasm at three-fifteen every morning—the acoustics of the Spanish-tiled court-yard allowing for maximum possible amplification—I would swear to God I live here alone. I like it that way. It gives me space to think, to plan.

"No," I said, after some consideration. "I'm not."

"Oh," said the girl, closing her eyes. "That's what I thought."

Time passed.

I shifted again on my recliner.

It was hot, and getting hotter.

"Any particular reason?" I asked, unable to leave the exchange at that.

The girl's eyes reopened, meeting mine. With a yawn, she said, "Most people don't wear jeans to the pool, I guess."

I looked down at my jeans. They were expensive and new and made to look as if they were cheap and old, but in a way that made it absolutely clear they were expensive and new. I looked up again and began to wonder how American girls get such perfect teeth, such perfect mouths, such perfect . . .

Don't stare at the bikini, I thought.

"*Chris,* by the way," I said, reaching over.

"Lara."

"Nice to meet you, Lara."

Lara smiled.

I stared at the bikini.

"You know, Chris, shoes and socks aren't a popular choice of pool attire, either. I wasn't going to say anything. It's just, you look so . . . *uncomfortable.* Then I thought you might be going somewhere."

"Right," I said, nodding.

"So I had to ask."

Now I was acutely aware of the sensation of my toes sweating. My socks were black, heavy, tight, elaborately ribbed. Come to think of it, it wasn't just my toes that were sweating. All the other parts of my body were sweating, too.

"Is that a wool sweater?" asked Lara.

"Cotton," I said.

"Oh, *cotton.*"

"You're right," I said. "I should change."

So now I crash through the door of my apartment and reach for the lights. It's a ground-floor unit, my bachelor bunker, and as such is in near permanent darkness. Blinking away patterns of ultraviolet, I thump upstairs to my bedroom, where I begin to throw clothes from a mirrored closet. I flinch as I catch my reflection. The creature in the glass isn't meant for Southern California, that's for sure. The creature in the glass is made for a cold and wet island, six thousand miles away.

I salvage what I can from the floor: goth-rock T-shirt, rubber-strapped Caterpillar sandals, tennis socks, Speedos.

It's been—what?—ten months now. Ten months in LA and my wardrobe still hasn't adapted. My anti-tan skin is largely responsible, although the memory of teenage acne has also played an undeniable part. The boils lasted until my parents finally sent me to the hospital, where I was given a jar of luminous green pills the size of tennis balls, which had truly extraordinary side effects. The treatment was experimental. There was talk of wild-eyed kids chopping up their grandparents. But I was a success story. The drugs dried up my spots along with every other gland in my body. My tear ducts welded themselves shut. My eyeballs turned to broken glass. My lips started to bleed, then disappeared entirely. But I was delighted, and I celebrated my newfound popularity with the opposite sex by taking up smoking.

But I never got over the fear of removing my shirt in public.

Another problem: I keep expecting the LA weather to turn. Every morning I awake to a cool ocean mist, fully prepared for a week of gray skies and drizzle. But it never turns out that way. By eleven o'clock the fog has always cleared to reveal an unchanging, untroubled sky. And where is this *smog* everyone keeps talking about? The sky shows no evidence of it—no evidence, even, of a functioning weather system. It is transparent blue, consistent in depth and tone, in all directions. Back in my hometown, back in the windy, bleating hills of the Scottish borders, you *are* the weather. It slaps you and it soaks you. It roughs you up and it shouts you down. All in all, it goes to an extraordinary effort to ruin your day.

Ah, yes: Wooler. Scene of my upbringing. I exited that little sheep farming town at the age of eighteen with all the speed and purpose of an intercontinental ballistic missile, stopping only for an education in sunless Humberside, then on to the bull's-eye of London, where I got my first job as a newspaper reporter, in the financial section. And now, at the age of twenty-eight, here I am. Yes, *here I am,* with perhaps the least-respected job title in my chosen field.

Hollywood correspondent.

Actually, the official title is Los Angeles correspondent, on account of my newspaper being too serious for show biz stories. Not that we avoid show biz stories, of course. That's where I come in. It is my job to ensure that the celebrity gossip is put into the correct sociopolitical context and recounted with the appropriate literary metaphors and allusions to Greek mythology. But it's not all gossip. I get the cautionary tales, too: the shotgun divorces, the bathtub suicides, the cocaine bank-ruptcies. They love these stories back in London. They love these stories *everywhere*—even here in LA. It seems that as much as we all want to be like these celebrity superconsumers, we're also relieved when it turns out their lives are largely violent and miserable. I stopped trying to make any sense of this a long time ago.

All of which, of course, is perfect cover for my real mission. Yes, I have another agenda, out here in LA. I remember outlining the plan to myself as my jumbo slammed into the tarmac at LAX in a fog of smoked rubber and jet fuel vapor. This is my last chance to make good on all those TV promises of my twentieth-century boyhood, I told myself. I am here to live a life of cars and gadgets and clifftop bachelor palaces. I am here to experience—to *consume*. Yes, I need to get all of this out of my system, while I still can. I need to max out; I need to go all in.

Girls, of course, are also a factor in this mission of mine. And how could they not be? The girls of LA are buffed and toned and scrubbed and shaved and moisturized and tanned and otherwise improved in every conceivable way to fit the heterosexual male's idea of perfection. Every homecoming queen in America, every cheerleader, every popular girl in high school—they all come to LA. There's only one problem: the men are equally perfect. And it's not just the gay men, who have their own miniature pleasuretropolis down on Santa Monica Boulevard: Boyz Town, where even the police cars are decorated with rainbow colors. No, the straight men are just as winningly muscled and groomed. Going to a restaurant in West Hollywood, where the actors and body doubles work the tables, is like finding yourself trapped inside a shaving-product commercial. They're charming too, the bastards, with their surfer dude smiles and unbreakable friendliness—*How y' doin' this evening, everything workin' out for ya over there, let me take care of that for ya*. I imagine them going home at night to Ralph Lauren bedsheets and *Marie Claire* cover girls.

Girls like Lara, in other words.

Do I have any chance with her? The odds aren't good, I'll concede. At five-foot-ten-and-a-half, with no discernible muscle tone, no skin pigment, and teeth like the ruins of a fire-bombed village, I barely qualify to compete. Did I mention my hair? Christ, yes, my *hair*. It has called a retreat on both fronts, leaving behind the vast and scorched no-man's-land formerly known as my forehead. I haven't yet found the courage to shave the remaining orange-blond fuzz to the scalp, so I'm starting to look like an out-of-work porn actor, or pre–*Captain Fantastic* Elton John. No, there can be no possibility of anything happening with Lara. I have as much chance with her as I would of taking Deep Blue's queen with an overlooked pawn.

And yet I do have one thing going for me: a steady job. Which means I can afford to live here in the Park Wellington—an apartment complex whose leisure facilities defy belief: swimming pool, tennis court, gym, and *two* hot tubs. I call my home the Leisureplex. Granted, it's not a particularly fashionable address: the beige stucco and gold fixtures haven't aged well, and the building relies on exotic plant life and a courtyard waterfall to distract from the concrete architecture.

But you can't beat the location.

One block north is the Sunset Strip—LA's very own interactive museum of human excess. Every night, Hummer limo convertibles guzzle down both lanes, the fist-sized pixels of the video billboards reflected in their white paintwork. The air is a hyperoctane cocktail of booze fumes, cigarette smoke, and Lamborghini emissions. The Lamborghinis themselves are positioned like art installations outside the ambitiously themed restaurants and guarded over by white-uniformed parking valets, the curators of LA's twenty-four-hour combustion exhibition. And all the while, blacked-out coaches cruise back and forth past the Sites of Historical Consumption. *Here is the Hyatt Hotel,* you can hear the megaphones shout. *Keith Richards once threw a TV out of the window of suite ten-fifteen! Look right, folks. John Belushi once coughed up a cheeseburger and milkshake right there in that minimall!*

Yes, everything has worked out perfectly.

I can hardly believe my luck.

On my way back to the pool I stop for a moment in the living room, where the TV is lighting up the walls like an aquarium. The news is on. "GREENSPAN LOWERS RATE TO FORTY-SIX-YEAR LOW OF ONE PERCENT," reads the caption. "SAYS MOVE WILL ENCOURAGE 'SUSTAINABLE GROWTH.'" Now we see the man himself, or rather we see a pair of giant black-rimmed spectacles, behind which are a pair of tiny, cryptic eyeballs. Yes, that's him all right: Alan Greenspan, chairman of the Federal Reserve. The screen now cuts to a correspondent. He's out in the desert, interviewing a home owner. The home owner says he has just cashed out his equity at a new low-interest rate and bought himself a sixty-inch TV and a Lexus convertible. "Can cheap money save the economy?" asks the correspondent, nodding seriously at the camera. Then back to the newsroom, where the anchor starts talking about the drought and the heat wave. I reach for the OFF switch and head for the door. As it closes behind me I wonder how I can get ahold of some cheap money, too.

"Wow, Chris, your life must be so *exciting*," said Lara, smiling. "I can hardly believe it. It's like a movie or a novel or something."

"Yeah, well, I suppose it sounds pretty cool," I chuckled. "But, y'know, it's just a job really, when it's all said and done."

So it went well by the pool—in spite of my outfit, which we needn't ever mention again—and Lara accepted my invitation to dinner. Until recently, of course, this kind of thing would have never happened to me. When you arrive in a new city, you are an observer; a ghost in the machine. It takes time to grow some flesh, to become visible to your fellow human beings. Take the Russian matriarch in my local coffee shop: she remembered me for the first time only two weeks ago. And now every morning we nod, we mumble.

Still, I can hardly believe it. I can hardly believe I asked Lara *out*.

"So when's your next assignment, Chris?"

"You never know in advance. They just call you and tell you to get on a plane."

"No *way*."

Before I recount any more of this, I should come clean. I have this . . . I have this habit. It's silly, really; embarrassing.

I exaggerate. I oversell.

I should make clear that this is a private habit, not a professional one (a result of a few hard lessons, early on in my career). But my tendency to overegg does come bundled with a few other vices, such as tendencies to overestimate and to overpromise. It's fair to say I have general aversion to reality in most of its popular forms. Yes, LA is in many ways the perfect place for me.

Too perfect, I sometimes think.

So I overegged my job a bit. I might have given Lara the impression that what I do for a living is a bit more . . . *interesting* than it really is. But I wouldn't have done it if the date had been going well. I wouldn't have done it if I hadn't failed to remember the rules of LA, the first and most important of which is this: a man *never* shows up to a date in a taxi. Especially not a minivan taxi, driven by an Armenian who plays techno music at the volume of artillery fire. In LA your car is your chariot, your castle, your piece of real estate in Gridlock City. I broke the rule largely because I intended to manage my nerves with vodka. Which brings me to the other rules of LA: drinking rarely gets in the way of driving; and if you're going to admit to taking a taxi because of your need to drink, you might as well go all the way and declare yourself a registered sex offender. This is why celebrities spend their lives dodging drunk-driving convictions when they could afford to hire their own fleet of chauffeured Bugattis. It's a control issue, a vanity issue, a credibility issue.

I knew from the second I saw Lara's face that the taxi had been a mistake. "Chris," she protested, neck tight, arms folded, "how are we going to get home?" With absolute confidence, I told her we would get another cab. Then came my next mistake: the restaurant. I chose it because it was on a rooftop, with a view over Hollywood. In fact, it was the only restaurant I could find in the online guide with any kind of view. I didn't realize that the rooftop in question was that of the Hollywood and Highland shopping mall, a place where coachloads of Midwestern tourists and Korean schoolgirls disembark every minute to admire a giant fake elephant. The food was billed as "fusion tapas." This meant that the portions were extremely small, thus forcing you to order a lot of them. And yet the size of the portions was in no way reflected in the pricing of them, thus turning the dining experience into a kind of consensual mugging. My eyes watered as I signed the bill, charged to the American Express Optima card for which I recently qualified. Still, I didn't mind so much. That's the thing with an AmEx card: it makes you feel like it's okay to pay over the odds. It makes you feel like you can afford it—like you're a *player*.

Over the miniature portions of dinner I discovered that Lara is from Louisiana, that her father is a shrimp fisherman and part-time alligator trapper, that she has two sisters, and that she sells advertising for a living. With that accent and that body, she could sell anyone pretty much anything. Lara doesn't actually live at the Leisureplex: she's the friend of a friend of someone who lives there, and the security guard, Steve, lets her in to use the swimming pool.

It was after we left the restaurant that the date threatened to become a genuine disaster. By eleven o'clock we were waiting for a nonexistent cab on the Walk of Fame, amid a hot spandex riptide of celebrity impersonators. Why do they have celebrity impersonators in Hollywood? Aren't there enough *real* celebrities? It seems to me like having a fake canal in Venice; a replica Eiffel Tower in Paris.

We watched in silence as a Jewish Elvis fought over his turf with an elderly Marilyn Monroe. Meanwhile, on a nearby curb, an exhausted Spider-Man sat with the *Los Angeles Times* crossword, eating a Whopper. I've read about these fake superheroes: they charge people a dollar to have their photograph taken with them—as a result, they're vicious about defending their territory. They're forever brawling, taking out restraining orders, getting sent to jail.

I noticed Spider-Man look up from his newspaper to admire Lara's legs, which glistened with expensive oils beneath a denim miniskirt. And then, perhaps fifteen or twenty minutes later, I felt something thick and hairy fall over my shoulders. I turned, and there in front of me was a small, perspiring Hispanic face, encased by a Chewbacca costume.

"Hey, amigo, that's a beautiful lady," said Chewbacca, with genuine concern. "Don't you have a *car* or something?"

"We're taking a taxi."

"You should buy a car," he said, helpfully.

Eventually, a cab pulled over. It was another minivan, this time converted for wheelchair access, so we slid around on a bench at the back as our second Armenian driver of the evening loudly scolded his phone. Not that we could really hear him over the techno music. Lara, being a good sport, let me kiss her good night. Or rather, she failed to react fast enough when I made my booze-induced farewell lunge.

Still, it was a kiss.

My chances of stealing another? Not good, I fear.

And now, after an early afternoon hot tub session, I hike up Alta Loma Road to the Sunset Strip—a lone sunburned pedestrian in a sweltering concrete universe. As I reach the crest of the hill I'm almost knocked off my feet in a blur of spokes and a clatter of gears. I yelp with fright and punch the air as a cyclist passes. I've seen this lunatic before. In purple leggings and scuffed body armor, he laps the block at Tour de France speed, oblivious to traffic. As he rides, he rants and curses about the end of the world. I sometimes wonder if he ever stops, or if he just keeps going all night, powered on by some supernatural, apocalyptic force.

You see a lot of them around nowadays: the babbling doomsday merchants, hawking their theories about the shitstorm to come. Perhaps they're the same people who go around blowing up Hummers and setting fire to luxury condo developments, leaving behind only the graffitied initials of the Earth Liberation Front—a so-called eco-terror group that doesn't officially exist.

Shaken, I crossed Sunset and kept bearing east to the Saddle Ranch, a bar made to look like a fake wooden barn, complete with fake wooden balconies, fake Wild West figures, and a fake coach and horses hanging over the entrance. The big attraction is a mechanical bull in the dining area, operated by an embittered waiter. I rode on the bull once and had to sit on a cushion for the next three days. The waiter found the whole thing enormously amusing. Everything in the Ranch is oversized: the Long Island Iced Teas come in "carafes" the size of flower pots and the steaks arrive on chain-sawed logs, with machetes instead of knives. The Ranch isn't so much a bar as an alcoholics' theme park.

Waiting for me in the coral outside was Jeff Rayner, a friend, expat Brit, and news photographer.

"I can't believe you did it," he said, as I approached.

"Did what?"

"You *know*."

"No, I don't *know*."

"I can't believe you told that poor girl you're a war correspondent."

"Oh, yeah," I said. "That."

Jeff never meant to end up in LA.

His real ambition was to work for *National Geographic*. In fact, he used to work in a wildlife park in England until the day he forgot to close the gate on his way home, resulting in a pack of wild Argentine pigs running free. Over the following twelve hours, the pigs went on a rampage, head-butting traffic, castrating pit bulls, and generally making, well, *pigs* of themselves until they were captured (four dead, one injured) by the authorities. Fortunately, Jeff came from an enterprising family, so he cut a hole in the gate of the pen and blamed it on animal rights activists, a claim that resulted in Jeff's emotional appearance that night on the national evening news. "I can't believe they did it," he sobbed, shaking his head at the gently nodding anchorman. "These animal rights people, *they don't love animals*."

This flicker of the media limelight was enough to inspire Jeff to reply to an ad in the *Press Gazette* seeking "LA-based photojournalists." He got the job, boarded the next flight to LAX, and within twenty-four hours was sitting outside an address in Bel Air with a seven-foot lens. The wannabe safari photographer had somehow become a paparazzo. But those were the old days. Jeff has gone legit. Now he does "proper" stories, for serious publications. He even takes portraits for magazines, sometimes of the same people he once hunted like game.

We pushed through the Saddle Ranch's swinging doors, passing the enclosure with the mechanical bull

"It wasn't a *complete* lie," I protested.

"Ayres, it was a whopper. You told her you're 'resting' between combat assignments. The nearest you've come to a combat assignment recently is having Brad Pitt's publicist fax you a press release."

"It was George Clooney's publicist."

"Whatever."

Jeff was being slightly unfair.

The real story, briefly, is this. A few weeks after I first moved out to LA there was a mix-up in London. Wires were crossed. Messages got lost. And somehow, for reasons best not further explored, I ended up on a press list at the Pentagon. Now if there's one thing you never want to get on before the invasion of a Middle Eastern country, it's a press list at the Pentagon. And yet that's precisely what happened. By the time I realized what was happening it was too late to stop it, and so I was promptly flown halfway around the world, handed a fluorescent blue-and-white flak jacket, and embedded with a forward reconnaissance unit of the United States Marines. I had never wanted to be a war correspondent. And now I can say with some confidence, some firsthand experience, that if there's one thing that can make someone who doesn't want to be a war correspondent feel even less enthusiastic about being a war correspondent, it is being a war correspondent. My stint on the front lines was brief, violent, and eventful in the worst possible way. It's a miracle I'm still alive. The only good thing to have come out of it is that no sane editor will ever send me into battle again. At the end of it all I was returned to Hollywood, possibly for good.

The war changed me, of course. I read once about Vietnam veterans, bored at home, who used to try to simulate the adrenaline of combat by driving on the wrong side of the road. I too have felt a certain swagger, a certain recklessness, since my return. I look in only one direction at pedestrian crossings now; I bowl along at thirty in the twenty-five-mile-per-hour zone. I've even started to talk to strangers by the pool, and invite them out to dinner.

Speaking of which: It's slightly disappointing, don't you think, just how well the war correspondent line worked on Lara? I've always believed that what women really want, what they *really absolutely long for,* is the very opposite of a war correspondent—a sensitive man; a man who prefers, say, home improvement to armed combat; a man who reads *The Nanny Diaries* for pleasure. But girls, they really want it both ways. They want the poet *and* the fighter.

Perhaps that's what Lara thought she was getting.

I should probably try harder to maintain this illusion. After all, I need all the help I can get when it comes to the opposite sex. Take my first-ever girlfriend: a German exchange student named Velma. It took me six months to kiss her, by which time she was in the airport, waiting for the final call to be made for her flight back to Düsseldorf. And I say kiss, but it was really more of a random chewing motion, directed at her face. Ah, yes, Velma. She had blonde hair that came down to her waist, green eyes, and she owned one of those close-fitting girls' denim jackets, which she wore with flared jeans and a long, knitted scarf. She looked like a teenage Brigitte Bardot. After she left, we composed melodramatic air mail letters to each other while secretly finding other people to practice kissing on. We reunited the following year—I took an excruciating forty-eight-hour bus trip to Germany—before realizing the impossible logistics of our bilateral relationship. Since Velma, my record with the opposite sex has been, well, patchy—to the point where there's actually very little data to analyze. In college, I once took a girl out for a curry, which seemed absurdly glamorous at the time. I paid for it with my first credit card. The girl in question seemed to enjoy the experience, although she dumped me the following week for her ex-boyfriend. "Sebastian and I had a reunion" were her precise words, spoken in posh schoolgirl and accompanied with the kind of face that you make when you stroke a terminally-ill puppy.

Then nothing, for years. Just heavy drinking, bad nightclubs, questionable wardrobe choices. Finally, on my first assignment to America—in New York, for the financial section—I met someone. It was a mismatch, but for a while it made me happy. The relationship struggled on for about two years until my ignoble return from combat, and in my postwar funk I ended it.

"I need a follow-up date with Lara," I announced when we reached the bar. "This time, no taxis, no elephants, no Chewbaccas."

"You're the show biz correspondent," said Jeff. "Take her to a Hollywood party."

"Los Angeles correspondent," I corrected. "And I don't get invited to Hollywood parties."

"That's because you don't *ask*."

"Yeah, well," I said. "Maybe."

A bartender appeared and we ordered.

On the whole, Jeff is better at living in LA than I am. He knows how to dress, for a start. Tonight's outfit was a pair of expertly faded jeans with a flare below the knee and an untucked white shirt with a rainbow pattern down one side. The ensemble was completed with a pair of white sneakers and a spiked 'hoxton fin' hairdo. Jeff is my age, but on nights like this he looks about a decade younger. If you had to guess, you'd say he was a member of a boy band.

"So did you hear about Jacko's birthday party?" he asked, casually.

He meant Michael Jackson.

Everyone's talking about Michael Jackson, as I'm sure you've heard. They showed that documentary about him the other night, the one made by the British journalist Martin Bashir. In the film, Jackson cheerfully admits to sharing his bed with other people's children and recommends that Bashir do that same. Not a good move, this, on Jackson's part. Or maybe it wouldn't have sounded so bad if Jackson hadn't looked as though he had recently relocated from Neverland to hell, what with his acid bath face and helium balloon voice. There are now rumors that the district attorney in Santa Barbara is going to try to put him away for good on child abuse charges, having failed with that other case ten years ago.

"What party?" I said, only vaguely interested in the answer.

"He's selling two hundred golden tickets for five grand a pair. It's like Willy Wonka all over again. We should gatecrash. We should do a *story,* Ayres. Why don't we find some scalpers on eBay?"

"And pay *five grand?*"

"Think of the story, Ayres."

"Jeff, if I filed a five-grand expenses claim for getting into a party, the editor would fly over in person to fire me."

"Suit yourself," said Jeff, sighing and looking over at a tanned girl in a bra top and miniskirt who had just straddled the mechanical bull.

I studied the wedge of lime in my drink and began to think about Lara, in her straw hat and her white bikini.

2

Early Symptoms

My hometown, Wooler, is closer to the North Pole than it is to Los Angeles. Or perhaps I should say it's closer to what's *left* of the North Pole—pending the North Pole's rebranding as something more marketable, something more climate appropriate, something like the North *Beach*.

Wooler is closer to the North Pole than it is to a lot of places. Not even the Romans could be bothered to go there: they left the place well alone, deep within the brawling cesspool of what was then Scotland, separated from the rest of the empire by Hadrian's Wall. As a result, Wooler's culture and dialect owe more to the Viking meatheads who butchered and vandalized their way down the east coast than it does to the tanned, sexy, cappuccino-making Romans. (Did they have cappuccinos in Roman times? I like to think they did.)

When I was a boy Wooler might as well have been on a different continent from the rest of Britain. When I think of the village now—two hours south of Edinburgh, six hours north of London—I think of stone houses, empty streets, cold sunlight through racing clouds, and that bawling, gobbing, never-ending bloody North Sea gale. Yes, on a windy day in Wooler you feel as though the Four Horsemen have bought their airline tickets and are on their way.

My parents—both retired schoolteachers—still live in the house that I grew up in (a thirty-year mortgage *means* a thirty-year mortgage in Wooler). They never had much interest in America, and until I moved here they had never crossed the Atlantic before, although I did have a great-great uncle Tom who had immigrated to Pennsylvania just before the Depression.

Every birthday during my childhood, I would get dollar bills from America, sent by one of Uncle Tom's descendants. I remember the first time it happened: the intense excitement of the strange green currency, followed by the intense disappointment of having it rendered worthless by the bank's commission and the Reagan-era exchange rate. This was my first introduction to the laws of economics, a subject I turned out to be good at, in spite of having no talent for mathematics. I loved the idea of studying money in the abstract, as if that's all it was—a series of concepts that could be manipulated, rewritten, abused. I was convinced that one day economics would make me rich.

Not that my parents didn't have money. They were comfortable— just not comfortable enough, as far as I was concerned. We didn't have what I thought were the essential things in life: computer, VCR, satellite TV. My father, on the other hand, could barely believe how far he had come up in the world: he was descended from Irish potato famine refugees who first went to London in search of work, then migrated north to dig the Manchester Shipping Canal. The "navvies," as they were known, were as poor as the shit they shoveled. Christ, what a way to make a living. Not that it could really be called a *living*. My dad spent the first two years of his life in the hospital because his mother was too sick to look after him. He was named Peter by the nurses and kept in a chest of drawers during the German bombing raids.

I once asked him what he was most proud of.

"Being middle class," he replied.

Aside from that first birthday card with the dollar in it, the other defining moment of my childhood probably came when I was sitting at my parents' kitchen table sometime in the late seventies. The shah of Iran was fleeing the Islamic revolution, oil prices were spiking, and scientists

were telling a largely uninterested world that something weird and scary
was happening to the weather. With my podgy face set into my best
Winston Churchill impression—I was good at these—I rose sternly
from my high chair and pointed a spoon at the street outside.

"Car!" I squealed.

This was my first word—or one of them, at least.

And then I vomited.

My fixation with the car—and the persistent, inexplicable nausea it seemed to produce—became something of a theme for the rest
of my life, helped along during boyhood by my toy collection. I'm pic-
turing here my little Texaco oil tanker, my Boss Hogg Cadillac, and my
Marlboro-sponsored Formula One car (ah, for the days when cigarette
companies sponsored children's toys). My favorite of them all was a
die-cast sports car, the color of custard, with plastic vents where its
rear window should have been and oval headlamps that pointed inward
and upward. After mastering the word *car,* I soon moved on to the word
Lamborghini. Cars even featured at mealtimes: my dad would coax me
into eating by pretending that a spoonful of mashed-up turnip was a
Porsche and that my mouth was a tunnel.

"Brum, *brum,*" he'd growl.

Soon enough, I had developed a healthy boyhood obsession with
the burning of prehistoric plant life in the name of zero-to-sixty acceleration times. Just the smell of combustion made me happy. I loved
being in gas stations. I got high on the fumes, the colors, the engine
noise, the rattle of the pumps. When I wasn't pretending to be a car, I
composed letters to car companies, requesting brochures. My dad was
pestered with follow-up calls from exotic dealerships in Knightsbridge.
I would hear him on the phone, saying, "No, I didn't write a letter . . .
ah, perhaps it was my *son,* Christopher . . . No, we can't quite afford
one of those, maybe when he's older . . . ha, ha . . . good-bye." At the
time, my father was the only man in England who kept buying French
cars: he insisted that comfortable seats were his priority. Meanwhile,
every morning, another parcel of automotive pornography would be
pushed through our letterbox, carrying the gold-embossed logo of a

leaping panther or a prancing stallion. I studied this material for hours, memorizing the important phrases: Connolly leather seats! Burr walnut veneer! Fuel injection! V12! Dual cam! Power steering!

My father finally broke the news when I was twelve years old. "The oil's running out, y'know," he announced one morning over breakfast. "It's running out and there's nothing they can do." The radio was on. I remember John Travolta and Olivia Newton-John singing "You're the One That I Want." The song had followed a news item about Ayatollah Khomeini. I remember the name because my dad found it amusing and would sing it around the house in the style of Elvis.

I was quiet for a very long time.

Oooh, Oooh-*Oooh,* chirped John and Olivia.

My father slurped his tea. He generally didn't pay a great deal of attention to politics or business. He was more interested in the cricket scores, or if Manchester United was going to beat Liverpool. He was, I suppose, a typical Englishman: content with the status quo, unless provoked severely.

"So the world is going to *end*?" I said.

Cereal was shaken from a box. More tea was poured. The kitchen windows were dripping with steam from the electric kettle. I could smell toast, melting butter, and my grandmother's marmalade. My grandmother's idea of relaxation was making marmalade. She organized her marmalade-making days like World War II military campaigns, complete with briefings, troop mobilizations, maps, inventories, predawn equipment checks, contingency supplies, you name it. And she made the stuff in military quantities, too. At the end of a successful marmalade-making day, derivatives traders on Wall Street would start dumping orange futures.

"Son," declared my father, "if the Americans can send a man to the moon, they can build a bloody electric car. Besides, oil is filthy stuff. We're better off without it. They say it's heating up the earth."

Oooh, Oooh-*Oooh,* went the radio.

"Suppose," I muttered.

Then a thought came to me.

"Wouldn't you *like* it if Wooler was hotter?" I asked. "Isn't that why we go on holiday to France every year?"

"It doesn't work like that, son. When you muck around with the weather, all kinds of bad things start to happen."

"Like what?"

"Hurry up and finish your toast. You'll be late for the bus."

There was only one main road, the A697, that ran through our village. Not a day went by without me giving serious consideration to the exact model of car most suited to the task of driving south on it, toward London, at speed. It was usually a toss-up between a Porsche (the one that could do almost two hundred miles per hour) and a Lamborghini (the one that came in lime green and was shaped like a wedge of cheese). At the age of twelve, both cars represented every notion I had about manhood, freedom, and success. Margaret Thatcher had summed it up perfectly: "A man who finds himself on a bus beyond the age of twenty-six can count himself a failure." I was very much on Maggie's side here. The bus journey from our village to my school was an hour of headlocks and sucker punches each way. Anyone who put himself through that as an adult would have to be an idiot. But what was the point of passing my A-levels and getting a job if there was no oil to buy, and no supercars to consume it?

My father, of course, had meant to be reassuring: electric cars would save the planet.

But I didn't want an electric car.

I wanted a Lamborghini.

3

Tinned and Sweating on a Broken Conveyor Belt

I awoke in a liquid panic at three-fifteen a.m. Sure enough, the woman in apartment 53B was going at it. That girl is an actress, no doubt about it. And a good one, too. A whimpering bass line held down the rhythm as she riffed, free-form, on a theme of human excitement. Two key changes later she launched into a rousing passage of atonal howling, interrupted only by a three-minute percussion solo from the bedsprings. But here's the strangest thing: I don't think there was anyone in there with her. I think she was faking it *alone*.

It wasn't the noise that had woken me. It was an idea. An idea so good, so brilliant, it couldn't wait.

Through a myopic haze I fumbled under the bed for the phone and dialed London. "This is Chris in LA," I croaked to the editor who answered. No one shares my name on the foreign staff, but I always feel the need to state my dateline. It helps me pretend my job is glamorous.

"Ah, Chris. So you've managed to leave the swimming pool."

I recognized the voice immediately: it was the foreign desk editor, aka the Beast. I call him the Beast because he must always be fed: news stories, features, columns, reviews, fact boxes, news-in-briefs. The Beast is always hungry. If you don't feed the Beast, the Beast gets angry.

The Beast is convinced that I spend all of my time by the pool. This happens to be true, but it's annoying nevertheless.

"What have you got for us today?" he growled. No mention was made of the unusual time. In London it was noon. The Beast expects me to remain vigilant for news events, twenty-four-hours a day.

Clearing my throat, I began: "How about this? A day in Neverland with Michael Jackson. An exclusive news feature."

I paused, allowing the ink to dry on an imaginary page.

"Color piece," I went on, in my best movie-announcer voice. "First person, naturally. Written from *inside* Jackson's birthday party, as the controversy over the sleeping-with-boys documentary rages."

Like I said, a brilliant idea. I would bribe my way into Neverland, just as Jeff had suggested, but take Lara instead. The perfect second date. And also, by happy coincidence, a story. An *exclusive*.

Jeff would get over it, eventually.

"Interesting," said the Beast. "But how do you propose to get into Mr. Jackson's ranch? You're not exactly his *type*." There was laughter on the line, sarcastic laugher. The Beast, as always, was skeptical.

"I've found a way."

More laughter, this time nastier.

"*Seriously,*" I said. "I can get into his birthday party on Saturday night."

There was a contemplative pause. The Beast was chewing something, and the sound was being carried with surprising clarity through jawbone to plastic, then down the telephone line. I felt as though I was inside the Beast's mouth, swilling around with all the mushed biscuit and instant coffee.

"Really?"

"Yes, really. But there's one . . . issue."

"Which is?"

"We have to pay someone five grand."

Something exploded in the Beast's mouth. Through the distortion on the line, I could make out only one word: "*Who?*"

"I don't know yet. I need to check eBay."

Another explosion, louder than before.

Flinching, I said, "Honestly, it's fine."

Muffled profanities followed.

I was asked to hold, presumably while a second opinion was being sought from upstairs in the executive suite.

At last, the Beast returned.

"The answer's yes, Chris. But this had *better* be good. We want the whole day, in detail, every single detail you can get, okay? I want to know what Jackson eats for breakfast, what kind of toothbrush he uses, what kind of sequins he has on his bedsheets, the color of his bloody pajamas . . ."

"Of course," I said, punching the air. "Everything."

"Chris?"

"Yes?"

"*Five grand,* Chris."

"Don't worry," I said, grinning. "You know me."

"We certainly do."

When I finally got out of bed I logged on to eBay, typed in the words "Michael Jackson" and "Neverland," clicked through a few pages, and sure enough there was a pair of golden tickets on sale for five thousand dollars. Still, I wondered if this was a con, designed to lure Jackson's most lunatic of fans. I thought of all those other dubious offerings on eBay: the human kidneys, the vacations on the moon, the auction of "nothing, absolutely nothing" that had once fetched one dollar and three cents. My blood carbonated with anxiety. If all this went wrong, the Beast would never agree to pay my expenses. And I could hardly afford five grand.

Five grand. Christ. The seller of the Neverland tickets appeared to be a charity: it called itself Togetherness and its motto was "Promoting the Togetherness of Humanity." Sweating, I clicked on the icon marked BUY IT NOW and entered my AmEx number. Line by agonizing line a new page loaded. I chewed on my pen. "Transaction approved," it said, eventually. I was instructed to wait for an e-mail from Togetherness with further instructions. I made myself an espresso and paced the apartment until I heard the double *plink* of an incoming message. I opened it to find the address of a house in Calabasas, a mountaintop suburb out near Malibu, where I could apparently pick up my tickets in person. In *person*? This was becoming more complicated than I had expected. I reached for a map and bolted from the apartment, car keys in hand.

Moments later, I emerged full tilt into the dusty netherworld of the underground parking garage. The garage taunts me with its cars. You wouldn't believe the vehicles kept by my neighbors—where do these people get the money? What do they *do* for a living? Two Rolls-Royces in Gatsby white, fifties' vintage. An AC Cobra replica, faster than the original. Four Porsches, three Ferraris, and several Japanese clones. The markings on their rear ends read like the things you would type into Google while searching for porn: all double Xs and triple injections. And then there are the eighty-grand shopping carts: the Range Rovers, the G-Wagons, the chromed-out Hummers with bull bars and searchlights.

The closest I ever came to owning such a car was in London, when I paid an enormous sum of money—all of it borrowed—for an early seventies MG convertible, manufactured at the precise moment when Britain turned from industrial power to leisure economy. With unknown mileage, a triple-engine transplant, and a body made entirely of putty and spray paint, the MG proceeded to stage a series of spectacular malfunctions at key congestion points throughout the capital, the most traumatic of which required a rush-hour crane-lifting operation on Tower Bridge. The resulting eight-mile gridlock through South London made the local BBC evening news. My confidence in the MG unshaken, I took on another enormous deficit to pay for repairs. A grinning mechanic proceeded to replace the fuel tank, upgrade the alternator, swap the body panels, and reroute the electronics. I congratulated myself on my financial savvy. This car, I told myself, it was an *investment*. It spluttered on for a couple more months until finally, after I had squandered a sum equivalent to a mortgage downpayment, I too suffered a breakdown. The next day I sold the MG to a bloke down in Croydon for two hundred quid and the train fare home.

Now I don't even have a car. The vehicle I use in LA is borrowed: a temporary loaner from my employer's American parent company, until

I establish a good enough credit rating to buy my own. The model was specified by an accountant in London, as were the factory-installed options, of which there are precisely none. As a result, I have the only car in LA without electric windows. I have the only car in LA without floor mats. Or power locks.

The walk to my parking spot under the Leisureplex is therefore one of anguish, and a daily reminder that I must carry out this plan of mine; that I must upgrade; that I must *do better*. I bow my head as I approach, trying to ignore all the smug Germans and mocking Italians, their grilles twisted into delighted sneers, their headlamps practically tearing up with laughter. My pace slows. And then . . . there it stands, alone in an oily, unlit corner. My Jeep. Not the open-topped, four-wheel-drive variety, but a miniature SUV: a car whose genesis, just like its purchase, could only have come from an accounting department.

With a printout of the e-mail from Togetherness in my mouth and the map in my left hand, I pulled open the door, being careful not to tip the vehicle over. It wobbled precariously, settling down to a gentle roll as I squeezed inside. There I was greeted with cloth trim and plastic, more plastic than seemed possible, and a dashboard of empty holes filled with rubber plugs and snap-on covers. These dashboard craters remind me of my dad's old Renaults. They remind me of the boyhood agony of knowing that in another vehicle, a better-equipped one, the very same holes would be filled with gadgets. Not that any number of gadgets could save the Jeep from its crapness. I once looked up the model in the back pages of *Car* magazine. "Old-fashioned and nasty," it advised. "Don't even *think* about buying one."

With a thunk and a whine from the remote-controlled gate, I bumped out onto Alta Loma Road, then wobbled east in molten traffic to Hollywood, where I took Highland to the 101. After an hour of bearing west I reached the exit for Calabasas, marked by a massive glass-walled Ferrari dealership. The population of Calabasas is twenty-three thousand: enough people, apparently, to sustain a market for million-dollar

Italian sports cars. Soon enough, I found myself on a pristine four-lane highway, banking up into the Santa Monica Mountains. On the way I passed a vast, low, black-mirrored complex, sunk into what appeared to be an English rose garden, kept alive by the mechanical rain dance of several hundred sprinklers. According to a low-key sign by the entrance, this was the headquarters of Countrywide Financial, America's largest mortgage lender. I wondered if it was the mortgage people, the creative debt men, who were keeping the Ferrari dealership in business. With interest rates at one percent, these people must be just about printing their own currency by now. Every morning when they come to work, having laughed themselves to sleep the previous night, they must pause in the lobby to salute a portrait of Alan Greenspan.

Next came the fortified green zone of the Calabasas Golf and Country Club, and then . . . and then nothing, just trees, scrub, and rock. A few miles later, the road dead-ended at a wrought-iron gate, next to which was a large wooden guard house. ARMED RESPONSE, read an unwelcoming sign.

Armed response to *what,* I thought. I pulled up alongside, wound down the window, and attempted a casual smile.

"Can I help you, sir?" said the guard, in a weary, skeptical tone, a tone that implied he almost certainly couldn't.

"I'm here for Togetherness," I replied, smiling again.

"Uh?"

"Togetherness," I repeated.

A smirk settled into the guard's face and made itself comfortable. "Eliot Ness?" he said.

"The charity," I elaborated. "Too-*gether*-ness."

"No charity here, sir."

"But this is the address I was given. Look."

I held up my printout of the e-mail. The guard ignored it.

"Contact name?"

"I don't have a contact name," I said. Again, I waved the printout. "All I have is this address."

"I'm sorry, sir, but you're going to have to go ahead and turn your vehicle around. You're blocking a fire lane."

"Look, there must be a way . . ."

"Like I said, sir, it's an offense to block a fire lane."

It was then I noticed the phone number on the bottom of the e-mail. "Hold on," I said, tightly. "I've got a number." I reached for my phone and began to stab at the plastic with my thumb before realizing there was no signal this far into the mountains. "No signal," I explained, showing him the empty bars. "But I have an appointment. Honestly. Is there any way you can . . . ?"

The guard took the printout, examined it, then looked up something in a thick directory on his desk. He picked up the phone on his desk and asked it: "You expecting someone? Male. Driving a . . . ?"

"Jeep."

"*Jeep*," he told the phone.

A long pause—I wondered if my contact at Togetherness was checking out the security cameras—then the guard asked for my name. I told him, and he repeated it.

Finally, the guard hung up the phone.

"Number 2180," he said, as the gate began to open.

So this is what a gated community looks like, I thought, as I pulled slowly forward. To the west was the two-tone horizon of ocean and sky; to the east, the sci-fi metropolis of downtown LA. Everywhere else there was canyon and brush. I began to pass houses the size of hotels: houses with multiple swimming pools, five-car garages, and spiral driveways leading to white-columned entranceways. I saw golden lions flanking marble fountains; Maybach limousines with gold-pinstripe detailing. I kept driving. Finally, I stopped outside number 2180. This house had probably the best view of them all: the driveway was cut into the rock face, far below which was the sequined hemline of the 101. What exactly was I supposed to do now? I kept the engine running and the printout in my hand and stared at the front door. I tried to breathe slowly. This had to be one of the weirdest days of my life. Then the door opened. A man wearing a drill instructor's hat, black sunglasses, black T-shirt, and black jeans emerged. He approached me at an efficient pace. He was holding something: a large brown envelope. Perhaps this wasn't a scam after all. I opened my door to get out but he held up his hand as if to say, No. Then he was right there in front of me. "Hello," I said. He said nothing and examined me, as if he were looking for clues. At last he held out the envelope, and I took it. Before I could say anything, the man had turned and was walking quickly away. I thrust my hand inside and felt two hard rectangles. As I pulled them out I felt the heat from the reflected glow.

The golden tickets. *The golden tickets!*

I heard choirs, birdsong, fireworks. I pictured Lara in her straw hat and her white bikini.

Hallelujah, the choir sang. Hallelujah!

And then the sun ducked under a cloud and gobs of hot, dusty rain began to pelt the windshield. I closed the Jeep's door and began to reverse carefully back down the driveway, a sheer drop to either side.

I couldn't believe it.

No, I just couldn't believe my luck.

I had expected Lara to at least sound vaguely impressed by the invitation to spend a day at Michael Jackson's ranch and celebrate his forty-fifth birthday. I mean, how often does that happen? All the time, apparently— if you're Lara. Through a long, cavernous telephone yawn, she told me that she had already been invited to the Neverland party by one of her "industry contacts" (was the event as exclusive as I had been led to believe?) but she couldn't decide if she wanted to go. The prospect of having me as a companion didn't seem to tip the balance in favor.

"I'm not sure, Chris," she said quietly, after I had told her about the tickets on eBay, the five grand, and my trip to Calabasas. I also told her I was writing a story, in an effort to make the date sound less contrived. "This is going to sound a little strange," she went on, "but I've just started taking these massage classes and they've given me some homework to do. I know, I mean, *homework*. It's like I'm in second grade. But it's due on Sunday. I've got to get it done."

Under different circumstances, the massage classes would have been an exciting development. As it was, this was bad news—worse than bad news. Jackson's party began on Saturday afternoon. Still, that gave Lara almost a week to do her homework, and how hard could it actually be?

"Ah," I said.

"I *know*," sighed Lara, with a sympathetic tone, the tone of a vet telling you that your dog needs to be either put down or given an emergency double amputation. Then I sensed a weakening in her breath. I suspected a calculation was being made: a female calculation; a calculation beyond the capability of the male brain. "But I could work in the car, right?" she ventured.

Too late. My attention had drifted. I was back in college, sitting on the bed of my dorm room. By my side was Katy, the girl I once took out for a curry. "Sebastian and I had a reunion," she was telling me, sadly. I knew all about Sebastian, the smug, freckled bastard. Now she was giving me the *aww* look. Then I saw Lara. She was wearing the white bikini. Now I was naked apart from Speedos and a pair of elaborately ribbed socks. Now I was running . . . running . . .

Noooooooo!

"Chris? *Chris?*"

I jolted forward in my chair.

Lara was still on the phone. Jesus, get a grip! "Sorry," I coughed. "I was . . . you were saying?"

"I could do my homework in the car, right?"

Ah yes, the homework. Perhaps this wasn't an outright rejection, after all. Still, you had to hand it to Lara: she knew how to make a five-grand date to the home of a celebrity sound like an inconvenience.

"It's nothing too complicated," said Lara. "Just some diagrams and a questionnaire. Shouldn't take long."

Can't you do the fucking homework the night before? "What a great idea," I said. I had, of course, already fantasized about our journey back from Neverland, and it didn't involve diagrams or a questionnaire.

"Don't let me forget, Chris. These classes are expensive."

"Lara," I said, with rising irritation. "Are you sure you want to come? I mean, you don't have to . . ."

"I'm *sure* I'm sure," she said, sounding unsure.

"See you Saturday then. I'll pick you up."

We arranged a time. As the phone clicked, I let my head fall into my hands: this was going to be another disaster.

I should have invited Jeff.

Saturday came.

I turned up outside Lara's house midmorning. The sky was all big, dumb, and happy. The LA sky wouldn't get along well with the Wooler sky, that's for sure. The Wooler sky is a brooding drunk, peeing into its trench coat, throwing up on the furniture, grumbling and spitting and raging and bawling, often all at the same time. The LA sky, on the other hand, is a cheerleader on antidepressants: blank-eyed, even-tempered, insistently optimistic.

Lara and the Jeep were similarly mismatched and took an instant dislike to each other. To be honest with you, Lara's old VW convertible, even with its dings and welts and rear seat landfill of CD cases, gossip magazines, hairspray bottles, and other girls' girls accessories, would have provided more appropriate transport. "What kind of car *is* this?" Lara asked, trying to find her balance on the bath sponge passenger seat. "I hope it won't make me *sick*." This seemed to upset the Jeep, which developed a sudden suspension problem, bucking wildly as it skipped over the grooves on the Sunset Strip, like a blunt needle on scratched vinyl.

If there's one positive thing to be said about my date with Lara, it is this: I learned a lot about how *not* to entertain a woman. For example, car journeys are a definite no-no. The stress factors of navigation, radio tuning, motion sickness, road rage, and those inevitable lapses into tense, weary silence combine to exert an almost unbearable pressure on both dater and datee. Another thing I learned: dating and journalism don't mix, either. From the second we got in the car I began to worry about the Neverland story. Would we get beyond Jackson's security? What would we *see*? What would be my intro? When would I file? If anything can shine ultraviolet on the flaws of your personality, it's an impending newspaper deadline. By the time we reached Ventura County—an hour from LA—Lara and I had developed the kind of mutual animosity usually achieved only after a long and expensive divorce.

The traffic, meanwhile, was stop-and-go; mainly stop. If the 101 is an artery, California should have dropped dead from coronary failure a decade ago. The drive up the Pacific coast is supposed to be a car commercial in its own right: all downshift switchbacks, clifftop vistas, and full-throttle straights. Not anymore it isn't. Now it's just another reminder that the previous generation had it so much better than us; that we are late arrivals at a party thrown by our parents—but the cops have shown up, the booze is gone, the drugs have been flushed, our hosts are in rehab, and we're left with only a trashed mansion with cigarette butts in the silverware, a corpse in the infinity pool, and a trail of blood and vomit up the stairs.

By Santa Barbara, the scenery had improved. The ocean had crept up to the highway, the palms were casting little bobbing pools of shade over the cars, and the mountains looked as though they had been upholstered in green velvet. But still, the *traffic*—thousands of people, all tinned and sweating on a broken conveyor belt. If it's like this on a Saturday, I wondered, what the hell is it like on a Monday morning? Then I glanced out to sea and saw the villains on the horizon: oil rigs, skeletal and gray, like warships, like diabolical invaders.

"You and Michael Jackson aren't so different, y'know."

I glanced over at Lara. She hadn't said a word since Ventura County. Now she looked cocked, as though she could go off at any moment. One more pothole, I thought, and I'm pink mist.

"How come?"

"You're from northern England, he's from northern Indiana. Small towns, not much cash. You both end up in LA. Jackson lives at the Tropicana Motel, you live at the . . . the . . . what do you call it?"

"The Leisureplex?"

"Yeah."

This was just what I needed: some amateur psychology. With her seat in the fully reclined position, Lara had rested a small, tanned foot on the dashboard. "Jackson goes on to sell millions of records and buys Neverland," she resumed. "*You* get a job as a war reporter, then you bribe someone five thousand dollars so you can take a girl you hardly know on a date to Neverland."

The word *date* unsettled me. So did all the other stuff. Perhaps it was time I told Lara the full story about my war reporting career. Or perhaps there was no need. Perhaps she already knew I was a fraud.

"One difference," I said. "I don't sleep with twelve-year-old boys."

"Jackson doesn't *sleep* with twelve-year-old boys, Chris. He just sleeps *with* twelve-year-old boys. Anyway, my point is: to other people, your life probably seems just as insane as his life seems to you."

"I don't see how we're alike, Lara. He's *black*. And he was a prodigy. When he was a kid—touring America, singing like a miniature Diana Ross—people thought he was a professional midget. People thought Jackson's dad had *bought a midget* and was passing him off as his son. He's insane because of the total corruption of his childhood. He doesn't know what's good for him."

"He's insane because he refused to grow up, and because he can get anything he wants, any time, without anyone telling him when to stop."

"Apart from the banks," I interrupted. "Everything is mortgaged and double-mortgaged with Jackson. I read somewhere that since the eighties he's spent close to a billion dollars on private jet charters, real estate, lawsuit settlements, zoo animals, divorces, you name it. Hence him selling tickets to his birthday party for five grand each. They say that if it wasn't for the fact he bought the Beatles catalogue, he'd be completely broke by now."

"Well, there you go. He's just like you."

Had Lara been reading my AmEx statements? That restaurant bill, by the way, for the tapas place: four hundred dollars.

Now Lara was laughing—unsettling laughter; the laughter of a Bond villain with a shark tank and a trapdoor. She leaned over so that her face was almost touching my shoulder. "Is your editor really going to pay for this, Chris?" she asked. "Or did you just put the tickets on your credit card?"

The date was now going worse than expected. Quite an achievement, really, given that I had *expected* it to go worse than expected.

"Look," I said, with more irritation than I had wanted to show. "I'm nothing like Michael bloody Jackson."

"Whatever you say, Mister Five-Grand Golden Tickets."

With that, we turned off the freeway and set about climbing through the San Marcos Pass to get farther inland. The Jeep rattled and whined. Lara kept opening her window to suck on the breeze. As we cleared the mountains, the fields yellowed into a sepia postcard. Horses grazed next to red barns. Tractors rusted by the roadside. Mexicans sold fruit from cardboard boxes at dusty intersections. *Mister Five-Grand Golden Tickets*? Lara had a bloody nerve. Couldn't she have at least pretended to be impressed? I began to wonder if we would actually meet Jackson, talk to him, shake his gloved hand. The thought seemed ridiculous. Then came a town called Los Olivos. Turning right, the Jeep battered its way up a potholed lane. I double-checked the directions. This place could not have been further removed from my mental image of Michael Jackson: in my mind, Jackson inhabited a low-resolution music video from the early eighties—a fake Manhattan backstreet with fake hoboes twirling on fake lampposts, while a moody, wet-permed woman provided the implausible love interest. We kept going. A signpost warned that we were now entering a bear reserve. A bear reserve? Jesus *Christ*. Was this how Jackson kept the paparazzi away?

I kept driving, trying to ignore the whisper in my head—you've been conned, you've been *conned*. Then I glimpsed a left turn with a gate at the end of it. Next to the gate was a guardhouse, a fleet of golf carts, a TV news crew, a security detail, a moonwalking Jackson impersonator, and a human wall of clipboard holders.

"My God," I said, with genuine surprise. "We're here."

Another day, another doorman; another St. Peter at the gates of paradise. These days I feel as though all I ever do is try to get into places I don't belong. In many ways, my eventual descent to hell will come as an immense relief: the ease with which entry will be granted; the speed at which the trapdoor to the burning lake of fire will open. None of this messing around with clipboards and lists and golden tickets and doormen's egos.

I steered the Jeep up Neverland's unmarked driveway and brought it to a halt in front of the gate, window open.

The Clipboard who greeted us was actorly and muscular, with a white polo shirt and a double-espresso complexion. Veins pulsed on either side of his neck, like the lights that indicate when an explosive device is armed.

"Hi," I said, shakily. "We're here for, er . . ."

"Michael Jackson's birthday party," interrupted Lara, smiling.

"That's right," I said. "Mr. Jackson's . . . event."

He was tall, this list keeper, and he appeared to have no intention of bending over to meet my eye, so I ended up addressing the embroidered horseman covering his thick left nipple.

"Need your ID," came the order from above. I watched as a big, dense hand tapped out an impatient rhythm on a big, dense thigh. That hand could do some damage, I thought. I looked over at Lara. She seemed to be straining to get a better look at something through my window.

"What about the tickets?" I suggested.

Again, I glanced at Lara. She looked as though she was . . . was she? . . . Jesus, yes, the *nerve*—she was trying to see if our interrogator was as good-looking as his sculpted midriff suggested.

"Just the ID," he said.

Shit. They were expecting ticket fraud. I pulled my driver's license out of my wallet and beckoned for Lara to do the same. After a minute or so of fumbling, two laminated mug shots changed hands. The Clipboard held them up against a printed list of names and began to whistle as he moved a pencil carelessly down the page. Halfway down, he was distracted by a call on his cell phone. By the time he finally hung up he was bored with the task at hand.

"Nope," he concluded. "Your name's not here."

"But I have the tickets."

"Like I said, we only need your ID."

"But . . ."

"Not my rules."

"Any chance you could check the list again?"

"Spell the name."

"It's written right there on the . . ." I sighed. Our driver's licenses were still in his hand. "It's A-Y-R-E-S," I said.

"Z-R-Y . . . ?"

Oh for Christ's sake. If only he would actually *bend over* so he could hear me. "No," I said, clearing my throat and addressing the nipple. "A-Y-R . . . Look, is there any way you can lean over a bit so that—"

"Not here," he repeated.

"Listen, it's Ayres. A-Y-R-E-S."

Now the Clipboard was strolling urgently away toward the guard-house. He said something to the other man inside. They nodded grimly. I felt a rash of fear on my face. I imagined awaking at dawn the next morning, alone in the bear reserve, naked aside from a pair of honey-soaked briefs.

"Sir?" said the Clipboard, walking back to the Jeep. His legs were like girders. You could build bridges with them.

"Look, we have the tickets right here. We paid—"

"Please pull forward and get out of the car."

"Sorry?"

"Pull forward and get out of the car."

"Why?"

"PULL FORWARD AND GET OUT OF THE CAR."

The tickets were fake. The tickets were bloody fake. I knew it. I'd been scammed on eBay. This was going to cost me five grand. This might cost me my job. This would definitely cost whatever statistical aberration of a chance I might have still had with Lara. Would the Clipboard call the police? Was there such a thing as attempted trespassing? Would we spend the night in jail? What about ticket counterfeiting charges? Oh shit. Oh *fuck*. I couldn't bare to look over at Lara. What must she have been thinking?

I did as the Clipboard asked. Lara also climbed out of the Jeep onto the dirt road. Now the other man from the guardhouse was approaching—the Clipboard's boss, I assumed. He was also wearing a polo shirt, but he was older, taller, wider, uglier: on the whole, a less sympathetic character. This was going to get nasty, very nasty indeed. Before I could say anything, however, Lara had strutted up to him. "Look, we were invited by the record company," she declared. "Tripp Purvis, global VP, based out of Nashville. He's a friend of mine, a good friend, and a client. Is there a problem? I can get him on his cell *right now* if you want. There should *not* be a problem."

Tripp Purvis? Who the bloody hell was Tripp Purvis?

There was a long, unblinking pause. Then the older man spoke. "Welcome to Neverland," he said. "We hope you have an enriching time with us here. And we'd like to thank you on behalf of Mr. Jackson for your kind support of Togetherness, working to promote the togetherness of all of humanity."

Exhaling gently, he put his hands together in the prayer position and gave a tiny nod.

"You've got to be kidding me," I muttered.

And then something awful happened.

Disclaimer

The following chapter describes how the author *imagines* his date in Neverland might have progressed under different circumstances. All details of Mr. Jackson's ranch have been taken from previously broadcast or published material. In no way should this chapter be confused with what *actually* happened, which remains a confidential matter between the author and Mr. Jackson.

4

Never-Never Land

Flushed with relief, and at last feeling as though it might have been a good idea to invite Lara, I climbed back into the Jeep.

"Nice work, Miss I-Know-a-Global VP," I said.

"Well thank you, Mr. Five-Grand Golden Tickets."

Then a tap on the window: gentle, but urgent.

It was the bloody Clipboard again.

"*What now?*" I groaned, reaching for the winder.

"Almost forgot," said our tormentor, holding up a sheet of paper and a pen. "You need to sign this."

"Sign what?"

"Mr. Jackson's confidentiality agreement."

"*What?*"

I began to wonder if Jackson's people had known all along who I was. They *must* have known. "It's nothing, nothing at all," he said, smiling. "It's just—y'know. We've had a few reporters, *assholes,* buying tickets on eBay and stuff, so we need everyone to sign this as a precaution. They spoil things for everyone, don't they, the press? Anyway, just a standard contract: you won't write about Neverland, photograph it, talk about it, video it, yada, yada. And if you see anything suspicious, just holler. If there are any reporters in there, they're going to find themselves in a world of shit."

"A world of shit."

"Always looking for something negative to say."

"Bastards," I said.

"Yeah, *assholes*," offered Lara, from the other side of the car.

"Please," said the Clipboard. "Sign at the bottom of the page."

He handed me the sheet of paper and the pen and gave me the same kind of tiny and yet somehow terrifying nod that his boss had just given Lara.

This was an extraordinary disaster. My career was over. I wouldn't be able to write a single word. I would have to pay the ridiculous price of the golden tickets myself. And how would I break the news to the Beast? I remembered the instructions given to me a few days earlier: *"This had better be good. We want the whole day, in detail, every single detail you can get, okay? I want to know what Jackson eats for breakfast, what kind of toothbrush he uses, what kind of sequins he has on his bedsheets, the color of his bloody pajamas . . ."*

Then I noticed something. "This is just a cover sheet," I said.

"Oh, you don't need the rest."

"Why not?"

"It's a big document."

I looked deep into the Clipboard's eyes, but there was nothing to be seen—just my own reflection, in miniature.

"A big document," I said.

"Any reason you need to see it?"

I wanted to beat my head against the Jeep's steering wheel. Actually, I wanted to beat the Clipboard's head against the Jeep's steering wheel. "No," I said. "And just for the sake of argument, if I don't sign?"

"We'd have to ask you to leave."

As I parked the Jeep in a field beyond the checkpoint it was hard to avoid dwelling on the progress of the date so far: I was probably out of a job, and almost certainly down five thousand dollars. Not bad for the first fifteen minutes. What's more, this remarkable personal and professional implosion had taken place right in front of Lara, which

meant that my odds of getting anywhere with her had gone from un-
likely to impossibe. Why hadn't I guessed that Jackson would pull this
kind of a stunt? This was a man who had learned the art of the contract from Berry Gordy's Motown Records. Of course he would have
a bloody confidentiality agreement. *How could I have been such an
idiot?* I suspected Lara was thinking the same thing as we got out of
the car and walked in silence up a dirt path to Neverland's rear entrance. Under any other circumstances I might have been excited
about what was to come. But I was paralyzed, and dreading my call
to the Beast the next morning. *Could I be fired for this?* At least the
date couldn't get any worse.

Or so I thought.

Neverland was deserted. After crossing a fence using wooden steps,
we reached a railway station with an elderly couple sitting on a bench.
At first I thought they were real: then I noticed their yellowing, milky
eyes and their dead, waxwork stares. They were waiting in eternity for
a train they would never board. A startled "Blimey" was the best I could
offer. Lara gave a low chuckle. *"Yeah,"* she replied. A pink flamingo tiptoed by. I could hear an elephant; then a tiger. Bloody Michael Jackson, I thought. Bloody golden tickets. Bloody Lara and her bloody bikini.

It was already clear that Neverland's owner was the victim of a
rare and possibly celebrity-induced psychosis. There were waxworks
everywhere: more elderly couples; a clown holding out a cooler full of
ice cream; a grandfather in Dickensian costume brandishing a platter
of English toffees. Their faces were all set into the same zombie glare.
I began to wonder if there were recording devices in the waxworks' eye
sockets. *Where had Jackson managed to find all this crap?* Above, cameras gleamed in the treetops. A Walt Disney sound track played through
loudspeakers disguised as rocks. The only real people we could see were
Jackson's radio-wired henchmen, buzzing around on the horizon in golf
carts. I felt like we were on a private island owned by some whacked-
out third world dictator.

Perhaps this was all a trap, I thought; perhaps we were about to be imprisoned, nipple-clamped, and forced to listen to Jackson's "Earth Song" for the rest of our lives. Adding to the general sense of unease were the statues of children everywhere, some of them partly clothed, others completely naked. Given Jackson's legal history, and the fuss over the documentary in which he talked about sleeping with other people's children, you would have thought he might have replaced them with something less provocative by now: bearded gnomes, perhaps. Then again, Jackson probably thought the Peter Pan theme justified it all.

Speaking of which. If Lara thought I had something in common with Jackson, she should have done some reading on Pan's creator, J. M. Barrie—also a British journalist. When Barrie was seven years old, his brother died in a skating accident. Barrie's mother never got over it. The author-to-be would dress up in his dead brother's clothes to please her. She told him she never wanted him to grow up; told him to stay *just like his brother* forever. Her wish came true: the trauma of it all left Barrie with psychogenic dwarfism. Now of all the things you don't want to get when you're a kid, psychogenic dwarfism surely has to come somewhere near the top of the list. Measles, you can deal with; whooping cough, you can tough it out. Psychogenic dwarfism? The game's pretty much over at that point. You become the man who invents the Wendy house and sets the theme for Michael Jackson's landscaping.

With nothing better to do we continued our odyssey through Jackson's ranch, eventually reaching the other side. By now it was late afternoon, and I had moved through four of the five stages of dating grief: denial (in the car); anger (at the checkpoint); bargaining (again, at the checkpoint); and now depression. All that was left was acceptance of my life-long bachelorhood. If I hadn't been so depressed, the other end of the ranch might have seemed almost pleasant. A collection of rustic-looking bungalows sat next to a little bridge and a flamingo pond. In one direction was an even larger train terminal (and, I assumed, Jackson's private residence), outside of which was a giant outdoor clock, dug into the side of the hill. Above was the word NEVERLAND, spelled out in yellow blooms. In the other direction was a paved driveway and the ranch's main entrance, at which stood a pair of huge gold-leafed gates featuring Jackson's fake royal crest and a silhouette of Peter Pan, gazing down from a painted moon. In a nearby bush was another statue of a naked boy, his little foot raised above a plastic slug. I kept looking around for other guests, to see how they were reacting to the lunacy of it all, but there were none to be found. Where the hell *was* everybody?

I wondered if Jackson had always been this unhinged—or if it was just mass adulation, unlimited wealth, and a staff of nodding flunkies that had driven him to it. I once read that Jackson had always loved to shock people; loved to pull stunts and confuse the press or lie to them. But at some point he *became* the stunt, and by then he'd forgotten how to even pretend to be normal. That's the trick, I suppose—knowing when normal is no longer normal. But is it possible to know? Or do we always assume that it's the world, and not us, that has changed for the worst?

We were disturbed by clattering steel and the shriek of a whistle. And then, as if from another dimension, a little red steam train appeared. It scared the hell out of me. I didn't even realize we had been standing on train tracks. The train's miniature cars were all empty. "All aboard!" shouted the conductor in a sickly tenor. He was some kind of circus midget, this conductor, and he was dressed like the waxworks in Victorian costume. To another shriek of the whistle we boarded. The train began to shudder forward. As the cars bucked and rattled, we passed the by now familiar sight of more nude children. Then came a stone bridge, a swimming pool, a video game arcade, another flamingo pond, a Native American village complete with wigwams and a waxwork chief, a wooden fort, and then, finally, a fairground with a Ferris wheel, carousel, bumper cars, and other rides. Everything looked slightly dilapidated, as though the machines hadn't been oiled or painted since the eighties, when Jackson was still earning more than he could spend. No doubt some fairground

contractor was ripping him off. "Is your editor going to be upset?" asked
Lara, as the train lurched and slowed. It was the first time the subject of
the checkpoint had come up.

"Don't worry about it," I said.

"Do you think they know you're a journalist?"

"I think the only people here are journalists."

"*We're* the only people here."

"Exactly."

We got off the train near the zoo, petted one of Jackson's elephants for a while, explored a dank outhouse in which a snake the
width of a tree hissed and squirmed in a filthy tank, and then ducked
into Neverland's cinema, near a basketball court. There was a glass window in the cinema's lobby, behind which was a wooden model of Jackson moonwalking. It reminded me of a Christmas window display on
Fifth Avenue—only a cheap, Chinese-made imitation. Perhaps Jackson had bought the wooden moonwalking doll from the same place he'd
bought the waxworks. "Can we *go* soon?" asked Lara. "I've got homework to do, remember?"

I'd been wondering when Lara's campaign to go home would begin.
I could hardly blame her. Here she was, trapped with a man she hardly
knew in a three-thousand-acre lunatic asylum, beyond which was nothing but dirt roads and a bear reserve. It was a four-hour drive back to
Los Angeles. A more considerate date would probably have left for the
parking lot at that very moment. For some reason, however, the thought
of leaving Neverland so soon irritated me.

"We should wait to see if Jackson turns up," I said.

"Chris, you *promised*."

"I know. But I need to see Jackson. For the story."

"What story? You can't even write anything!"

"Just in case."

"What about my homework? You *promised*."

"Lara, we'll go soon. Don't worry, chill out."

"DON'T TELL ME TO FUCKING CHILL OUT."

"Jesus, Lara. Chill . . . I mean . . . Jesus, I'm sorry."

"No, I'm sorry. I just hate being told to chill out. There's this guy at work, he's always telling me to chill out."

Maybe that's because you need to chill out, I thought. "Thirty minutes?" I said. "Can you give me thirty minutes?"

"Then we leave?"

"Then we leave."

"Fine."

With that, I stalked off to the bathroom, letting the spring-loaded door catapult into the face of the man behind me.

"Sorry," I muttered.

But I wasn't sorry at all.

To be honest with you, I can barely recall the details of what happened next. Only two things I know for sure: we stayed in Neverland for longer than thirty minutes and, since that night, I've never seen Lara again.

The time line of the evening went something like this: I left the bathroom to find Lara standing outside, in an even worse mood than before. It was now dark and I noticed that half the bulbs on Jackson's Ferris wheel were out. It was a wretched sight, that Ferris wheel. But Lara had other things on her mind. In a sharp, hurried whisper, she informed me that the man who had followed me into the bathroom was none other than Mike Tyson: former world heavyweight boxing champion, convicted beauty queen rapist, ear biter, recently declared bankrupt, and, it turned out, friend of Michael Jackson. "Wow," I said, distractedly. "I thought he was still in jail." Lara told me that I wasn't getting it. Wasn't getting *what*? I asked her. It was Tyson's face, Lara explained, that had absorbed the impact of a certain double-sprung bathroom door, a door that I had released from my grip in a moment of spite because of my unreasonable irritation at being asked to drive back to LA. Lara went on to observe that from her vantage point in the lobby I had failed to demonstrate any meaningful remorse for this lapse of judgment; that if a situation ever called for remorse *this was it*. She cited news stories about Tyson assaulting autograph hunters in Brooklyn and being sued by his own bodyguard for allegedly punching him twice in the face, breaking his left orbital bone. She inquired about my psychological health and wondered aloud if there was any way that I could turn our trip to Neverland into an even bigger disaster. She briefly pondered the existence of an Ayres curse. Then she pointed discreetly to Tyson, who was now looming ten yards to the north, flanked to the east and west by minders or friends of terrifying proportions. They brought to mind a mountain range: an impassable terrain of flesh and muscle; a terrain that no ordinary man could ever hope to cross. In their eyes, I glimpsed the "world of shit" the Clipboard had promised.

Lara suggested we move to a more populated area, so we speed-walked to a nearby circus tent, where a buffet dinner was being served. Tyson and his crew rolled along slowly behind. More people were now arriving at Neverland: busloads of people, in fact. I heard someone mention that Jackson had been giving away golden tickets as part of a competition organized by an LA radio station. The narrow road that ran alongside the fairground was now a gridlock of white luxury coaches, which groaned and hissed as if in protest at their destination. I looked up and saw ecstatic faces peering out from behind the tinted glass. What were these people so fucking happy about? Jackson was insane, didn't they know that? I wondered if the competition-winners had been asked to sign confidentiality agreements, or if that privilege was reserved for the idiots who had paid five grand for admission.

At the buffet we dined without enthusiasm on chicken and vegetables. One of Tyson's minders began to elbow my chair every time I took a sip of beer. At one point I practically swallowed the entire Heineken bottle. In an effort to catch my surveillance detail off guard, we bolted halfway through dessert. For a few euphoric moments it seemed to work. But soon enough they were back: this time, minus Tyson. Out of options, we got on the Ferris wheel. With a belch from the diesel generator, our creaking gondola swung up and out. Christ, this thing was *old*. It was at that moment Lara disclosed her fear of heights. Equations of velocity and mass became suddenly visible in her brow. Silent and rigid, she clung to the safety bar. When the gondola reached the top of its arc I told her the worst was over, that we'd get off soon. That was when the ride broke down. Far below us, Tyson's people huddled with the Ferris wheel operator, laughing. In another universe, Lara might have sought reassurance in my arms, might have clung to her manly suitor. Instead she seethed. "Don't fucking move an inch," she warned me. "If you move this gondola, I'm gonna tell Mike Tyson you called him a bankrupt rapist."

Ten minutes passed, perhaps twenty.

Finally, the machine slowly lowered us back to earth. Or at least as close as you can ever get to earth in Neverland.

On numb legs we fell out onto the grass. It was getting cold. We allowed ourselves to be carried by the swell of the crowd into another circus tent by the merry-go-round. Tyson's crew still seemed to be marking their target. The tent was packed. Young girls were sobbing with joy. Grown men were dancing to Kylie Minogue. And then, perhaps inevitably, a uniformed children's choir emerged. They swayed and clapped their way into the center of the room, then performed a chorus about children, hope, and the future. The tent darkened when the music ended. Lasers swooped. Fake thunder boomed. And then in a burst of light Jackson emerged, Jesus-like, on a steel platform, ten feet above the crowd. *Was this as close to him as we were going to get?* I was struck by his tiny figure: it was that of a teenage girl, not a middle-aged man. He wore a black sequined suit. But no amount of sequins could distract from his terrible, broken face. From somewhere behind his flame-retardant hairpiece—or perhaps it was real—Jackson squeaked out a thank you and riffed with merciful brevity on the themes of children, hope, and the future. Then he hung back as Tyson joined him on the platform and began to cut his birthday cake.

It seemed like a good time to leave.

As we fought our way to the back of the tent, Tyson scooped up some cake and threw it at Jackson.

"Food fight!" yelled someone from the floor.

"Yeah, food fight!" yelled someone else.

It brought the house down.

Somewhere out in the gloom of the estate we found a shuttle to take us back to the parking lot. I sat next to a doctor in a black leather jacket. He said he was Michael's dermatologist and started to tell me all about Bubbles, Michael's chimpanzee. It turned out that Bubbles had been evicted from Neverland after turning inexplicably violent. I knew exactly how the poor chimp felt.

On the backseat there, Lara took my hand and gripped it.

What was *that* for?

Reunited with the Jeep, we wobbled our way back down Neverland's driveway, then headed southwest, back to the San Marcos Pass and the relative sanity of LA. Lara switched on her map-reading light and opened one of her massage school textbooks. Two miles later she snapped it shut again.

"Stop the car," she said. "I'm going to throw up."

5

The Desperate Period

Doughboys café, Third Street. Doughboys serves porn food; food that should exist only in fantasy. It takes meals remembered from your childhood and remakes them with bigger budgets. The results are described by the menu in a low, masturbatory whisper. This is the peanut butter sandwich: "Chunky peanut butter, bittersweet chocolate and banana on our *pan de mie* bread, dipped in egg batter and grilled, and served with raspberry dipping syrup . . . *pure decadence!*" Today, after twenty minutes of indecision, I had ordered the French onion soup from a waiter with a white man's Afro and only one pant leg, the other removed to display a knee-high tattoo. In Doughboys, everyone has tattoos. Apart from me, of course.

And Jeff.

"Ayres, what *happened*?" he groaned, from across the table. He was wearing a lime green "Mr. Fantastic" T-shirt.

"I don't want to talk about it."

Spread out in front of us was Monday's edition of a popular British tabloid. On the front page was a photograph of a female journalist—one of my rival Hollywood correspondents—standing next to the gates of Neverland. She looked triumphant. Above her was the headline: WE GO BEHIND LOCKED GATES OF JACKO'S WEIRD HOME. Inside was a beautifully written twelve-hundred-word color piece, outlining every detail of Neverland, including a few I hadn't noticed ("In a giant seashell two stripped stone babies lie smiling"). Clearly, I hadn't been the only newspaper reporter to find Neverland tickets on eBay. I *was* the only journalist, however, to pay five grand for them, then write nothing— although "nothing" wasn't entirely accurate, as the Beast had let me rehash some copy about the party from the wires.

"I don't understand," said Jeff. "I thought you bought the tickets. I thought you got in? And you didn't write anything?"

"I *did* buy the tickets, Jeff. Then some nodding bastard at the gatehouse made me sign a confidentiality agreement."

"Nodding?"

"He kept nodding. Like he was a Buddhist or something."

At this point my soup turned up in a ceramic vat with a loaf of bread on the side. Viewed from Jeff's side of the table the soup must have almost completely obscured my upper body. No normal human being could eat such a meal. No normal human being could eat *half* such a meal. The Emmentaler cheese was several fathoms deep; beneath it lay a crouton big enough to support the foundations of a small house. Below that was a landfill of stewed onion. As for the broth, it wasn't so much a broth as a beef stew in its own right. I imagined the chef dropping an entire Aberdeen Angus cow, unskinned, into a cauldron the size of a swimming pool. As I attempted to penetrate the cheese with the back of my spoon I looked around. There was more fat in my soup than there was on any of my fellow diners. How could this be possible?

"And you fell for all that?" said Jeff, as he was presented with a basil chicken salad of similarly gargantuan dimensions.

"Fell for it? I signed the bloody thing."

"It was a confidence trick, Ayres. I bet they didn't even let you see the terms, did they? Did you get any legal advice? How can they claim that Neverland is confidential when it's been on TV about a million times? They even broadcast part of the birthday party on *Entertainment Tonight*. I watched it at home in my pajamas. Kept trying to catch a glimpse of your enormous bald head."

"They *broadcast* it?"

"*Entertainment Tonight,* Ayres."

"Well no one in London wanted to take the risk."

"I hope you at least got somewhere with that girl, Lala."

"Lara."

"Well?"

"No, it didn't go well."

"Oh, Ayres."

"She hated every second. Wanted to go home. Almost vomited in the car. I'm never calling her again. It's over."

"You should have taken me. None of this would have happened. I hope you at least got your five bloody grand back."

I stared into the black ocean of my onion soup.

"Ayres," said Jeff. "You *did* get your five grand back?"

I can see them now: a team of archaeologists, several millennia into the future, digging for relics on Sunset Boulevard. There's a commotion over at the northeast corner of the site. The ruins of the Leisureplex have just been discovered. An unshaven man in a cowboy hat and open-necked shirt, sweat gushing from his brow, holds aloft what is left of my skull. "Interesting," he murmurs. "Bipedal primate, a late *Homo Sapien*. I believe this could be from the Desperate Period."

It would be fair to say that things aren't going entirely to plan. The debacle in Neverland has left me broke and demoralized. Five thousand dollars, those tickets cost me. Divided into affordable monthly payments of two hundred dollars, plus interest, it will take me two years to pay it off. *Two years.* How in the name of Christ did I manage to screw up a date that cost five thousand dollars? Another question's bothering me. If I failed under those circumstances, what chance do I stand now? What better gimmick can I come up with than an evening at Michael Jackson's ranch? A night in the Oval Office? Lunch in *space*?

I've lost my confidence.

I haven't left the Leisureplex for days.

Yes, I have entered . . . a Desperate Period. And there's no stopping a Desperate Period, not when a Desperate Period is already under way. That's the whole point: desperation is contagious; it infects everything. You just have to buckle down and try to ride it out. But I fear the Desperate Period will do what all self-respecting Periods do. I fear it will go on for a very long time.

Have I mentioned the weather?

Even by the standards of the desert in summer it is unbelievably hot. The walk from air-conditioned building to air-conditioned car is now almost unbearable. Perhaps someone should invent a head-mounted air conditioner. Is LA seriously planning to keep this up? The temperature continues to climb as autumn fades and winter approaches. Admittedly, the seasons in LA are subtle events, and you have to concentrate hard to notice them (unlike in Wooler, where each one tries to outdo the other), but surely they shouldn't be operating in *reverse*. Every day, another suburb out in the San Fernando Valley bursts into flames, shutting down important porn Web sites and causing the traffic to set like concrete. Cars are spontaneously combusting. You can see them out on the shoulder of the 101, melted into the tarmac like swatted bugs. As for the Los Angeles Department of Water and Power, it can't take the pressure anymore. For the past month now, thirteen million people have been running their air conditioners, 24/7. Every other minute, a new transformer blows, a new circuit breaks, a new fuse shatters. The blackouts at the Leisureplex last for hours at a time. Up on Sunset the traffic lights have been out for days.

If the weather is bad in LA, it's downright apocalyptic in Europe. In the green and pleasant town of Faversham, Kent, it is currently registering a Sahara-like one hundred degrees. The crew of an airliner from Jamaica almost called off its landing at Heathrow yesterday after looking at the temperature gauge and wondering if they had navigated to the wrong country. In France, fifteen thousand people have died from heat exhaustion. In Italy the body bag count is twenty thousand. Thousands of others have come to a hot and sticky end in Britain, Spain, and Portugal. For the British, who invented tin-foil sunbathing and twenty-quid flights to napalm islands, there is at least some irony in this. The way things are going, Wooler will have to stop breeding sheep and start growing coffee beans. Yes, England is changing. A couple of months back, I flew to a friend's wedding in Oxford and rented a hotel room without air-conditioning. "Who needs air-conditioning in *Oxford*?" I guffawed to the receptionist, with maximum LA smugness. I spent most of the night on the floor, moaning and sweating, with an ice bag between my thighs and my head in the minibar.

The heat won't last forever, says the news. On the contrary: so much ice from the North Pole will soon have melted into the Atlantic that the warm Gulf Stream currents will have all shut down. That's when we'll finally get some cooler weather—as we always do, when an ice age arrives.

Meanwhile, the sun keeps up its work . . . without thought, without feeling. Why is it we consider this dying star a friend? Personally, I've never liked it. Me and the sun, we've always had our issues. I take one look at the sky and I go red in the face. And now, with everything getting *hotter* all the time—with the sun putting in all this extra work—I feel like a canary who's gone to live in a gas chamber. I read once that in five billion years time, the sun will begin to simultaneously expand and implode, its outer layers boiling away the oceans and most of our atmosphere. Yes: the sun is out to get us. But no one's blaming the sun for our planet's broken thermostat. Of course they're not. Why blame the dying star above us, with its nuclear moods and its polar swings, when they could just as easily blame themselves?

So now I'm in the Jeep, wobbling and thumping down Sunset Boulevard to a party in Beverly Hills. Watch as I make that difficult left turn onto

Beverly Drive while glancing up to admire the tall, illuminated palms, like cheerleaders' pom-poms, against the darkening sky. Then comes the five-way stop sign, which forces the cars to gather like a geometric puzzle in the intersection, each one jerking forward and backward in search of a solution. My destination is an art gallery called the Mammonian, off Little Santa Monica Boulevard. The reason for tonight's event? The launch of a new five-hundred-horsepower Bentley. Yes, only in LA can you find a Bentley on display at an art gallery. My invitation arrived this morning from the office of Sally Worthington-Haynes, a noted publicist and the owner of an absolutely terrifying English accent. I know very little about Sally Worthington-Haynes, apart from the fact she once worked for the *New Yorker,* and that her former boyfriends and husbands have included Hollywood actors and billionaires.

I slowed as the Mammonian came into view. The building was lit up like a glowing cube of ice, and the street in front of it was lined with parking valets, each one dressed in black, as if they were taking part in the military parade of a fashionable Latin American dictator. It's taken me a while to come to grips with LA's parking culture. The first time I pulled up outside a restaurant in this city, I thought I was being carjacked. I quickly learned that having a gang of Mexicans open your doors and snatch your keys is one of LA's great conveniences. It's also a way to demonstrate your place in the city's hierarchy. It makes sense, when you think about it: what's the point of spending three grand a month on a car if you have to park it out of sight, in a concrete high-rise with a broken elevator? With valet parking, you get to climb out of your car at the front door, *with other people watching*.

I once looked up the word *valet:* it comes from the fifteenth-century French word for manservant. Those French aristocrats would have loved LA, what with its manservants standing on every corner under their little curbside umbrellas—like ice-cream sellers on an as-phalt beachfront.

After the mistaken carjacking incident I spent a few weeks trying to avoid valets. But parking without them—and their five-dollar fees— is like parking without looking behind you: almost impossible. After dusk, the valets rule the parking meters. Even if you do find a legal spot, you'll almost certainly end up violating one of the dozen or so clauses on your nearest parking sign—which will be written in an extraterrestrial language of colors, abbreviations, hieroglyphics, and calendar markings, understood only by the parking enforcement officials, who patrol the streets in their white space cruisers, looking for cars to abduct, to beam up and transport back to their own parking planet, many millions of light-years away.

In front of me now was a Ferrari the color of a crime scene; behind me a Range Rover the size of a country estate. I watched as the chief parker pointed at the Jeep and shouted something to one of the men in black, who turned and ran to the car, beckoning for me to get out. He must have been Mexican, Salvadoran, perhaps Guatemalan. I smiled at him, while thinking: how much more can the Hispanics *take* of white people? When are they going to start throwing their weight around, like the blacks did after the Rodney King beating? The Latinos, after all, are good at coups. They have revolution know-how—just like they have construction know-how, gardening know-how, car-parking know-how. And how will the whites defend themselves, when all they know how to do is order complicated lattes?

"Bentley party, señor?" he asked.

I nodded, still smiling.

By now the Ferrari and the Range Rover—the stallions of LA's tribal chiefs—had already been positioned outside the gallery's illuminated entranceway. I put the Jeep in park and climbed out. The moment my foot touched the ground, the valet jumped in behind and squealed away in a rubber fog, sparing me the embarrassment of being seen with my own car. Head down, I passed through the vortex of clipboard holders and into a square room with a concrete floor, white walls, and a high ceiling. The noise was incredible; like canned laughter in an echo chamber. For a moment I thought the place must have recently hosted a children's event, as there was paint thrown all over the walls. On closer inspection, however, the splatters were framed and had small white stickers underneath. Each one displayed an unfamiliar name, a cryptic title, and a large number preceded by a dollar sign. The more obvious work of art was positioned in the center of the room: the Bentley. Yes, *that* was more like it. I peered through a tinted window and into a better, more expensive dimension: the Swiss mantle clock, the walnut dash, the suede headliner fabric, the heavy, polished controls. According to the sticker on the dashboard, all that stood between me and ownership of this vehicle was one hundred and fifty thousand dollars—not including sales tax, delivery, and registration fees. Suddenly I was back in Wooler as a nine-year-old: Connolly leather seats! Burr walnut veneer! Fuel injection! V12! Power steering!

I stood back and surveyed the crowd. Beverly Hills princesses, plum-cheeked hedonists, journalists with notebooks and bad breath, fleets of android publicists, the rich, the very rich, and the troops of assistants employed by these feudal lords to perform just about any task, no matter how exotic or simple. Together we circled the Bentley while teenage girls in long black aprons held aloft trays of red wine, raw tuna, and deep-fried wontons.

It was then, without warning, that gravity football-tackled me and tried to drag me down. The noise of the party went into reverse. I saw sun spots and shadows. Spilling my drink, I attempted to move in the direction of the door. Bad idea. What the *hell*? I stood there and felt the blood circle and drain from my head. Panic attack, I thought. Great, a panic attack. *One hundred and fifty grand,* a voice behind me was saying. *The fuckin' thing is a dinosaur. It weighs as much as a house and it does twelve fuckin' miles to the gallon, what's the fuckin' point? They should retire it, just like they retired the Concorde.* I turned to locate the source of this monologue, but the voice had moved out of range. Now I felt hot and sick. Why a panic attack *now*? A strange woman smiled in my direction, her teeth stained with wine and tuna. For a moment she looked like a gargoyle, like a leering prophet of death.

I'm pleased to report that things improved dramatically as the evening wore on. There I was, quietly palpitating, when Sally Worthington-

Haynes seized my arm. Her outfit was Jackie Onassis goes to Carnaby Street: short white skirt, matching jacket, knee-high boots, and the kind of jewelry that usually comes with an extradition request and a body count. The ensemble could have been flown in from Paris that very night. Meanwhile, her hair was blonde and bobbed and hung with expensive softness over her tiny frame. As for her age: impossible to guess. Sally Worthington-Haynes is one of those LA women who slip into an alternative dimension sometime after their fortieth birthday. It works the same way with men in this city. You think you're talking to a college student, what with his rock 'n' roll T-shirt, his skateboard, his bong collection, and his extensive knowledge of low-fi British indie music, then you find out he's fifty-eight, with six kids and three percent of Google. What do these people *do* to themselves? Is it just superior DNA technology, higher-octane blood? I look around the room at a party like this and I feel as if I'm aging in goldfish years, on time-lapse video. When I tell people my age in LA, they can't believe it. *But you look so much older,* they try hard not to say.

"Ah, Chris," declared Sally, with an accent that was somehow even more frightening than I remembered from the last time we met. "Glad you made it. How are you? Now, have you found courage?"

All this was delivered at military speed, but I didn't have a clue what she was talking about. Courage? Perhaps this was a joke about my combat tour, which had recently earned me some unflattering blog coverage. "I never had any to begin with," I said, deadpan, trying to play along.

Sally looked impatient and annoyed.

"Not *that* kind of courage," she hissed. I sensed Sally didn't approve of self-deprecation, especially when it came to journalists and their wars. "Courage Macleod," she went on. "She's *British*. Her grandfather was an admiral, great man, lots of medals, wounded in action." She went on to list a number of sirs and barons and lords and viscounts and princes who were related to Admiral Macleod and, by extension, to his brilliant daughter, Courage Macleod. You spend a lot of time with Sally trying to recognize names you *should* know but don't. Sally is so well connected, her six degrees of separation are more like one and a half. She enjoys demonstrating this by referring affectionately to some of the most important people on earth by their first names, as if she just had them over for dinner the previous evening. You quickly find out this is probably because she just had them over for dinner the previous evening. Incidentally, this makes Sally's dinner parties uniquely perilous. You spend the whole time telling the person to your right about your Great-Aunt Nelly's fungal armpit problem and then you find out he's the king of Tonga.

For once, however, this name did sound familiar.

Macleod. *Courage Macleod*. It brought to mind Scottish estates, glossy magazines, and a naked female torso, photographed in black-and-white. Jesus Christ, yes: Courage Macleod, wasn't she a . . . didn't I just read about . . . I remembered a headline in *Town & Country,* something to do with blue blood and black ink, how Courage had made a fortune as the face of some French perfume brand. Yes, Courage Macleod, *the supermodel*.

"Why on earth would I know *her*?" I said. "She's a supermod—"

Before I could finish this sentence Sally was leading me toward the door, where she was now making loud and urgent inquiries as to the whereabouts of Courage Macleod. I was suddenly overcome by the horrible realization of what was about to happen. Please stop, I wanted to say. I'm not ready to meet a supermodel. I'm from Wooler. *I'm in a Desperate Period*.

"Outside. Valet," ordered Sally, after gathering some new intelligence. I shuffled along behind her in silence.

Beyond the glass double doors, we saw a blacked-out Ford Mustang, fashionably out of date, just about to pull away.

"Courage!" shouted Sally, waving her hand as if hailing a cab.

What was she thinking?

The Mustang glowed from the rear and stopped. A tinted window was lowered. And there, across from the empty passenger seat, sat a creature as pale and delicate as a work of origami. Her dark hair was tied up and her impossibly fragile arms were stretched out to grip the thick, hot rod steering wheel. Schoolmarm glasses failed to disguise the mathematical perfection of every bone in her face. I glimpsed the top of a tiny dress, now wrapped in a black cardigan. Something inside my chest was inflating. I began to feel very odd.

Then Sally said, "Leaving so early? I didn't get a chance to introduce you to Chris Ayres. The writer. He's here to cover LA."

Somewhere behind my cheeks, a plutonium rod was lowered into a vat of water, which began to boil furiously.

"Nice to meet you, Chris," said a voice that was at once posh and informal, an English hymn with a blues rhythm.

I made an unusual noise. A noise of thwarted longing, of hopelessness.

Sally glared at me.

"Hi," I corrected.

Courage lowered her head so our eyes could meet. I noticed the top of a stockinged leg, extended fully to reach the brake pedal, and I imagined the Italian-made stiletto at the end of it. "So how long have you been in LA?" she asked, a stray hair falling like a pendulum against her steeply angled cheek. She brushed it aside, but it swung down again, keeping time.

"Chris has just come back from the war," boomed Sally. "Embedded with the Americans on the front lines."

"Still in one piece?" asked Courage, with the nonchalance of a girl for whom many men had probably gone to war.

"Just about," I confirmed, in my lowest, most manly tenor.

"We should have lunch," offered Courage. "Fellow Brits and all that." I made a note to find a church the next day and make a lengthy apology to God for all those years of atheism. Whatever you want, Big Guy, I would say, I'll get it done. Anything, really. But please, *please*: just keep this up.

"That would be splendid," I said.

Splendid? Who says *splendid?* To be fair, this whole situation—this whole organizing-lunch-with-a-supermodel-outside-a-Bentley-party thing—was so far beyond my experience that I was surprised I was holding up so well. In fact, I was wondering if I had actually died over there in the Middle East, amid the dust and the gunfire, and if this were all part of some divine reward.

"Great," said Courage. "I'll be in touch."

I imagined myself waiting for a week by the phone before finally making a shaky call to Courage's assistant, who would make me spell out my name three times before putting me through to another assistant's voice-mail, where I would explain that I had met a supermodel at a Bentley party and was awaiting her call so that I could take her out for lunch and tell her all about the war.

With an elegant wave, Courage disappeared behind rising glass. She reminded me of Audrey Hepburn. Or perhaps I just wanted her to remind me of Audrey Hepburn. I wondered if I was star struck— model struck?—or whether she was as exquisite as that framed glimpse through the Mustang's window suggested. Until a few minutes ago, of course, I had barely recognized her name. There wasn't much chance of me forgetting it now. I watched as the blacked-out Mustang leapt forward, all eight cylinders growling and popping, and swung right onto Little Santa Monica Boulevard. Thank God she hadn't seen me turn up in the Jeep.

"Are you all right?" demanded Sally, as I stood there, looking as though I'd just met the ghost of Christmas future.

"Astonishing," I said.

"Don't be silly," scolded Sally. "Courage has a wonderful boyfriend. Big in hedge funds, or something."

Sally folded her arms, a visual clue as to the absolute impenetrability of Courage Macleod's romantic life.

"Astonishing," I repeated, as my stomach crept out onto a ledge and took a long, fearful look at the scene below.

6

Lacking Courage

My bedroom, the morning after the Bentley party. Make that lunchtime, possibly early afternoon. It's best if you look away now. I seem to be losing my talent for hangovers. I just can't *do* hangovers anymore. My tongue is a brothel carpet. My head is a box full of broken mirrors. My stomach is . . . I think something is *alive* inside my stomach. What happened last night? What did I *do*?

I open my eyes and groan. I feel terrible, worse than terrible. My head shakes to a distant African rhythm.

Boom-ba-bum-ba. Boom-ba-bum-ba.

You know, when you look closely, my apartment isn't as great as it sounds on paper. You begin to notice the cottage cheese paintwork, the ants marching in double file along the baseboards, the sad pink of the fluorescent-lit bathroom, and the brass faucets that have turned green—the same color as the water they produce for the first minute or so. Yes, my apartment is in need of some love. Like its occupant, my apartment is going through a Desperate Period.

After the party I must have driven back to the Leisureplex, abandoned the Jeep, and hiked up to the Saddle Ranch. I went there to meet Jeff, who I found by the bar holding court with a carafe of booze in his hand. I needed to tell him something. I was excited, shouty, borderline jabbering. I ordered a carafe of vodka for myself. And when

I was done with that I ordered another. Then a beer. The beer was a mistake. I remember Jeff shouting at me, telling me not to be so stupid, not to be so ridiculous. "Ayres!" he said, "It's not even worth *thinking* about." I accused him of being jealous. He said something about Neverland.

Boom-ba-bum-ba. Boom-ba-bum-ba.

By my bed the phone rang. I grabbed it quickly to shut it up, a decision I instantly regretted. Ah, *shit.* Why hadn't I just let it go through to voice-mail? This was probably London. I was in no state . . .

"Oooh!" squeaked a female voice.

It was a delicate sound, pure, and intimately close. *Boom-ba-bum-ba* went the hangover drums.

"Did I disturb you?" it continued.

I heard a breath being taken, a breath that made me feel strangely light-headed. Slowly, the memories returned.

Could it be?

Nah.

It's a PR, I thought.

"It's Courage," said the voice, sensing confusion.

Oh, *fuck.*

Now I was out of bed, jumping, shaking my legs, smoothing down what was left of my hair, making myself presentable for the phone. I remembered what had made me so excited last night. *I had met a supermodel.* She had invited me out for lunch. It had seemed almost cruel in its implausibility and timing, coming as it did on one of the most desperate days of the Desperate Period.

"Courage!" I said, too loudly.

"Yes?"

"I mean, ha-ha, great. Great to see you. Hear you. Splendid." *Stop bloody saying "splendid."* I needed to cough, spit, urinate—and perform several other unspeakable yet essential hangover wake-up routines.

"I didn't get a chance to ask you last night," said Courage. "How do you like living in LA?"

Oh no. She expected conversation. This was very bad news, given my condition. Such a broad question required a catastrophically witty answer, an answer so funny, so incisive, so colorful, so erudite (should I reference Twain, Wilde . . . Descartes?) that she would have to repeat it endlessly to her colleagues and friends. She would of course get it slightly wrong, and have to apologize for not being able to do my inimitable delivery any justice. The answer to this question could set the tone for our relationship. It could eventually be repeated at our wedding—cited as the moment when Courage Macleod realized that, in spite of his baldness and his acne and his sunburn and the fact that he wasn't very, well, y'know, "my type" (laughter from friends, recalling celebrity ex-boyfriends), he was just so . . . *brilliant*.

"Yeah, LA's okay," I said.

The drums kept beating.

The crowd in my head booed and groaned.

There were more questions. My answers continued to fall like lead bricks into a cold ocean. I needed to take radical action. I needed to terminate this call before Courage terminated this acquaintanceship.

"Why don't we have lunch?" I finally shouted.

". . . today?"

Of course not today. I had an appointment with my bathroom floor today. "No, no," I coughed. "Maybe later in the week?"

"Thursday? I can move a meeting."

Christ, she was really serious about this.

There had to be a catch.

"Thursday's great," I said, wishing I knew the catch.

"Why don't we meet outside the Mammonian at noon. There's free parking next door. We can go somewhere nearby?"

Was this the catch? Did her billionaire boyfriend own the gallery? Was Courage going to bring her boyfriend to lunch?

"See you then," I said, now sweating.

"Can't wait," said Courage.

The phone clicked then purred.

*   *   *

I have a confession to make. I'm in no shape to start dating a supermodel. Not that our lunch is a *date*, of course. But whatever it is I'm in no shape for it. Since arriving in LA I've filled out, I've chunked up. My flesh is designed for the winters of Wooler, not the summers of Southern California. Like a polar bear, I hoard fat for survival. And when my body isn't busy hoarding fat, it's busy trying to get me to eat fat. Go ahead, my body says, have a nut. Have a hundred.

It's always been this way. When I was growing up in Wooler, my favorite meal was a chip buttie: thick-cut fries in a white bun, sunk under ten fathoms of beef gravy or, even better, curry sauce. Ah, yes—the marvel, the achievement, of the chip buttie with curry sauce. It's right up there, I think we can all agree, with the genius of the battered saveloy, the majesty of the pork faggot, and the outstanding contribution to world cuisine represented by the pickled egg. And what do they eat here in LA? Fruit salads. Alfalfa sprouts. What *are* alfalfa sprouts? Giving my body this kind of food is like giving an elephant a desktop computer: it has no idea what to do with it. Every morning when I wake up in LA I can feel the panic, the bewilderment, in my genes. *Where the hell are we? What are we doing here?*

And so, in tracksuit and running shoes, I jog slowly past the pool of the Leisureplex and down the stairs to the tennis court, where I make a right to face a key-coded door, beyond which is the gym.

The gym. The air-conditioned capsule where I fake my labor, where I attempt to fool my genes. Hey look, I say to them. It's cold and I'm running, how are we going to find the energy to keep this up? What's that over there? It looks like . . . Hey, it's fat! Can't we burn some of *that*? But my genes, they're not idiots. You don't get to be a gene for nothing. After two hundred thousand years of evolution, these genes know what they're doing, and they're not going to be tricked by a bit of air-conditioning and a treadmill. No matter what I do in the gym—running, lifting, bending, jumping—my genes remain unshaken in their belief that sooner or later LA is going to suffer a winter of such Arctic severity, that my survival will be impossible without the warehouse of lard they have so thoughtfully constructed in my belly.

And so I run, and while I run I wonder if the modern male, like the five-hundred-horsepower Bentley, is nearing obsolescence. Perhaps this is our last century, our big farewell. The other day I saw a news item about women buying vials of frozen sperm online, from catalogues where the donors are sorted by Ivy League college, by height, by muscle tone. The babies created through this process are more advanced than ever before: they're custom designed, kitted out with optional extras, performance packs, superpowers. And when they're born the doctors store the blood from their umbilical cord, for future upgrades to their DNA.

They say it's only a matter of time now before scientists make the really exciting breakthrough: synthetic sperm. Then again, perhaps it's reproduction itself that is becoming obsolete. In a laboratory in Michigan, a genetically enhanced mouse called Yoda has just reached its fourth birthday. This would make it 136 in human years. Soon, say the scientists, this same technology will be applied to us. Yes, soon the Final Generation will be here—immortal, beautiful, superhuman. But what about the people *without* the very latest in gene technology? I exhale loudly and stare out the window. I see a Mexican man, about my age, digging in the garden. I keep running. The readout of the calorie counter ticks slowly upward. *One hundred. One hundred and one. One hundred and two.* The Mexican wipes his brow. He doubles over and coughs. I catch his eye as he looks up and give him a startled wave.

He stares back at me, then resumes his work.

"Gosh," said Courage on Thursday, taking a gentle sip of sparkling water. "And you were attacked by *how* many tanks?"

"A whole company of them. It was dark and we were lost, somewhere in the marshlands, and our GPS didn't work. So we just had to sit there in our Humvee, ahead of the front lines, waiting to die."

"Wow."

"It was no big deal, really."

"You must have been very frightened."

"I was more angry than frightened, y'know? Angry that I might die so young. But it was the job I'd chosen."

"Well, I suppose, but *still*."

"Thing is, when you're that close to death, you feel so alive."

"Really?"

"It's addictive. You crave the danger."

"And do you . . . *crave the danger*?"

"Sometimes."

"Gosh."

Courage frowned while lifting an impaled leaf of arugula to a soft and slightly glistening mouth.

I probably don't even have to tell you what a load of bullshit this is. The truth is that I almost died of fright out there in the desert. There was no glory in my combat tour. As far as I know, the poor bastards I was embedded with are still out there—still taking rocket fire from insurgents posing as goat herders. I deserted them after nine days. Not that a British journalist can *technically* desert a unit of the U.S. Marines. Still, that's what it felt like. I've been thinking about trying to absolve myself with a memoir of some kind. *War Reporting for Cowards,* I'm tempted to call it.

"And how long were you over there, Chris?"

"A few months."

"Think you'll go back?"

"Yeah, probably," I said, with a slow, nonchalant yawn. "Maybe I'll do a bit of Christmas shopping in Baghdad."

Courage laughed. I immediately wanted to make her laugh again.

We were in Beverly Hills, at a little courtyard restaurant with white umbrellas and waiters who spoke Italian. In an attempt to look high-fashion, I had bought a brown-striped Hugo Boss polo shirt, which was made out of a shiny material and had a V-neck instead of buttons. It was half a size too small. I couldn't decide if it made me look European playboy or Boyz Town gay. The rest of my outfit was business as usual: jeans, socks, brown slip-on loafers. I can't remember what Courage was wearing because I was trying hard not to look. A look could turn into a glance, which could turn into a full-blown stare, which could turn into a hasty request for the bill and another lost opportunity. Nevertheless, I got the impression that Courage was playing down the whole supermodel thing. In a city of women who dress to be noticed, she was practically in camouflage. Those schoolmarm glasses weren't enough to fool me, however. Oh no. On the few occasions our eyes met I felt as though something inside me were whimpering and clawing, desperate to get out.

Over a lunch of immense personal restraint—I turned down the Kobe blue cheese burger for a beetroot salad, and left the heavy, leather-upholstered wine list unbrowsed on the table—I found out that Courage retired from modeling a few years ago and now works full time for an interior design firm, which she eventually plans to leave so she can set up her own business. I also discovered that Courage graduated with a double-first from Oxford. A *double*-first? Wasn't one enough? No wonder Sally Worthington-Haynes loves her. The pair of them could run the planet. By the end of our lunch Courage had compiled for me a reading list of instructive LA-themed books, which she promised to send me in the mail: they had titles such as *Play It as It Lays*, *The Day of the Locust*, *Oil!*, *Ask the Dust*, and *The Last Tycoon*.

"The journey to LA is usually one of seduction and horror," she said. "Look at Evelyn Waugh, Aldous Huxley . . . they were transfixed and appalled. Huxley stayed here, of course, even after he'd written *Brave New World*. Englishmen can be the biggest hypocrites in LA. They come here and bang-on about the excess, then they go out and buy the biggest SUV they can find."

"I love it here," I announced.

"Really?"

"I feel at home," I said, and began to wonder when I would be able to replace the Jeep with a real car, like Jeff's giant SUV.

The conversation soon turned to Courage's boyfriend, a subject I'd been trying to avoid, for reasons of morale. Mercifully, he remained unnamed. The abridged version of his résumé goes something like this: musician, boxer, Yale graduate, philosopher, photographer, philanthro-

pist, record label owner, actor, linguist, gourmand . . . Christ, it's excruciating. No doubt Courage forgot to mention the part about him being a
Pulitzer-winning war correspondent at some point during his hugely successful, continent-spanning, supermodel-dating career. Naturally, he's
exactly my age. A week younger, in fact. The leisure economy, the global
economy, makes you believe it is possible to follow any career you want,
free from such tedious constraints as performing a necessary task or earning money to feed and accommodate your family. Courage's boyfriend is
one of those rare hyperachievers who proves this is possible. The only
consolation is that he is almost certainly not a billionaire as Sally suggested. His fortune probably extends to a mere hundred million or so.

Regardless, I attempted to show a respectful interest in my rival's
brilliance while desperately thinking of a way to see Courage again, pref-
erably in the evening, when anxiety could be tamed by booze.

That was when the subject of the new Walt Disney Concert Hall
came up. My mind blanked at the first mention of it, then I remembered the details: The Disney Hall was the work of the celebrity architect Frank Gehry and had been built at a cost of nearly three hundred
million dollars amid the crackhouses and twelve-lane freeways and sky-
scrapers of downtown LA. It would soon open with one of the most
flamboyant inaugral galas in the city's history.

Everyone would be there.

I put down my napkin and cleared my throat. "Oh, Courage," I
said. "If you want to go the gala I've got a spare ticket."

"Really?"

"Yes, really."

Our eyes met, and didn't move. I gripped the table. What was I
doing? This was insanity. Stop, I told myself. Please, *stop*.

"Don't tease, Chris."

"I'm a journalist," I chuckled. "We always get invited to these
things, and they always give us plus-ones. *Come*."

Not in my entire career have I ever been given a plus-one. Incidentally, I made the "come" sound supercasual, as though I were invit-
ing her to an after-work pub quiz, rather than a black-tie event full of

A-listers, at which we would be photographed together on the red carpet, looking like a couple.

Courage allowed herself a smile. My last date had cost five grand.
I wondered how much this one was going to cost. Not that there were
any tickets on sale for the event. Come to think of it, how *was* I going
to get two tickets? One name came quickly to mind: Sally Worthington-
Haynes.

"Oh, that would be amazing," Courage was now saying. "Thank
you so much Chris, I can't wait. How exciting!"

She appeared genuinely delighted . . . and yet, I had to admit, a
little hesitant. I didn't blame her. Assuming I did manage to get two
tickets to the Disney Hall gala, how would this look to her boyfriend?

Maybe she knew I was bluffing.

"Oh, no problem at all," I blustered, signing the check.

I felt a trickle of saltwater run from my forehead into the corner
of my eye. Yes, it was hot out there in the Desperate Period.

"You'll call me?" asked Courage.

"Of course," I replied, catching the sweat with my cuff.

7

Upgrade Everything

Something has to be done.

The situation is getting out of hand. I mean, enough's *enough*, goddammit.

It's my TV.

There it is: a twenty-four-inch model from the previous millennium, so comically obsolete it could be a prop from an episode of *Star Trek*. The screen bulges outward like a goldfish bowl, as if it's being pushed from behind by the impossibly long cathode ray tube. If you get up close it smells of damp static, white noise, and multicolor afterburn. As for the remote, it's almost bigger than the TV itself and goes through an eight-pack of batteries every week. The TV has become a metaphor for my lifestyle: in urgent need of upgrade.

The prospect of a date with a supermodel has certainly brought the shortcomings of my zero-capital existence into focus. It has also reminded me that the nonromantic elements of my mission in LA are advancing slower than expected. Yes, the TV will *have* to go. I've already spent two days straight on the Internet, browsing the latest generation of flat-screen models—TVs big enough to beam messages to visiting extraterrestrials; big enough to broadcast the score at the Super Bowl. But how to choose between them? The difference of just one digit on the spec sheet (these things read like extracts from *Quantum Mechanics IV: Advanced Theories for Astrophysicists,* only less accessible to the general reader) can mean

a difference of ten grand. *Ten grand.* How can a TV be so expensive?
What the hell *is* plasma, anyway? The fifty-inch model I've settled on
comes with a higher price tag than my grandparents' first house. I'm going
to need a TV mortgage—a structural TV deficit.

   Just the thought of a major household purchase exhausts me. All
that research; all those calibrations of need and want, mainly want. Then
there's the alleged convenience of the Internet. In the old days you went
to a shop, you got ripped off, and that was that. These days, you stay
indoors, hunched over a flickering terminal, studying the kind of data
once available only to Wall Street derivatives traders: price, tax, shipping,
insurance, packaging, handling, finance, currency movements, interest
rates, the NASDAQ index, weather statistics . . . astrological factors. The
product reviews alone contain enough words to fill a *Best of Dostoyevsky*
volume. And then, only after two days of missed work and interrupted
sleep—your eyeballs practically bleeding with the strain, your brain swollen with overload—do you finally, inevitably, get ripped off anyway. This
is why people think they have no leisure time. They think shopping is
work. The trouble is, I'm as addicted to this twenty-first-century consumption ritual as everyone else is; I love to suffer this hard leisure. And the
Internet has become my dealer—always pushing more of the same, just
the way I like it. I fear the flat-screen TV will be my gateway product to
other, more complex audiovisual equipment. Before long, I'll be experi-
menting with Blu-ray, dabbling in surround sound.

Now I glance around the room at my only other possessions: the fake-
steel floor lamp, purchased from the Ikea in Studio City during an afternoon of profound existential despair; the plywood tables and chairs,
also purchased from Ikea, during another afternoon of profound existential despair. And how could I forget those fake-steel Ikea racks, of
indeterminate purpose. I almost lost a finger to those racks during a
violent all-nighter with the assembly instructions, which featured no
actual assembly instructions, only abstract diagrams. Doesn't anyone
grow out of Ikea? I long to give it up. It's the *cheapness* of everything, I

think, that feeds the Ikea need. How do they do it? How can a kitchen cost ninety-nine dollars? I suspect the answer is that it *doesn't* cost ninety-nine dollars. We just haven't worked out who's paying for it yet.

The time has finally come, I think, to get Ikea out of my life.

Everything must be upgraded. I will start by putting my floor lamp for sale in the furniture section on Craigslist.org.

But not everything in the apartment can be sold.

The sofa bed, for example.

This was a gift from my grandmother, on the occasion of my move to America. She gave me the cash, and I chose the style myself from a showroom in Manhattan, back when I was on assignment in New York. I chose badly. Victims of the Tower of London have been strung up on more comfortable equipment than my sofa bed. But I can't sell it. No, I can never sell it. In my grandmother's world, not even death cuts it as an excuse to sell something as valuable, as permanent, as a piece of living room furniture. I think of my grandmother every time I look at the sofa bed, with its creased sandy-brown covers and its cast-iron frame—a frame so heavy you would need eight men and a winch to rotate it three degrees closer to the TV.

My grandmother's commitment toward material possessions is the only explanation I can come up with for my otherwise inexplicable decision to buy a lifetime "stain insurance" policy for the sofa bed. It didn't occur to me that I could simply remove the covers and put them in the washing machine. Instead, I accepted the logic of the saleswoman—fortyish, pant suit, cake batter foundation—that it would make more sense to pay four hundred dollars to keep a crack team of stain removal experts on a lifetime retainer, so that in the event of a stain disaster they could speed their way over to my apartment, anywhere in the world, analyze the precise nature of the blemish, then advise me on emergency measures—measures such as removing the covers and putting them in the washing machine.

Still, the sofa bed is the only thing of any value in my apartment, so perhaps my instinct to protect it was correct. Which raises the question: why don't I *own* anything? It's not like I never had cash. I just wasted it on the MG, valet parking, bottles of champagne in Hollywood night-clubs, expensively labeled V-neck sweaters. And so, at the age of twenty-eight, I own nothing. My apartment is rented. My car is borrowed. My furniture is Ikea. My TV is a joke.

Something must be done.

Have I mentioned the smell?

Christ. The *smell*. It's as though a horse has died in one of my air-conditioning vents. To describe the odor as disgusting would be to do it a favor. There's a sweetness to it, like intestinal gas after a night of heaving drinking. I marvel at the sheer ambition of its assault on the human senses. It could go places, this stink. It could have a big future in biological weapons. There—you can almost *see* it, a yellowing mist above the TV, like last night's cigarette smoke. It's messing with my sense of balance; my sinuses; the taste of my meals. And nothing will get rid of it. The other day I boiled cloves and cinnamon sticks (as rec-ommended by Martha Stewart). They didn't stand a chance. Neither did my electrical air freshener, which short-circuited after twenty min-utes. I've scrubbed the floors, doused the ceiling, sprayed half a dozen varieties of orange cleaner and liquid bleach into the air. After long periods indoors, my nose self-anesthetizes: it learns to ignore the hor-ror. And when I go back outside, I barely notice the difference. Then I come home and—*bam!*—I'm doubled over, head down, palm flat against the wall for balance, tears streaming from my eyes. The spasms come hard and fast. Yes, it's *bad*, this stink. It reminds me of . . . despera-tion. Male desperation. Perhaps that's why the women of LA won't come anywhere near me.

Perhaps they can *smell* the Desperate Period.

"Sally. Huge favor," I said, tightly. "Can you get me a couple press tick-ets to this, er, Walt Disney concert thing?"

It was the morning after the lunch with Courage, and I was still in my apartment, wearing only boxer shorts. There will come a time when all business is conducted by home workers in their underwear. I tried to make the question sound offhand but I felt adrenaline surge through my body like storm water in a hurricane. By the time I got to "thing," my throat had contracted to the width of a flea's armpit. I wondered if the smell of desperation could travel via telephone.

Eventually, Sally stopped laughing.

Then she said, "I can't believe you did it."

"Did *what*?"

She couldn't possibly know about the Courage situation.

More laughing, then Sally said, "Oh, I know about the Courage situation."

A heated vial of embarrassment now spilled into my bloodstream, fizzing and smoking as it mixed with the adrenaline.

"Courage told you?"

"Courage Macleod thinks very highly of you, Mr. Ayres," said Sally, the laughter now long gone. "Your ears would have been burning. But from what I gather, she's going to be very disappointed."

"I was hoping you could help me with that."

"She certainly enjoyed your war stories. The tank attack, in particular. We agree that you should write a book."

"Sally, you *must* be able to get me press tickets."

Sally either didn't hear me or wasn't interested in listening. "Are you really going to go back?" she asked.

"Uh?"

"To the Middle East?"

"Yes. No. I mean . . . the tickets, Sally. What about the *tickets*?"

"No chance, I'm afraid."

"What?"

"Look, there's no press. I wish I could help. Besides, Courage was under the impression you already *had* tickets"

"I could pay."

"Ten thousand dollars each. And they're sold out. In fact, I've just seen the waiting list."

"Who's on it?"

"Bono."

I groaned. "Come on, Sally. There's always press tickets. That's why they built the damn thing in the first place. To show it off, to prove that LA has culture, to tell the world they're not a bunch of . . . you *know*."

"Airheads. And that's nonsense. There are airheads in every city." There was a rich pause, during which I sensed Sally might be about to break. Then she exhaled and said, "I suppose I can get you red carpet, with the paparazzi. But you couldn't take Courage. Not unless she posed as a photographer. But I hear she spends an awful lot of her time avoiding photographers."

I began to marshal a final plea but called a retreat at the last moment. Sally's firepower was overwhelming. Perhaps my date with a supermodel was as doomed as my date in Neverland with Lara.

"I warned you," said Sally, sharply. "Courage has a boyfriend, and a very wealthy one to boot. From what I hear, it won't be long before Dickie makes it onto the *Forbes* billionaires' list."

Dickie? His name is *Dickie*?

I wanted to start beating the phone against my desk but restrained myself. Then Sally's tone finally warmed.

"Just give up on this one, Chris. Make an excuse. Say you've got to leave town for a news story. She'll understand."

"You think?"

"Of course she will."

Give up? No chance. I clung to hope like a mother clings to a newborn. I cradled hope, nursed it. The upside of desperation, at least, is that it makes you try harder. Fortunately, I am also an experienced ticket scavenger. In London, I used to devote weeks with my friend Glen to penetrating the fortified entranceways of every event on the social calendar, from Madonna's birthday party at some cobwebbed pub in Notting Hill to the latest James Bond premier in Leicester Square. We became experts at deploying tuxedos, vaulting security fences, bribing doormen, and enlisting posh friends to double as assistants. I know the deal with these big events: there are always tickets reserved for celebrities who never show up, along with backup seats for their flunkies, which remain unfilled until the final hours before the show. The custodians of these tickets are usually publicists, working either in-house for the venue or for an outside firm, usually hired by a sponsor or some affiliated organization. But whom to call? Sally clearly wasn't going to help, and I had no idea which PR firm was involved with the opening gala. Then I remembered once meeting the woman responsible for publicity at the Los Angeles Philharmonic Orchestra, which would be taking up residence at the Concert Hall. She seemed as good a place as any to start.

I began to throw open the draws of my plastic Ikea filing cabinet, flinging out household bills, expense forms, medical records, blank discs, paper clips, photographs, parking tickets . . . ah, here we go: business cards. I thumped the pile on the desk and fanned them out, searching for the raised blue logo of the Philharmonic. I saw Sally's card, Courage's card, and several other cards from Aston Martin and Range Rover salesmen, trophies from fantasy weekend car-shopping trips. Then, finally, I glimpsed it: the Philharmonic's logo, underneath which was written the name "Bianca Sweetingham, PR Director." It was followed by several phone and fax numbers and an e-mail address. Holding the card aloft like a sporting prize I performed a brief victory dance. The dance is essentially the same as my childhood excitement dance, which involved a frontward arm waggle, like a squirrel on amphetamines. A particularly good car brochure could provoke the excitement dance. That, and a new Lego set. Over the years, the dance morphed into more of a drumming motion, like air guitar, but easier to mistake as the onset of an epileptic seizure. The routine is typically accompanied by the vocal simulation of a snare drum. No one has ever seen or heard me do the dance as an adult, and I'm happy for it to stay that way.

Shaking, I picked up the phone and dialed Bianca's number.

It rang. Then,

"Hello?"

The voice was harried and sour.

"Ah, yes. Hello. I'm looking for Bianca."

"This is she."

Think posh. Think posh.

"This is Christopher Ayres."

I pronounced Ayres like Aay-*ahs*, with a lingering "s," and followed the introduction with the name of my newspaper, ending it with "of London," for maximum snob appeal.

"Ah, Mr. Arse. Hello."

"Aay-*ahs*. It's Aay-*ahs*. I'm calling about my tickets, to the gala." It was a bold move, this. But I had no choice.

"Your tickets?"

"Oh. I thought my assistant, Annunziata . . ."

A baffled silence. Then Bianca said, "Hold on, let me take a look."

I congratulated myself on coming up with the name Annunziata. It sounded terrifyingly upper class. Nevertheless, I wasn't entirely sure how to continue this ruse. Clearly, my name wasn't going to be on the seating plan. I felt my mouth go suddenly dry. The electricity had gone out again and the air conditioner was down. My entire body now had a saltwater glaze.

"Can't see you here," said Bianca, clicking her tongue.

"Really?" I said, faking astonishment. "And you're looking under the correct name, Christopher Aay-*ahs*?"

"Yes. But you don't seem to be—"

"I'm the one doing the piece on LA's emergence as a capital of global culture. The architecture correspondent."

"Architecture correspondent?" said Bianca, now sounding genuinely concerned. Music critic would have been the more obvious title, but also easier to check. And I didn't want her checking anything.

"Recently appointed," I added.

"I'm sure we can get you on here somewhere. Let me see." I imagined a seating chart spread over her desk, like battlefield intelligence.

"Yes, right here! Okay, you're good. I've got you two seats, upper balcony, near the back. It's all we have left available, I'm afraid. Does that sound okay?"

I couldn't believe how easy this had been.

"Mr. Aay-*ahs*?" said Bianca.

"Thank God," I said.

"Sorry?"

"I mean, er, thanks. Good."

"You're welcome. I'll messenger the tickets to your bureau today. Call me if they're not with you by five o'clock. We look forward to seeing you on Thursday, Mr. Aay-*ahs*. And have a safe flight."

Flight? She didn't know I was calling from LA?

"Will do," I said, as a smile tugged at unfamiliar muscles in my face.

Bianca allowed herself a brief giggle. "It's going to be very exciting."

She had no idea.

Everything seemed to be going suspiciously well. I had two tickets to the opening gala of the Concert Hall. I had a date with a supermodel. I even had a new plasma TV, en route from an online megastore up in Seattle. I could sense a tension, a knot, in the very fabric of the Desperate Period. Even the smell in my apartment was waning. Was this the beginning of a new era, a new me?

My immediate concern was getting into shape for the big day. And where better to do this than Los Angeles? In LA, you are only ever a couple of phone calls away from a science-fiction rebirth. A credit application here, a down payment there, and, yes, I'll take the platinum teeth please; sure, give me all the hair you've got. I imagine ticking off items on an options list: bulletproof skin, X-ray vision, he-man chest, drumskin buttocks . . . and at what angle would you like us to set your new jaw, Mr. Ayres? Then there are the nonsurgical options: the whitening, tanning, bleaching, scrubbing, dyeing, conditioning, toning, and so forth, offered by those exotically scented boudoirs down in Boyz Town (the Face Place, the Leg Locker, the Buttock Bunker), the ones next to those unfamiliar-smelling supermarkets, where men in shorts and string vests buy food that puts science over any form of human pleasure: wheatgrass soybars, beancake pastries, wholegrain fruitstrips, multivitamin gelsteaks. Christ, it doesn't even *look* like food. Nevertheless, I'm all for self-improvement: a bit of rewiring here, supercharging there. I suppose I should be grateful to the gay men of Boyz Town for making this possible, or at least socially acceptable. Nevertheless, much of this manly preening remains beyond my comprehension. Anal bleaching, I'm told, is the latest Boyz Town gimmick. What's up with *that*? How much time do people spend looking down there, anyway? I'm told the porn business is responsible for this new craze—this explosion, you might say, in the anal improvement market.

After much internal debate I decided to limit my predate overhaul to a thirty-five-dollar spray-on tan. And so I made an appointment at Sunset Tan, located on the top floor of a strip mall on Sunset Boulevard, next door to a taco joint. They certainly went to town on the decor, over at Sunset Tan. The brochure describes the style as "evocative of a futuristic boudoir, with plasma screen TVs, brushed steel walls, frosted glass doors, silk drapes, candles, and a custom designed water sculpture." A futuristic *boudoir*? What is it with LA and these throwbacks to the pre-guillotine French aristocracy? If Louis XVI were still around, he would feel right at home here, what with the *valet* parking, and the *boudoir*-inspired tanning facilities.

The word *boudoir,* incidentally, means "sulking place." Not that anyone at Sunset Tan was sulking. Quite the opposite. They almost wept with excitement while telling me about the life-changing potential of modern tanning technology, and their belief that I should buy twenty sessions, at a bulk discount, instead of one. I too almost wept with excitement while being told about the life-changing potential of modern tanning technology. And so, trembling with anticipation, I was led beyond the reception and into a science-fiction maze of glowing plastic corridors. The tan itself was administered in a blue shower cubicle, in which I was instructed to stand naked aside from blue hairnet, blue slippers, and white gel on my fingernails. I emerged shivering violently, to an overwhelming stench of manure.

This stuff can't be good for you, I thought. And then the chemicals got to work. Ever so slowly, I turned from white to off-white, from off-white to light peach, and then, at last, from light peach to dirty orange.

There was no doubt about it.

It was a *miracle*.

And now to Tony's Tuxedos, at the other end of Sunset Boulevard, for galawear. The eponymous owner of Tony's is a big man, extravagantly Italian, and a few baked zitis short of morbidly obese.

"*Signore,*" he declared, after a long and exhausting frown. "We don't hava the panta short enough for your size."

"What?" I said, looking down at a U-shaped bald patch.

Tony lifted his face out of my crotch and said, "No pants in your size. *Sfortunato.*" Then he began to stand up. Again, this really took it out of him. I wondered if I should drive him to the hospital.

"I'm not that short," I protested. "I'm five eleven and a half." (I'm five ten and a half, actually, without shoes, but I've lied so often about this statistic that I now believe the fabricated number to be true.)

"*Signore—no, no,*" said Tony, waving his arms in apology. "Not so short. Ha-ha-ha. We just had whole orchestra to fit for tuxedos, for concert downtown on Thursday night."

"A concert?"

"Mrs. Disney pay for it all. Big event. *Very fancy.*"

Tony was now coughing violently into a fist the size of a meatloaf.

"That's where I'm going, too!" I protested.

The coughing stopped, and Tony said, "You play instrument?"

"No. I'm—"

"And we have no thirty-two-inch waist, *Signore.*"

"What?"

"Only thirty. Or forty-two." Tony gave another shrug, and the skin on his neck folded like the bellows on an accordion.

Oh, *bugger*.

I wondered if I should just buy a bloody tuxedo. The trouble was, I had already maxed out my credit card with the TV. There are only so many things you can upgrade in one week. This left me with the option of spending the evening in a ball vice or wearing my pants ghetto-style. Now Tony was holding out a pair of long-legged and tiny-waisted dress pants, perfect for a rock star. The jacket, meanwhile, was boxy and oversized, with padded shoulders. I put it on. As far as I'm aware, I've never looked good in a tuxedo. Clearly, this time wasn't going to be any different. Tony then produced a silk tie, in a light pink color, instead of the usual black bow tie. "Signore Clooney wear this tie," he said, with a strangely mournful smile. "Here. You should try." I held it up against the white shirt. It looked . . . slightly odd. The pink of the tie somehow made my spray-on tan appear fluorescent. Still, it was better to look like a bad imitation of George Clooney than a waiter on a Disney cruise liner. "I'll take it all," I said to Tony. Any further browsing seemed futile. Tony nodded graciously. He was now sweating so much his head was steaming. It was then, as I gave myself one last pitying glance in the full-length mirror, that my phone rang.

"Chris?"

Shit—the Beast.

A call this late in the day meant some old-timer had died, and they needed me to write up the late-edition obituary. Usually, I've never even heard of the celebrity and have to crib shamelessly from various fansites.

"Hi," I said, warily.

"Just to let you know . . ."

"Yes?"

"About this Walt Disney Concert Hall opening."

I laughed. For once, I was ahead of the game. It hadn't occurred to me that the Beast would actually be interested in the Concert Hall as a *story*. For once, my self-interest had done me a professional favor. "Already done," I declared, with a smug chuckle. "I'm going."

"Oh—you got tickets?"

"Yes!"

"Ah, well, jolly good. But just to let you know, you probably won't have to write anything."

"Eh?"

"We're sending over the architecture correspondent."

Oh for Christ's sake.

The Beast continued: "The desk wants him to do a piece on LA's emergence as a capital of global culture."

Silence.

"Chris?"

"We *have* an architecture correspondent?" I managed.

"He's trying to get tickets now. Talking to someone in your neck of the woods called Bianca, with the Philharmonic?"

I could only imagine the conversation. This was excruciating. "Ah, right," I said, as a pressure began to develop in my chest. I tried to let it out but the pressure kept building, as though I were a human blimp.

"Just wanted to give you a head up."

"Much appreciated," I gasped.

"Now you can just enjoy yourself. Get *pissed*." The Beast seemed to find this final thought extremely amusing (the Beast doesn't get out much). With an unhappy prod of my thumb I ended the call.

Fuck.

Now the damn phone was ringing again, buzzing and rattling and singing its annoying little strangled tune. This was probably Bianca, in need of some urgent answers. The number came up as "unknown."

Squeezing my eyes shut, I accepted it.

"It's Courage," said Courage.

"Oh, thank God," I sighed, blinking again. It was dark in Tony's Tuxedos, and what sunlight had made it through the blinds was hanging in the air, lighting up every last molecule like a science experiment.

"You okay?"

"Oh—yes," I coughed. "Fine."

"I have a question."

"Shoot."

"Do you happen to know which table we're on?"

"Table?"

"For the dinner?"

"Dinner?"

"You *know*. The after-show dinner, outside in the marquee, the one with the band and the midnight fireworks show?"

"Oh, *that* dinner," I said. I was beginning to wish I was back in the Middle East, being attacked by tanks. *Why hadn't anyone mentioned the fucking dinner? What's the point of going to the opening gala if you don't have a seat for the dinner?* It's always the way with these VIP events—you think you've skipped over one velvet rope, only to be presented with another, then another. I should have known from my experience in London: no VIP area is complete without its own VVIP area, which inevitably has another VVVIP area.

Courage sensed a problem. "Chris, don't worry," she said. "Honestly. It's great just to be going to the gala."

Her voice was pinched with disappointment.

"Don't be silly," I laughed, wretchedly. "Of course we're going to the dinner. Let me find out about the table."

"No, really, don't worry. You're so kind just to take me. I'll see you on Thursday."

"Want me to pick you up?" I offered.

"Great. At my office. Six?"

"Sounds good."

I hung up. Then I remembered the Jeep. I surely couldn't take a supermodel on a date in the Jeep. Still, it might not matter. Given the developing situation with the architecture correspondent, I'd be lucky to keep my tickets at all. *Bugger*. This was turning into Neverland: The Sequel.

*   *   *

Drunk, alone, his face ruined by booze and weather, the homeless man on the corner of Wilshire Boulevard and Alvarado slapped a filthy palm against the Jeep's window and opened his mouth, displaying a tongue like an ancient swamp creature, its skin cracked and bleeding and bathed in a green curd.

"God bless," he mouthed.

A red light, on my way downtown.

For a moment, we held each other's gaze: the privileged and the destitute, the consumer and the consumed. "God bless you sir," he mouthed again. From my anecdotal research, I've found that the simple, plaintive blessing is by far the most popular begging strategy of LA's homeless. There is, after all, a nuclear reactor of guilt in this city, and the blessing taps right into it, creating a brief but overwhelming current of yuppie shame. Hence the reason I was now reaching for my wallet, scavenging for a twenty. Yes, the guilt here runs strong. So too does the self-loathing: the autophobia. And as the world heats up—as the apocalypse nears—it gets stronger by the day. Now I could see something in the man's trembling hands: a scrap of cardboard on which he had listed his every woe, like a kind of anti-résumé: homeless, alimony, cripple, bankrupt, government, AIDS. I blinked and saw green. And then I was off. That's the thing with guilt: it requires a captive market.

Now heading southeast on Wilshire Boulevard I looked up. The sky was suffering from indigestion, probably brought on by the heat wave and the Santa Ana winds, which suck hot air and dust from the Mojave Desert and spray it over Los Angeles, like a giant leaf blower. LA goes to pieces during these grittiest days of the Santa Ana winds. The streets begin to feel like a nightclub the morning after: used, disheveled, somehow ashamed. Not that the far-eastern stretch of Wilshire ever looks anything but ashamed. In the twenties, this street was known without irony as the Champs-Élysées. Today, one of the few remaining landmarks is the Ambassador Hotel, opened on New Year's Day in 1921 and closed in the eighties, twenty years after it had hosted an election party for Bobby Kennedy. The party ended with a bang, but of the wrong sort: Kennedy was shot dead in the kitchen. They're bulldozing the place now to make way for a school.

As for the rest of the Champs-Élysées, it's all low-rise Korean barbeque joints, street hustlers, Laundromats, dive motels, and the black lake of MacArthur Park, in which city workers found several hundred rusting handguns when they drained it as part of the Red Line subway construction project. MacArthur Park is now making an effort to look respectable, but the effort isn't convincing: like a mugger in a suit at a pretrial hearing. Strange to think that America's millionaires once came here to holiday, to lounge poolside at hotels long since demolished to make way for unsmiling men in fluorescent-lit booths, offering paycheck loans.

The Jeep banked left and upward as it rolled onto the concrete tightrope that links Wilshire to downtown LA. With the car balanced high above the rapids of the 110 freeway, I took in the scene ahead: LA's mock-Manhattan, like a life-sized movie set. But where the actual Manhattan teems and crawls and howls and barps, downtown LA just sits there, hypnotized by the drone of several thousand industrial air conditioners. I've long suspected that downtown LA exists only so Angelenos can look New Yorkers in the eye and say, *Yeah, we've got one of those*. The first time I went down there I could hardly believe it. Amid the upended razor blades of the skyline, several thousand street people huddle in the boarded-up lobbies of what were once the city's most fashionable hotels: the Alexandria, the Rosslyn . . . the Million Dollar Hotel. *The Million Dollar Hotel*? These days, you could barely build a garage in Bel Air for that kind of money, never mind a hotel. The facades of these ruined landmarks stare out at the filth and the madness with all the melancholy of a king reduced to sweeping his own servants' floor. At least the film crews provide a daily distraction, flying helicopters through tunnels, machine-gunning pedestrians . . . blowing up cars. I once read—or perhaps it was Sally Worthington-Haynes who told me—that the exodus from downtown began before World War II, when a cheap and seemingly inexhaustible water supply gushed into the swimming pools of Beverly Hills. The water had been diverted to LA from Owens Valley, two hundred miles to the northeast—all thanks to the genius of Bill Mulholland, LA's chief water engineer. *Genius* is a subjective term, of course. Up in Owens Valley there is now a moon-sized crater where a lake used to be. You don't hear much about it, apart from the occasional weather alert, caused by the millions of tons of toxic dust blown up from the lake bed during high winds. Yes, the people of Owens Valley know a thing or two about the price of a Beverly Hills swimming pool.

I swung hard left onto Grand Avenue as Wilshire dead-ended, my progress slowed by the force field of the traffic lights. It was then I finally looked up to see where I was going. And there it was—a giant steel butterfly, its wings lit from the street below, perched on the tip of Bunker Hill.

The Walt Disney Concert Hall looked as though it had landed on its foundations to rest; as if at any moment it could flutter upward and outward, swooping down over the ruins of downtown, causing the crack addicts to point up in wonder at the strange, mechanical creature emerging from the translucent sky. Up on Grand Avenue I could trace the outline of the after-show marquee, constructed from a tube of see-through plastic, presumably so the guests could watch the fireworks later on. Not that I'd be seeing the inside of that marquee—not after my failure to get tickets to the dinner. I felt a cold liquid anxiety spill into my gut.

But I had more urgent things to worry about. Perhaps you've already noticed something wrong with this picture.

I'm alone in the car.

That's right: Courage Macleod is not with me.

So there are a few things I haven't told you. Perhaps I should begin with my journey to Courage's office in Beverly Hills, where I'd arranged to pick her up at six o'clock. The traffic was bad, or at least worse than usual, and I was running late. Sweating in my tuxedo, I drove with my fist buried in the horn, swerving to avoid a head-on collision with a blonde in a Corvette. The narrow waistband of my pants was squeezing my intestines so hard I could feel them pushing up against my kidneys. This caused my face to redden, creating an unflattering contrast with my pink tie, which now didn't seem like such a great idea. It was going to be a long night. Finally, after another near-miss—this time a rollover as I swung down an alleyway behind Rodeo Drive, my right wing mirror cracking into a restaurant Dumpster—the Jeep emerged with surprising velocity into the one-way system of Roxbury Drive, shuddering to a halt outside Courage's building. I stopped in a no-parking zone on the right side of the four-lane street and switched on my hazards, a brilliant ploy to exempt me from a ticket. I wished I was driving a better car. In fact, I'd considered hiring a limo for the evening, but after the experience with Lara and the Armenian taxi driver I just couldn't do it. Tonight was far too important. Picking up my phone, I dialed Courage's number.

"I'm outside," I said, trying to ignore the pain in my crotch.

"Yes, I think I see you," replied Courage, in an unfamiliar tone. "Hold on, I'm coming out. I'll be two seconds."

Something was wrong. Something was definitely wrong.

I chewed on breath-freshening gum and fixed my stare on the glass doors to my right. As promised, they soon opened and out came Courage in a black cocktail dress, black stockings, and black heels. I wondered how I could possibly get away with standing next to her at a party. It would be like parking a rickshaw next to a Roman chariot. Courage was now doing that tiptoe run that girls in heels do when they're in a hurry. The pain in my crotch was becoming unbearable. When Courage reached the car she tapped urgently on the passenger-side window, motioning for me to open it. It was then, in a moment of abject horror, that I remembered that the Jeep didn't have electric windows. Courage knocked again, and I saw a frown develop on her otherwise flawless brow as I unfastened my seat belt and leaned over the center armrest, ducking down in search of the winder. With my threadbare scalp now bobbing inexplicably in front of her, I attempted to generate enough torque from my contorted position to lower the window. The pain in my crotch was now officially unbearable: my pants had my balls in a grip so excruciatingly tight I began to fear for my unborn children. Finally, the window began to move. It lowered in a slow, jerky movement, accompanied by an awful scraping noise, like a rock caught in a wood chipper.

"Aren't they electric?" she asked, when it was over.

"No," I explained. "They're not."

Courage smiled, the same smile that had once appeared above a free sample of French perfume in *Harper's* magazine.

At least there didn't seem to be a problem.

"Chris—there's a problem."

Oh for Christ's sake.

"Really?" I said, trying not to sound devastated. At least the pain in my crotch had now triggered a pressure hose of endorphins into my bloodstream. I was beginning to feel lightheaded, borderline delirious.

"I can't leave my car here overnight," said Courage. "I'm going to have to drive myself. Do you mind, terribly?"

It was an awkward moment. Suddenly the politics of our relationship had been exposed. If I drove her to the Concert Hall, it meant I had to drive her home. Or at least drive her back here to Beverly Hills, where she could pick up her car and drive herself home. Did Courage already know that this evening was intended as a clumsy date? Had Sally spoken to her? *Had Dickie been asking questions?* I began to realize the massive delusion I'd been under all along.

"Not at all," I said through a weak smile.

"Why don't you wait here for me, and we can drive down there in convoy? I'm not entirely sure where I'm going."

"Good idea."

The abrupt change in plan almost made me forget about the navigational challenge ahead. The parking lot of the Concert Hall was deep within the belly of Bunker Hill and therefore virtually impossible to find.

On an earlier reconnaissance trip, I'd ended up halfway to Palm Springs. To be honest, my internal compass has never been a reliable instrument. I have to think long and hard before remembering which way is left. In fact, I have to imagine a particular street in Wooler, the street where I first learned which way was left. Often, there's no time for this process, which means I have to guess, which means there's a fifty percent chance I end up going the wrong way, even when following specific directions. Once, in a rented car on an out-of-town news assignment, Jeff refused to speak to me for two hours after my repeated failure to follow his instructions. "Ayres, you're the world's *worst* driver," he kept saying, as he headbutted the dashboard. Nevertheless, I could hardly ask Courage to lead the convoy, so instead I watched as she tiptoed back through the gallery door, reemerging a few minutes later from the parking lot next door, at the wheel of her blacked-out Mustang, which gave the Jeep an unfriendly snarl. *This is romantic,* I thought. I imagined the alternative scenario, in a nondesperate universe: Courage and I, snug together in the cabin of a Bentley convertible, our laughter mingling with the soft notes of a Mozart piano concerto.

It took us more than an hour to get there.

This was largely because of the route I took, which ambitiously bypassed downtown's one-way system leading us directly—at least in theory—to the Concert Hall's subterranean parking structure. After passing the same intersection in Korea Town for the third or fourth time I glanced in my rearview mirror and saw Courage raising her hands in exasperation. Overall, however, I like to think my navigation was confident and precise—masterful, almost. Nevertheless, I was surprised to find the Concert Hall's underground garage almost completely empty. Where the hell had the other guests parked? Perhaps they'd all arrived in stretch limos, I thought.

Stiff and yawning from the journey, we climbed out of our cars and faced each other under the medical scrutiny of the fluorescent lighting.

"Isn't there valet?" asked Courage, her voice bouncing off the concrete walls.

"Don't think so," I said.

"Strange."

"Yeah."

"Oh well."

That smile. Oh, that *smile*.

"You look great," I offered.

"So do you," said Courage, with a look of sympathy.

Now we were late, speed-walking toward a stainless steel elevator,
which hummed efficiently like an expensive kitchen appliance as it
pulled us out of the parking garage and up to the Concert Hall plaza.
Seconds later, the doors opened to reveal a vast and empty red carpet
—a red sea, almost—on which stood several hundred abandoned tri-
pods, like plastic tree stumps. Christ, we were *really* late. I was briefly
taken aback by the scene, but Courage kept going, cantering forward
on thoroughbred legs. Trying not to worsen the damage to my crotch,
I shuffled quickly to catch up. Terrible agony. A lone paparazzo stood
guard at the hinged glass entranceway: not a real paparazzo but a hired
one, to make the noncelebrities feel important. He was bored, guzzling from a can of soda, his camera and elaborate flashgear hanging
loose around his neck. I suspected he was wondering if he had time
to sneak a cigarette, or maybe finish the last half of a chocolate bar.
Behind him, I could see a woollen-hatted mob jostling for attention,
holding up a sign that read, "For the Rich Overabundant Opulence,
for the Poor the Boot." Couldn't they have come up with something
catchier? Behind the protesters were several dozen Mexicans in red
jackets with the word VALET emblazoned on the back. I hoped Courage hadn't noticed them.

The fake paparazzo became briefly animated as we approached,
then seemed to lose interest at the last minute. "Picture?" he offered

lazily, as we neared the door. Courage either didn't hear him or didn't care to hear him, and her pace quickened, approaching a gallop. I half expected her to swing the door in the paparazzo's face, sending him crashing into his equipment.

I was trying hard not to dwell on the situation with the architecture correspondent—who I assumed was already seated inside the auditorium—or the after-show event to which we hadn't been invited. I would almost certainly have called Bianca Sweetingham to beg for seats at the dinner had it not been for the colossal embarrassment of the Foreign Desk sending over the exact same journalist whose identity I'd clearly stolen. My strategy with the tickets that Bianca had already couriered over to me was simply to keep them, maintain a dignified silence, and hope to God they hadn't been canceled by the time we made it to the door. Only now was I beginning to recognize the magnitude of the potential disaster if this gamble didn't pay off.

On we went through the echo of the foyer to a pair of grinding escalators, like inverted Caterpillar tracks, which we rode up to a carpeted public area, where a bank of elevators stood, open-mouthed. Courage was maintaining an almost superhuman speed and hadn't looked behind her once. I was breathing heavily, my balls now trapped somewhere in my left pant leg. There was no way I could tend to them in public, so I tried to ignore the pain. Soon we were being winched upward again, the elevator plinking softly as we passed each floor. It was a long ride. How many floors did this place have, anyway? My ears popped. Finally, after a jolt of high-altitude turbulence, the elevator came to a giddy halt. From this height, I thought, we'd be lucky to see the stage, never mind the musicians.

A frowning usher greeted us. She beckoned aggressively for our tickets. Courage struggled to hide her impatience as I pulled the two heavy cardboard slabs from my jacket pocket in slow motion. My heart was now thumping in a relentless techno beat, and a poison was gathering in my gut, demanding to be set free. The usher's frown became more complex as she studied the tickets. She looked up, revealing an unsympathetic face: flat, wide, the angle of the cheekbone suggesting great skepticism.

And those eyes: Christ, those eyes! They could probably see through lead, never mind the bogus legitimacy of my credentials. "Together?" she growled, making it clear that her examination of the tickets had entered only its initial phase. We nodded yes. The usher now unclipped a walkie-talkie from her belt and mumbled something into it, her mouth almost touching the plastic. *Just let us in,* I kept thinking, *just let us in.* Other ushers, bigger ushers, were now walking quickly toward us. Should I just make a run for the door? Now we were surrounded on all sides: gate-crashers at a billionaires' ball. I was beginning to wonder if we would end up spending the night in a skid row jail. "Take me, not the girl!" I imagined myself begging. "The girl's got nothing to do with it!" And then, in an instant, it was all over. The usher pulled open the door to the auditorium and practically shoved us through.

"Last guests arrived," she told the walkie-talkie. "Doors closing. Repeat, doors now closing."

So there we sat—the reporter and the supermodel, the frog and the princess—on this strangest of evenings. I felt a shudder of vertigo. Nerves hadn't bothered me for a while, not since that incident at the Bentley party, but now I felt them return: a familiar molten dread, accompanied by a paranoid fantasy of nausea, of throwing up on the blue curls and spangled dress of the woman in front of me, which prompted more dread, then more paranoia, then more dread, and so on, until it became a virtual certainty that I would throw up on the blue curls and spangled dress of the woman in front of me. The acoustics of the hall weren't on my side. Every shift of my buttocks, every curl of my toes, was amplified and broadcast in three-hundred-million-dollar clarity to the hushed crowd of industrialists and socialites. I had also become acutely aware of the smell of my fake tan, which I noticed was leaving an orange stain on the cuffs of my shirt. There it was again: like fertilizer, like plant food. I tried to focus instead on the giant organ behind the stage, its rectangular wooden pipes gathered together haphazardly, like firewood, like a bag of McDonald's french fries.

"What do you think?" asked Courage.

"Of what?"

"The *hall,* silly."

This was our first conversation since the parking lot.

"Oh, it's . . . nice."

Nice? Was this the best architectural criticism I could manage? Courage widened her eyes and rearranged her stockinged legs, so that the tiniest part of her thigh was now resting against the tortured fabric of my pants. No doubt this was unintentional. Nevertheless, I become suddenly concerned about the effect any lower-abdominal swelling could have on the crotch situation, which was already pretty serious. I feared my pants might actually explode.

Courage leaned closer to me and said, "You know what I think?"

I gave an expectant shrug.

"I think . . ."

"Yes?"

Courage hesitated, and I could see a decision make its way tentatively across her face. "It looks like a *vagina,*" she said.

With the word *vagina* I let out a tormented moan. It might have been the pants, or it might have been something else, something more complicated. Fortunately, the noise escaped at the precise moment a woman onstage began to perform "The Star-Spangled Banner." As she sang I looked around me, at the convex walls and the swollen ceiling, and for a moment I imagined myself trapped inside a giant wooden birth canal. It was then I noticed Courage giving me one of those lip-sucking faces, as though she found my squeamishness privately amusing.

The acoustics of the hall made it impossible to talk during the rest of the first half. As a distraction, I looked at the program, which informed me that we were listening to Charles Ives's "The Unanswered Question." I began to wonder why composers' biographies are always so *depressing.* The format is always the same: the promising youth, the euphoric yet fleeting creative period, and then the slow decline, the mental breakdown, the syphilis, the bankruptcy, the divorce, and of course the slow death, usually from something involving boils. Weren't there any *happy* composers? Not that Ives had it so bad: he went to Yale, founded his own insurance company, and suffered only occasional psychotic bouts ("heart attacks," as his family called them). Nevertheless, the program noted that Ives's music was ignored during his lifetime, and that he eventually gave up hope, fell ill, and died. I concluded that it was simply the inevitability of death that depressed me, the laughable brevity of our ambition.

Now I was consumed by "The Unanswered Question," which sounded as though it had been composed for a synthesizer, with the disadvantage of having been written several decades before the invention of the synthesizer. It hovered and pulsed, bleeped and clanged, as if a gospel choir had been abducted by a UFO and its members had their vocal cords replaced by superior alien technology. Ives was certainly ahead of his time: one part of "The Unanswered Question" was performed in surround sound by a trumpet behind us. The program noted that the trumpet "posed the eternal question of existence." This was an appropriate theme. Ives's gloomy biography, the agony in my crotch, and the stress of the date with Courage had caused me to question my own existence. What exactly was I trying to achieve this evening? What did I want from Courage Macleod, anyway? I looked over at her. She was also reading the program. Then she looked up and our eyes crossed paths, prompting urgent diversions. Perhaps we'd end up being friends, I thought. Not that friendship was ever part of this plan, this *mission*. Then again, it was almost certainly the only option.

An intermission followed, during which I gulped two glasses of champagne as Courage was approached by several older men, all of whom seemed to know her well. "Where's Dickie?" they asked in turn, before pummeling her with several follow-up questions regarding Dickie's recent achievements in various glamorous, exotic fields. I realized at that moment that I never, ever wanted to meet Dickie. Courage tried her best to manage the discomfort of the situation, avoiding any specific description of our relationship when introducing me to her interrogators. Soon enough a bell rang and we began to file back inside. That was when I turned and glimpsed a familiar outline behind me: female, thirtyish, puzzled. Slightly annoyed, perhaps. Then she waved. "Mr. Aye-*ahs*? Mr. Aye-*ahs*?" Oh no. I tried to hunch down, to sink below the riptide of tuxedoes, but the harpoon had already been fired. Fear pulled at my intestines. "Christopher!" she bellowed. Courage now shook my arm. "Someone's calling you," she said. Trapped, I turned to see Bianca Sweetingham elbowing her way furiously toward me: a tiny, poised, glittering creature—glittering but *sharp*, like an industrial diamond. "Ah, Christopher," she said. "I thought it was you." I turned to Courage and beckoned for her to go on without me. But Courage had already stepped aside from the crowd and made a face signaling that she would be happy to wait, at a respectful distance. Bianca's face soured as we shook hands. I waited for her to make the first accusation, to let off the first round, but nothing happened, and she just stood there, studying me as a young boy might study an insect trapped in an upturned jar.

"How are you enjoying the performance," she asked, eventually.

"Oh, it's, er, good," I said.

"Good, good," Bianca nodded, seriously.

"Yes, it was very good," I added.

"Oh, that's *good*."

This was getting ridiculous. Couldn't she just get it over with? Then Bianca seemed to remember something.

She frowned and said, "I just talked to your colleague."

Here we go.

"Colleague?"

"Your fellow architecture correspondent," she said, with a surprising lack of sarcasm.

"Really?"

"Yes. A very interesting man. We're so pleased you could both make it. Are you working on the same story together?"

It was then I realized that American newspapers, far wealthier than their British counterparts, often assign multiple journalists to cover the same story. To Bianca, there was nothing at all unusual in this situation;

clearly, my newspaper would have *two* architecture correspondents, who would both be sent over to write an eight-thousand-worder on the Concert Hall. "Yes," I said, suddenly awash with relief for the first time in days. "But I'm working more on the, er, social angle. The scene. The *architectural* scene. The color. The . . . *excitement*."

"Interesting," said Bianca, again looking very serious. "And you're coming to the dinner, aren't you?"

"Dinner?"

"Didn't anyone call you? You're on the Disney table."

"*Disney* table?"

With that, the bell rang for the final call. Bianca produced two seat numbers from her purse before elbowing her way back to the other side of the room. I turned to Courage, who took my arm.

"Good work," she whispered.

I would love to tell you that the dinner changed everything, and that under that million-dollar marquee, with its see-through roof that exposed the stars, an awkward evening turned into a profound meeting of two weary souls. In another book, a less desperate book, I would describe how at that huge circular table, with its silken tablecloth and platinum knives, we talked for hours, sharing histories, cross-referencing friends, recalling parties attended years ago ("Oh my God, you mean *you* were there too?"), and uncovering all those coincidences that men and women uncover soon before they become more than friends. By now you would be imagining the physical choreography between us: the mimicked postures, the unbroken glances, the scraping on the floor as our chairs edged closer together. I would tell you how I had led Courage by the hand to the dance floor in front of the jazz band, where the harmonies were as far removed from Charles Ives as candy floss from foie gras. Smiling, I would recall the scene that followed on the plaza: Courage checking her watch and saying a reluctant farewell, amid an explosion of color in the black stadium of the downtown sky. And I would tell you that it was then, under that fake gunpowder apocalypse, that I grabbed Courage by the waist and pulled her toward me, as she uttered her soft words of capitulation: "But Dickie! What shall I tell him? He's a *good* man . . ."

But of course I didn't steal Courage away from Dickie. The only thing I managed to steal from anyone was a breadstick, from the eighteenth cousin removed of Walt Disney, who was sitting next to me. Dinner was interminable, and the breadstick theft partly revenge for my having to shout meaningless observations into my neighbor's hearing trumpet—"I'm from England. No, *England!*"—while Courage was wooed aggressively by the man to her right, who couldn't have been a day under ninety-five. Meanwhile, in front of me, Warren Beatty kept throwing his head back and laughing at something the blonde across his table was saying. Why couldn't I have been on *his* table? As far as I could tell Beatty was the only recognizable celebrity at the gala, and he was enjoying the attention immensely. The other guests weren't the kind of people who appeared in the press. They were the kind of people who owned the companies that owned the companies that owned the press. The most satisfying moment of the evening came at about ten o'clock, when Sally Worthington-Haynes shimmered past the table. Her dress might have cost as much as the marquee itself. When she saw me, she had to steady herself against the back of Courage's chair. Then she saw Courage and became even further disabled by laughter. "You're something else, Mr. Ayres," she said, shaking her head.

"No press, eh?" I replied, with as much restraint as I could manage.

"I don't know how you did it."

By now, Courage was being approached by another one of her elderly male admirers, and Sally pulled me aside

"Are you sure you know what you're doing?" she asked.

"I know, I *know,*" I hissed. "Dickie's a very rich man. Don't worry. I don't think Dickie has anything to worry about."

Sally studied me for a moment, then laughed some more.

*   *   *

It was just after midnight—and just after the fireworks—when Courage made her inevitable move. "I must go," she said, with sudden urgency. "Thank you so much, Chris. We must have lunch again soon."

With that—and with a brief, transactional kiss on the cheek—Courage Macleod was gone. I drained my wine, stared at the back of Warren Beatty's head for a while, then decided I needed a cigarette. A packet of cigarettes. When I was sure that Courage had left the Concert Hall, I walked back to the Jeep and edged it out onto Wilshire Boulevard, this time heading west, toward Beverly Hills. I was in a curious mood. Something was happening, I could feel it. Forces were at work. Events and people were streaking toward me like meteors, like weather. I wound down my window and let the air burn my face for a while. It was then I spotted the fluorescent oasis of a gas station and pulled over to buy the cigarettes I no longer wanted. By the time I was back on the road I realized why I was feeling so odd.

I was drunk.

And yes, there was a police car behind me.

8

Ah-Ha Kwe-Ah Mac
(The Place Where it Rains)

My plasma TV arrived this morning, along with a new, ultra-violent weather system from the desert. When the man from UPS rang the doorbell, the wind was blowing so hard outside I thought he had come to announce the apocalypse. Yes, these Santa Ana winds could make a thermonuclear blast seem like a light ocean breeze. The weather people are blaming it all on a high-pressure bubble out in the Great Basin, which is pushing air downhill toward LA, where it is being funneled through the mountains and dried out and superheated along the way. Whatever the problem is, it's serious. As I signed for the delivery the lights buzzed on and off in my apartment, and chunks of stucco dropped from the wall in the courtyard, smashing into the fountain below. The UPS man winced and clutched at his hat.

"New TV?" he shouted through the gale.

"Yeah."

"*Big.*"

"Yeah."

"Can you smell smoke, by the way?"

"No," I said. "Why?"

"Thought I could smell smoke."

"It's the wind," I told him. "It's making you paranoid."

The box for the TV was so big I could barely get it inside. When I climbed on top to knife open the lid I found that it was designed like a

Russian doll, with several outer layers and a delicate, foam-cushioned core—to protect the giant TV during its odyssey across the Pacific. The bigger surprise came when I tried to lift the thing out of its cardboard cocoon: I couldn't. Flatscreens might look slim and delicate but they're heavier than lead dipped in concrete. I was planning to hang the TV on the wall, but now I feared for the wall. How much *is* a new wall, anyway? Three hours and four trips to Radio Shack later, I managed to get it fired up. Every conceivable input of color and sound required its own special triple-insulated cable with its own special platinum-coated dongle. The manual even recommended a separate two-hundred-dollar power conditioner, to ensure that only the purest, finest, most succulent electricity enters the TV's high-maintenance, Chinese-made circuitry.

Sweating, stripped to my boxers, and matted with dust from lying on the floor, I finally located the ON button. I will say this: the picture is dramatically different than that of my old TV. For example, it's a lot bigger. Tuned to CNN, I can now see every pixel in Larry King's face. The manual tells me that if I want to make the pixels smaller—and the picture sharper—I will need to buy a new high-definition receiver and a new high-definition cable subscription. And then, after I have acquired both of these things, I will need to buy a new high-definition TV. Say what you want about obsolescence, but it doesn't waste any time these days.

I sat there in the living room for a while, flipping through channels until I settled on a local news station. It told me that the winds were doing their best to take out the entire LA power grid, which was already in trouble because of the heat and the number of things plugged into it, which had apparently reached a new record this year. Customers of the Los Angeles Department of Water and Power were being advised to switch off energy-inefficient devices, such as plasma TVs. Eh? I could have sworn that my TV was an energy-efficient model. Not so, said the news: the average plasma TV uses as much electricity as a refrigerator (it certainly *weighs* as much as a refrigerator, I thought).

Then an environmentalist came on to accuse the LADWP of getting its electricity from coal-fired power stations, which release millions of tonnes of carbon dioxide into the atmosphere every year, thus trapping heat from the sun and worsening the drought in the southwest. Sooner or later, said the environmentalist, California would simply begin to combust, resulting in fires worse than those inflicted on Dresden during World War II. "Do you think the average American is aware," he asked, "that a plasma TV runs on *coal*?"

He looked upset, this environmentalist. Come to think of it, I was starting to feel pretty upset myself.

The item ended with a professor of some kind talking against a backdrop of the LA skyline. He explained that it was actually possible to *bury* the carbon dioxide produced by coal, but that if all the carbon dioxide produced by the world's consumers were buried the earth could theoretically inflate to twice its size—especially if people kept getting richer all the time, and buying more stuff, which needed electricity, which came from coal.

I reached for the OFF switch, but the LADWP beat me to it. With a bang and a reverse whine, the power went out.

All of which gave me more time to contemplate the other two things that arrived for me this morning: a bill from American Express and a book from Courage, *The Day of the Locust* by Nathanael West. The book was wrapped amateurishly and had an unusual postmark. I knew it was from Courage only because of her promise over that long-ago lunch in Beverly Hills to send it to me—a promise I hadn't believed for one second she would keep. Does the book mean there is still hope? Probably not, judging by the dust jacket: it promises a tale of "the would-bes, the never-wases, the hopefuls, and the pretenders . . . and the lies by which they live."

Yes, I think Courage had me figured out all along.

The AmEx bill was arguably more troubling. Added to the five-grand charge for those Neverland tickets was now a four-grand charge for a plasma TV. Which means I'm almost ten grand in the hole. Divided into affordable monthly payments of two hundred dollars, plus interest, it will now take me four years to pay all this off, unless I can find a way to make some money on the side. Still, there's always the prospect of raising cash by selling furniture, even though the proceeds from that were supposed to go toward buying *new* furniture.

Which reminds me. I must put that lamp up on Craigslist.

By early evening the power was back on, but Armageddon was still in progress. The front door was being shaken on its hinges as though a jealous weather God were trying to break in. The windows were closed, but grit blown up by the wind had still made it inside, leaving a tiny layer of dust on the furniture. I was reading *The Day of the Locust* and waiting for my dinner, which was on its way via LAbite.com, a new restaurant delivery service. I should have just called my local Chinese but I didn't have the energy to repeatedly shout my name, address, credit card number, and expiration date to the deaf, non-English-speaking woman who inexplicably takes the telephone orders. The people at LAbite must know all about this woman, otherwise I doubt they would have the nerve to charge not only for delivery but also for convenience, as though these two elements of its service are entirely unrelated. Not that *service* is included, mind you. No, this is billed at ten percent, on top of which you are more than welcome to make an additional gratuity. Gratuity is certainly the right word for it: it feels gratuitous. Still, you get your money's worth. The last time I ordered from LAbite my cheeseburger arrived in a blacked-out BMW driven by a blonde in a suede miniskirt and knee-high go-go boots.

I shuffled awkwardly on my grandmother's sofa. It really is *exceptionally* uncomfortable. Every day I find myself reaching down and removing a few more razor-edged feathers that have somehow worked themselves through the fabric of the covers. Where did they *get* these feathers? What breed of mutant duck did they find that could produce such deadly plumes?

At nine p.m., the phone rang.

"Ayres, can you smell smoke?" asked Jeff when I answered. I could barely hear his voice through the noise on the line.

"Why is everyone so paranoid about wildfires?" I said. "They're all all in San Diego, aren't they?"

"Turn on the news."

I did as Jeff said and found myself watching a massive column of fire leaping over an eight-lane freeway out in the valley, causing the cars to explode like Molotov cocktails. "WORST FIRES IN CALIFORNIA HIS-TORY," said the caption. "WINDS CARRY EMBERS FOR MILES."

I continued watching as the newscopter gained altitude and backed off from the blaze. Flames writhed for miles in either direction, like a purgatorial ocean. The news reported that the fire had started in the Cleveland National Forest but had merged with a dozen other fires across the state, resulting in a superinferno that was burning from San Diego County to Ventura County, north of LA. The fire was now a weather system in its own right: a tornado and a hurricane in one, feeding on the oxygen of the winds and meeting no resistance as it stormed through parched forests and wood-framed mansions in gated communities. With every minute it became wilder, more unstoppable. The smoke was already visible from space: plumes as black and filthy as the smoke from the burning oil wells in the first Gulf war.

Outside, another gust of wind assaulted the door, sending more dust through the cracks in the windows.

Smoke, I thought.

I could smell *smoke*.

We had no choice but to get closer to the fire. The Beast would get into the office at midnight, our time, and he would want a story. I could just imagine him sitting down with his morning tea and switching on the BBC, only to see the view of California from one of the weather satellites, which made the entire state look like a volcano, mid-eruption. The fires were so powerful, pilots were having to avoid burning debris at fifteen hundred feet. Reports were also starting to come in about casualties. In one mountaintop village, the bones of a woman had been found in her charred bathtub, along with the skeleton of her dog. A dozen others had been burned alive in their cars or where they stood. A volunteer firefighter had been killed when a flame the height of a ten-story building, traveling at a rate of one and a half acres per second, suddenly changed direction, overrunning his position. The other three members of his crew escaped, but with injuries—one of them had his goggles literally welded to his face, and his esophagus turned almost to charcoal.

So this was the plan: Jeff would meet me at the Leisureplex and we would drive to a former gold mining town called Julian, which was about two hours south of Los Angeles, in San Diego County. Julian was encircled by fire, and the firefighters had gathered there as though it were a modern-day Alamo, preemptively hosing down buildings and cutting back brush, in what everyone feared would be a futile effort to halt the progress of Armageddon.

It seemed like the most obvious place to go. The thought also shamefully occurred to me that it would be something to tell Courage about later: something to keep up the illusion of the war correspondent.

From the maps I had studied on TV, I guessed we could approach Julian by coming at it from below—first by driving south on the I-5, then east through what was left of Cleveland National Forest, and finally north up Highway 79. Theoretically, this would ensure we were moving through places where the fire had already been, rather than where it was going. We would get to Julian just after midnight, find some firefighters to interview and photograph, get a couple of hours' sleep in the car, then file a story sometime before breakfast.

After that, we could head back to LA.

And hope it was still there.

It took us an hour on the freeway to escape the gravity of Los Angeles and its endless, interchangeable boomburb, while a violent crosswind kept trying to force the Jeep into oncoming traffic. Finally, the electric glow of the city dimmed and became scattered, fuzzy pinpricks. The smoke was thickening all the while, seeping through the vents and reflecting the Jeep's puny headlights back into my face. My eyes kept watering. I was rubbing them when I saw the exit to Cleveland National Forest. The traffic lightened as we left the I-5, then disappeared altogether. I found myself strangely aware of the dark; the depth of it; the utter blackness.

The smoke had suffocated the moon.

"So what happened on your date with the supermodel?" asked Jeff, after a thirty-mile silence.

"Nothing happened. I got drunk. Then I drove myself home."

"You *drove*."

"I know, I know."

"And you got home okay?"

"A squad car followed me for a while. I didn't realize that a sweating man in a tuxedo driving at a quarter of the speed limit with all the windows open might look a bit suspicious. But they lost interest eventually, thank Christ. I wasn't *drunk* drunk. But I was over the limit. I could feel it."

"Ayres, stop *braking* all the time. You're making me car sick."

"It's the smoke. I can't bloody see."

It wasn't just the smoke. It was nearly midnight now, and I was getting tired. The road kept ducking and twisting and it seemed to be taking us nowhere. This area had almost certainly been evacuated over the past forty-eight hours. I wondered what lay beyond the blackness: what wreckage, what casualties. I was so consumed by the thought that I barely noticed the hooded shape when it appeared in the road. And then, with a terrible jump, I saw it: a human outline, staring right at us, holding up its hand. What was wrong with his face? It was . . . *covered* in something. Instinctively I braked and swerved, and for one hallucinatory moment I thought the Jeep had lost its balance, that we had been freed from the grip of the pavement and invited to explore the most violent laws of physics in the trees to our left. Instead we skidded to a halt in the middle of the road. *"What the fuck was that?"* I shouted. Behind us, something was moving in the white noise of the gale. I twisted to look but could see only the Jeep's taillights staining the smoke through the rear window.

"What *was* that?" I asked again.

The answer came with a heavy tap on the window and the sound of metal clicking against glass.

"Oh *shit,*" said Jeff, sinking into his chair.

I turned my head slowly. A filthy hand was pressing a sheriff's badge against the window. It belonged to a police officer. His face was a mask of ash. It looked like cake icing, as though he been in a food fight. Ahead, I could now make out the blue pulse of a squad car's lights, dulled by the fog.

Breathing again, I wound down the window.

"This road is closed," said the officer. "What the hell are you boys doing out here, anyway?"

"Highway Seventy-nine is closed?" I asked.

The officer was now leaning in so close I could practically tell what brand of cigarettes he smoked. He was examining the Jeep's cabin, as if hoping to find a corpse on the backseat.

"Evacuation area," he said.

"Ah, right," I nodded.

The officer shone a flashlight at Jeff. "Tell me," he said, slowly, "where are you fellas headed?"

Perhaps he thought we were looters, here to scavenge from empty houses.

"We're reporters," I said. "From LA."

"From Los Angeles, eh?" The officer laughed. "They have funny accents over there in Los Angeles."

"Accents?"

The flashlight almost blinded me. "If that's a Los Angeles accent, son, I'm a Tahitian showgirl."

Ah, yes—the accent.

"We work for the British press," I explained, fumbling around in my wallet for my press badge, which had expired. I handed it to him through the open window. "We're based in LA. I'm a reporter and my colleague here is a photographer. We're here for the fire."

"*Media*," he said.

"Is it safe for us to drive up to Julian?" I asked.

The officer laughed again.

"Be my guest," he said.

We drove on: a tiny hurtling mass of noise and light in an otherwise empty universe. The officer told us that we could use Highway 79 as long as we realized that we were on our own. At least the wind had calmed a bit, now that we had changed direction, although I was still aware of its proximity.

It was one o'clock now, and I was surprised that the Beast hadn't called. I looked down at my phone. "NO NETWORK," it told me. *Shit.* The towers must have been caught up in the blaze. I would have to call him later. And then I noticed something strange. It was the road. It was turning *white*.

"What's that?" said Jeff, sharply.

"What's what?"

I stomped down with my right foot to shift gears. Jeff switched off the map-reading light and leaned forward, squinting at the road. "Ayres! Stop!"

"*Eh?*"

"FOR CHRIST'S SAKE, STOP!"

The Jeep wiggled and shrieked.

The headlights struggled to penetrate the dust. Nevertheless, in front of us I could make out a dip in the road filled with water, the source of which appeared to be a pipe leading to a house on our left—the first house we had seen in a while. Only it wasn't really a house: just the naked structure of a chimney, some bricks, and what appeared to be a mound of black slime. In the driveway was a puddle of steel and four melted tires. It had never occurred to me that a fire could get hot enough to actually *melt* a car. It might as well have been made out of ice cream. In the darkness, we hadn't been able to appreciate the annihilation around us. Now it was becoming horribly clear. On the street there was another puddle of steel where a signpost should have been. Next to that was the charred stump of an electricity pole. It still throbbed orange in the wind. The high-voltage cable that had once been attached to the pole lay in a heavy tangle in front of the car, one end of it disappearing into the water.

"What happens if you drive into floodwater with a power cable running into it?" I asked, quietly.

I looked over at Jeff. His face appeared almost translucent in the dull glow of the cabin.

"Something very bad," he said.

We sat in silence for a moment, staring into the black water.

"*Shit,*" I said.

The moonscape illuminated by the Jeep's headlights reminded me of World War II footage from Dresden, just as the man on the news had predicted earlier in the day. What few trees remained had turned white and jagged, as if from the shock of what had been done to them. Most things, in fact, had turned white: the ash from the fire was as pure and as deep as snow. And yet hot embers continued to fall, glowing in the dark like fireflies. It was a strangely peaceful sight: a nuclear winter wonderland.

Somewhere around here, I reminded myself, entire families had suffered unimaginable deaths. I began to feel overwhelmed by sadness. Had they even managed to recover all the bodies yet?

"I wonder if they had a swimming pool," said Jeff, still looking at the ruins of the house next to us. "That's what you're supposed to do in a fire, y'know—jump into a pool."

"That's what they did in Dresden," I said. "They jumped into the water towers. They ended up being boiled alive."

"Jesus *Christ*, Ayres."

"You brought it up."

"I was talking about *survival* techniques. I wasn't talking about people being boiled alive, for fuck's sake."

"This is ridiculous," I said. "Let's head back."

"Look," said Jeff, handing me a crumpled printout from Mapquest. "The Cuyamaca firehouse isn't much farther. We can't head back now. It's one o'clock in the morning and we're already here."

I sighed and closed my eyes. Jeff had a point. "What kind of a bloody name is *Queer Macca,* anyway?"

"It comes from the Indians. Ah-Ha Kwe-Ah Mac."

"How do you know that?"

"Read it online. You'll never guess what it means."

"What?"

"Literally, 'the place where it rains.'"

We looked at each other for a second, then at the blizzard of ash outside. Perhaps it *did* used to rain when the Indians lived here. Perhaps it rained all the time.

"Bugger it," I said, as I swung the Jeep onto what was once someone's front lawn. The wheels spun in the ash, but we churned forward eventually, bumping our way around the water to the other side.

"Ayres?" said Jeff.

"Yeah?"

"Watch out for power lines this time."

Three minutes later I drove over a power line. It was impossible not to: they were everywhere. By the time we heard the thump it was too late. Perhaps the electricity had been switched off, or perhaps the rubber of the Jeep's tires was thick enough to absorb the shock. Whatever the case, we were still alive—and after driving over the first power line, the others didn't seem like such a big deal. Power cables weren't the only things in our way. There were more liquid street signs; more cars turned to puddles of metal; even animals, grilled on the spot where the flames had caught them. These charred obstacles kept looming out of the ash, forcing last-minute diversions. We made it to the firehouse by two o'clock. By then the wind had returned, even worse than before. I could barely get the car door open.

We weren't the only reporters there.

A TV crew from a national morning show had already set up its equipment inside the small wooden cabin, and an anchorwoman on a TV monitor—I guessed she was in New York—was doing an interview via satellite with the firefighters, most of whom were apparently volunteers and had been trying to save other people's property while their own homes burned. I learned from the interview that the fire had been work of a novice deer hunter named Sergio Martinez. The mug shot of Martinez on the TV monitor seemed to say it all: mid-thirties, weight problem, glasses with inch-thick lenses. Armed with his new rifle Martinez had made it only a quarter of a mile from his pickup truck before becoming hopelessly lost in the Cleveland National Forest. Scared, alone, and dehydrated, he did what he had been told to do in his hunters' survival course: start a "signal fire." Martinez hoped that the fire would attract the attention of a helicopter, but the flames spread too quickly and he ended up flapping around trying to put them out. Remarkably, he succeeded.

That was when Martinez made a very bad decision—a decision that surely ranks alongside some of the Very Worst Decisions Ever Made.

He started another fire.

It caught the attention of a helicopter, at least. It also caught the attention of anyone living within 440 square miles of his position, as this was the area utterly annihilated by the resulting blaze. So far, said the anchorwoman, the fire had killed fourteen, injured two hundred, caused eighty thousand to be evacuated, and destroyed four thousand buildings.

I almost felt sorry for Martinez. He had failed to realize a number of crucial facts about his environment before starting that second fire. For example, it never rains any more in the Place Where it Rains. The soil is dust and the trees are being eaten alive by a plague of sap-drinking beetles. Meanwhile, there has been a construction boom in the forest, which has brought with it fire departments and fire-extinguishing techniques, which means that the brush has been allowed to grow around the parched and infested trees, more brush than ever would have been allowed by Mother Nature—which would have kept it in check with smaller blazes caused by lightning, blazes that would have simply burned themselves out.

All of which explains how a solitary deer hunter, in a solitary moment of stupidity, was able to destroy an area ninety times larger than that destroyed by the nuclear weapon dropped on Hiroshima.

While the broadcast went on I moved over to the coffee machine at the back of the room and started talking to a battalion chief named Carl Schweikert. He wore the same icing cake as the police officer who had stopped us earlier, and his right arm was being held up in a sling. Schweikert's loss to the fire was total: his home, his business, everything he had ever owned. I felt like an idiot, standing there and asking him how he felt, jotting down his reply in my spiral notebook.

Schweikert asked me who I worked for, and I told him.

"The guys up in Julian have got a couple of Brits on their crew," he said, suddenly grinning. "Good guys. Funny accents."

"Brits?" I said.

"Yeah."

"*British firefighters?*"

Schweikert laughed. "That's your story, right?"

"What are they doing here?"

"Ask them," said Schweikert. "They're up in Julian. One of 'em married a local. The other's a contractor, I think."

"We're on our way to Julian tonight," I told him, now impatient to leave. Suddenly I was relishing the thought of calling the Beast. This story could be good enough to make up for Neverland.

"You should wait until morning. The fires aren't out yet. Those Santa Ana winds can change direction in a second."

I nodded blankly and thanked him again.

We couldn't wait until the morning.

Deadline was sunrise.

Julian, three o'clock in the morning.

There were no firefighters anywhere to be seen. No people at all. In the tunnel vision of the Jeep's headlights, we saw evidence of hasty evacuations. Photographs had been spilled from boxes onto front lawns. Clothing was strewn in hedges. Cars had been abandoned with their doors wide open. There were no streetlights, no traffic lights, no respite from the dark whatsoever. We found a parking lot next to an empty police station and sat there, listening to the wind and waiting for dawn. Would the Brits ever show up? I was beginning to doubt it.

"Do you ever get the feeling that everything's moving backward?" I asked Jeff, after ten minutes or so.

"Like what?"

"Like technology. We used to go to the moon. We used to have the Concorde. We used to have so much hope for technology. But now it all seems so obsolete. My plasma TV runs on coal, for Christ's sake."

"Ayres, if you bought a plasma TV that runs on coal, then you got even more badly ripped off than I thought you did."

"It's the *electricity* that comes from— Ah, never mind."

"Why are you worrying about this when we have a deadline in four hours and no sign of these bloody firefighters?"

"Because maybe we did it. Maybe we broke the weather. Maybe the heat wave isn't just some random cycle of the sun."

Jeff said nothing and prodded the radio awake. It buzzed and swooped for a while, then found a local news channel.

"The fire is the size of Rhode Island," said a distant male voice.

Another voice, also male, whistled in the background. "Are the firefighters getting it under control?" it asked.

"Not yet. Over there in Julian, the whole town has been evacuated. The firefighters are in a defensive position."

"Anyone still there?"

"No one in their right mind."

"Tell us about the forecast."

"The Santa Anas are still blowing at forty, fifty miles an hour. This is compressed and superheated air we're talking about. And just to make things a little harder, this part of California hasn't had a drop of rain in six months. *Six months*. Not a drop. And this is coming on top of a drought that has been going on for years. These are the worst possible conditions for fire season, Bob."

I reached for the OFF switch.

"No rain in *six months*," I said.

"Ah-Ha Kwe-Ah Mac," said Jeff.

There was nothing more to say, so we stared out the windshield into the blackness ahead of us. And then I saw it: a reddish-orange flicker on the horizon, getting brighter by the second.

It wasn't the sun.

9

We Are Liquid

Thick, brown, and streaked with yellow, a ring of smog made itself comfortable above the Hollywood Hills—a toxic sunbather, camped out in an otherwise pristine sky. With an uneasy smile, I looked down from the spoiled horizon and into the creamy pulp of my chicken Caesar salad. This was a late lunch—it would soon turn three o'clock—but I had lost my appetite.

This smog has come out of nowhere. At first they blamed it on "supercommuters": those wild-eyed carbon junkies, priced out of the Greenspan real estate bubble, who spend six hours a day guzzling coffee from armrest cup holders and being shouted at by FM commercials. But not even the supercommuters could account for so much crap in the air. Blame was quickly redirected to the *extreme* commuters: the briefcase and roller-bag crowd, the lunatics who leave their cars at the airport and fly on discount airlines. And yet the smog still made no sense. Climatologists were summoned. They double-checked their blimps, recalibrated their vanes.

Eventually, they found the problem: the city is *importing* smog—great plumes of it, each one up to three hundred miles wide. These killer clouds start out as dust blowing over the Gobi Desert. When the dust travels east over China it picks up soot from the factories and the coal-fired power stations, and together the dust and the soot cross the Pacific until they reach California, where they come to a rest over the Sunset Strip. Yes, the LA smog, like everything else now, is made in China.

I've been trying not to worry. Ever since the fire I've been making an effort to ignore problems beyond my control: debt, pollution, the "peak oil" scenario, the warming Atlantic, the cooling dollar. If America decides to close its factories and buy everything half-price from China, only to have China fuck up the sky in return, it's none of my business. What can I do? Besides, I have enough stress in my life as it is; stress such as Courage Macleod.

From the other side of the table she said, "Gosh, Chris. And then what happened?"

"The fires were coming for us," I sighed, with an expression that I hoped would convey a great resolve, a nerve unshakable in the certainty of death. "The flames were two hundred feet high. We didn't know if it was safer to stay or to leave. So we just sat there, in the evacuated town, *waiting*."

"To die?"

"It was a possibility."

"Gosh, Chris."

Lunch was Courage's idea. A thank-you for the night at the Walt Disney Concert Hall, she said. I wanted to ignore the invitation, or at least claim some kind of calendar clash, but deep down I knew this was never going to happen. Male egos just don't give up that easily. The invitation made me wonder about Dickie. Had Courage broken up with him? Had there been more to our date than I had imagined? Had I failed to decipher some kind of female code of attraction, back there in the Disney hall? Yes, male egos can take pretty much anything you throw them, and still they'll keep running back for more.

Courage told me to meet her at the Ivy on Robertson Boulevard. A strange choice, I thought. The Ivy is perhaps one of the least welcoming establishments in the world. You could dance into a kebab joint on the Gaza Strip draped in the Israeli flag and singing "Hava Nagila" and you'd

probably get a warmer reception. The waiters at the Ivy are so sensation-
ally unpleasant you're practically reduced to tears of gratitude when they
slam a plate down in front of you instead of smashing it over your head
and gouging your eyes out with the broken shards. The reason for the
attitude is the number of celebrities who use the restaurant's picket-
fenced patio—which is exposed to the street, and therefore to the
paparazzi—as way of getting into *People* magazine. The entrance to the
Ivy resembles that of a movie premier. Photographers, valets, bodyguards,
drivers, reporters, publicists, managers, and personal assistants can be
found clambering over one another like hamsters in a cage, while a stack
of violently hued Lamborghinis howl and barp in a holding pattern along
the curb. In theory, anyone can make a reservation at the Ivy, but it's
strongly discouraged. You hear horror stories, possibly exaggerated, about
unimportant diners being hustled by a bellboy through the Cape Cod
dining room (threadbare rugs, weathered antiques, crooked paintings,
and peeling woodwork) and on into a back room, then another back room,
then down three flights of stairs to a basement, through another door,
across a parking lot, and into a converted utility shed, in which a solitary
table sits directly in front of a workmen's Port-a-John.

Yes, you have to watch yourself at the Ivy. And you have to watch
the bill, too. A lobster salad and a bottle of sparkling water could max
out the King of Saudi Arabia's American Express black card, and you
don't want to sit there on your cell phone, next to Tom Cruise and a
delegation from the Church of Scientology, explaining loudly to a cus-
tomer service representative in India why he should authorize the transaction. Fortunately, Courage appeared to be on pretty good terms with
the restaurant's management: she had reserved a table in the prime real
estate of the patio, in full view of the paparazzi.

It was like being on TV.

"So what happened?" she asked.

"We just fell asleep in the car," I said. "What choice did we have?
What could we do? If we had left Julian, we might have driven

into the fire. So we stayed. And when we woke up—you'll never be-lieve it."

Courage widened her eyes with anticipation.

"*What*?" she whispered.

"It started to snow."

"Snow?"

"Snow." I snapped my fingers. "The weather changed, just like that. All of a sudden it was freezing bloody cold."

"And the snow put the fires out?"

"Pretty much immediately. Someone up there had obviously de-cided that enough was enough."

"What about your British firefighters?"

"About as British as Willie bloody Nelson. They'd gone completely native, accents and everything. Not that it mattered for the article. They showed up in a fire engine just before dawn. One of them took us up to see his house. There was nothing there, just the bricks around his chimney and a lump of metal that used to be his outdoor grill, all of it covered in ashes and snow. He was laughing it off but you could tell he was devastated. His wife was in tears."

"Poor thing."

"Yeah. The Beast loved it."

"The Beast?"

I explained. When I was done, Courage excused herself, and I tried not to look uncomfortable, sitting there on my own. I pretended to study a text message on my phone, even though it had no signal. I tapped my feet. When Courage returned she glanced around conspiratorially.

"So how have you *been*?" she asked unexpectedly, leaning in closer than before. Today Courage had abandoned her schoolmarm glasses and let down her hair. Today she wasn't ashamed of being a former supermodel.

"Busy," I lied. "But good."

"Chris," Courage ventured, biting her lip. "I've got something to tell you."

"Okay," I croaked, as the atmosphere around the patio seemed suddenly to lose its oxygen.

"It's . . . well . . ."

"Yes?"

A tanned and muscular man brushed past the table and Courage gave him a tiny, intimate wave. He grinned in recognition. "My friend Tony," explained Courage, proudly. "He owns a record label."

I nodded irritably. Tony moved on.

"You were saying?" I said.

"Ah, yes. My epiphany."

"Your epiphany."

"I want babies, Chris."

I felt an urgent relocation of blood to my face.

"It came to me the other day," Courage went on, oblivious. "I want them *now*, Chris. I'm twenty-six, you know. Why sit around and wait? I've never understood this modern theory that you should hold out for as long as possible. Have your babies early, that's what I say. Take off a couple of years. Then you're free to get on with whatever it is you want to do in life."

I emitted a strangled gulp, which Courage took as agreement. In fact, her baby strategy was the very opposite of my mission when I first came to LA. My plan was to max out on leisure, binge on self-gratification, until I could take it no more. I had wanted to get it out of my system. But what if you never get it out of your system? What if at some point you just have to make the decision to stop living for yourself? Are we even capable of this anymore? Look at Scott Peterson, the Californian fertilizer salesman. He was so upset by the thought of his pregnant wife ruining his lifestyle that he killed her on Christmas Eve, put their house up for sale, signed up for cable porn, bought a Mercedes, took up golf, grew a goatee, and started to spend a lot of time with a masseuse at Modesto's Sweet Serenity Day Spa. For a while I thought Peterson was just a statistical anomaly—the rare but inevitable boomburb sociopath. Then, when I was writing a story about the case, I discovered that homicide is the second most common cause of death for pregnant women.

"So there you have it, Chris," said Courage. "I'm ready." She laughed. "Never thought I'd hear myself say that."

"Courage," I said, feeling as though the organs in my chest might implode, "there's something I should—"

"Do you want babies, Chris?"

"I love babies," I declared, with unnecessary volume.

"*Really?*" Courage gave me a look of amused skepticism. "I hate the little buggers. They say you love your own."

"Look, Courage. There's something—"

"Um?" Courage looked up. My words had been rendered silent by a roar from a nearby table of celebrity basketball players. "Dickie's very excited," she said. "He's going to make a wonderful father."

I dropped my napkin. "Jesus Christ, Courage," I said, thickly. "I just can't stand it anymore."

The room seemed to go silent. I heard a whine in my ears like a subway station. I was about to jump in front of the train.

Pushing away her plate Courage frowned. Now I had her full attention. "Can't stand *what* anymore?" she said, slowly.

"Well . . ."

"Yes?"

"It sounds stupid, but . . ."

"Go on."

"No, it's nothing."

"Tell me!"

"It's . . ."

"Yes?"

"Carbon dioxide emissions," I spluttered. "The world's ending, Courage. Those fires were just the beginning. Global warming—it's going to get worse. Do you know where California gets all its drinking water? From the snow in the Sierra Nevada Mountains. And what happens when the snow starts to disappear? They're saying California will be uninhabitable by the year three thousand. Uninhabitable! If the race riots were bad in ninety-two, wait until we get the water riots. And soon everyone in China will be driving a car. That's a billion cars, Courage. *Shitty* cars, with no fuel injection, no catalytic converters. And that's before they start using air conditioners and buying plasma TVs. Then the Indians will get in on the act, and then maybe the Africans. Did you know the Indians are planning to build a car that will cost three thousand dollars? That's the same price as a DVD player in a Lexus! And why shouldn't they build it? How can *we* tell *them* that they're not allowed to live better lives? We're fucked, Courage. Everything's totally *fucked*."

"Gosh," said Courage, stiffening. "You've certainly got a lot on your mind."

"Yeah," I agreed, now slightly out of breath and staring dejectedly at my final forkful of lettuce and Caesar dressing.

I really did have a lot on my mind.

It was quite an outburst, I agree. The thing is, at the exact moment I decided against revealing my true feelings to Courage, I had to really *commit* to my diversion. I had to go all in. In the end, the effort was so convincing I began to wonder if it really *was* fear of the end of the world that had been bothering me all along. I began to wonder if it was Courage who was the real diversion.

But why the sudden change of plan? What signal had Courage given that caused me to finally accept defeat? I think it might have been something in the weariness of her tone, the anticipated disappointment of "can't stand *what* anymore?" As though the revelation of any romantic ambition would be considered professional flattery, of the most inconvenient, the most unhelpful kind. I felt like a ball boy at Wimbledon, about to stop play to congratulate the top-seeded player on his magnificent forehand. Coming from the other side of the net, the compliment might have meaning. But I wasn't on the other side of the net. I was crouched down behind the baseline, without a racquet, balls fizzing here and there above my head.

As for my spiel about global warming, Courage's response was typically academic. As my father might say, she's read more books than I've had hot dinners. Fear of a climate apocalypse, said Courage, is like fear of anything: it can be used to manipulate. For this reason she maintains a concerned agnosticism about many of the more terrifying apocalypse scenarios she hears or reads about. Meanwhile, she suspects that a good deal of my self-loathing is related to generational guilt, to the knowledge that what would have been considered criminally profligate during my 1980s childhood in Wooler is now considered relatively mundane in LA. All of this apparently makes me highly susceptible to the charge that human excess is bringing about the end of the world. This makes sense, I suppose. Then again, I can't help but feel that the main reason I'm susceptible when it comes to the charge that human excess is bringing about the end of the world is the fact that human excess really *does* seem to be bringing about the end of the world.

The lunch ended with a brief and unsettling discussion of *The Day of Locust*. Courage told me that Nathanael West—who was killed in a car crash while allegedly on his way to F. Scott Fitzgerald's funeral—was also fixated with the apocalypse. For West, however, it was "Okies"— the refugees who came to LA during the Dust Bowl and the Depression— who posed the threat. When West saw the Okies weeping and screaming on Hollywood Boulevard over a minor celebrity, he saw a plague of locusts that could bring to power an American Mussolini. I wondered if this was supposed to make me feel any better.

And then the check arrived, and I began to feel much, much worse.

No luck with selling my lamp on Craigslist. Perhaps this is because there are another 3,217 other lamps for sale on Craigslist. I've also noticed that the people who use Craigslist are, for the most part, completely insane. Take the posting I came across yesterday.

I have a bunch of junk in my fridge that I want to get rid of. I figure that instead of dropping everything in my trash can, I can get some guy to come over, get him naked in my bathtub, and I'll pour my rancid crap all over him.

This was followed by a thoughtful description of the items on offer, including "lots of beans, something I think was ham, red-now-green tomato sauce, spinach surprise, you name it." The posting concluded with an assurance that sex was absolutely not part of the deal. Oh, and there was a disclaimer: "You must be an extremely desperate and pathetic male to answer this post."

At least the garbage dumper was actually offering something, mind you. Other Craigslist postings seem comprised of nothing but rants, crazed theories, lunatic advice. I wasted a good ten minutes, for example, reading an essay entitled "Stop Patting My Fucking Head" by a short woman who apparently has to put up with a lot of people patting her head. This was followed by a posting under the self-explanatory headline "Do Not Handle Jalapeños and Then Have Sex." Clearly, I am not the only resident of this city with some extra time on his hands.

And yet I find something oddly exhilarating about Craigslist. There is a sense, amid all those billions of terabytes of human want, of human need, that almost anything can now be instantly traded: furniture, houses, friends, lovers, cars. These things, they didn't used to be so *liquid,* did they? They involved some kind of commitment, some kind of putting-up-with. No longer. Everything, everyone, at any point in time, can be liquidated.

Sometimes I wonder if I should just post something in "misc romance" and be done with it. Is there a readily understood abbreviation for "bald, ginger, and desperate"? I can already see the headline: "Male, twenties, BGD, seeks twenty-six-year-old supermodel." But I worry about personal safety. You probably heard on the news about that man in Glendale, the one who found himself tied to the bed in a motel room while his online date recited Satanic poetry and stabbed him twenty-two times with a ceremonial sword. In my current state, I'm not sure I could handle a night like that. No, I just don't have the *energy* for an evening of ceremonial stabbing.

Perhaps I would be better off in "casual encounters," the more gropingly honest subsection of Craigslist, where the postings are comprised largely of characters and numbers, indecipherable to the layman, yet nevertheless unmistakably obscene. Craigslist, of course, isn't the only marketplace for such uncomplicated trades. While skulking around in "casual encounters," I found myself directed to another Web site, AdultFriendFinder.com, which greeted me in a flurry of multicolored pop-ups, each one groaning and panting in its own little pornographic universe. It's a zoo in there—a wildlife documentary, with humans as the subject. Among its many boasts, AdultFriendFinder claims to be "the world's largest sex and swinger personals community," with more than 1.5 million listings in California alone. If this number is correct, then five percent of the state's population is searching online, *right now,* for casual sex with strangers.

Only five percent?

Whichever way you look at it, the Internet has given the twenty-first-century male the kind of sexual opportunity, the kind of sexual liquidity, once available only to sultans, pharaohs, kings, and the various members of the Rolling Stones. If Craigslist had been around a couple of millennia ago, perhaps even Khosrau II, of ancient Persia, might have thought twice about the expense and general inconvenience of his traveling harem of ten thousand wives. After all, the modern male, with his computer and his Internet connection, can now explore every whim, every kink, every twist, every preference—every vague curiosity—at any hour. Yes, while women have been busy ordering their Ivy League sperm from mail-order catalogues, men have been working on their own way to render the opposite sex obsolete.

Is any of this a good thing?

I suppose we'll find out, either way.

* * *

All of which raises the obvious question: Why do I continue to chase the impossible promise of Courage Macleod?

My failure with her has certainly been getting to me, perhaps more than I've let on. Late at night, to the sound track of the woman in apartment 53B, I've been seeking the advice of the closest thing I have to a life partner these days: the smell. Like a dutiful wife, the smell is always there to greet me when I come home; always there to kiss me good-bye when I leave. The smell talks to me during the day and whispers to me at night. I ask the smell if I should leave Los Angeles, leave America. I ask it if the Desperate Period will go on forever.

Not that I *want* to leave. Where would I go, anyway? London? Wooler?

I feel at home in this city. In LA, the future seems . . . so close. In one century, LA has gone from a town of one hundred thousand to a city of thirteen million. *Thirteen million*. It took London two millennia to grow to half the size. Compared with London, LA is on its first draft. Think of the revisions, the edits, the epiphanies to come. Stand on a street anywhere in this city and you can watch as the cranes erase and rework—correcting spelling, inserting punctuation. LA is flat and ugly, say the Londoners and New Yorkers. Yeah, well maybe *they* should try to build a city of thirteen million in half the time it took the Normans to put the roof on St. Paul's Cathedral. Of course, this onslaught of the future—helped along by Alan Greenspan's one-percent interest rates—brings with it a certain amount of apprehension. How much more can the city *take*?

But like I said, I've been trying not to think about things beyond my control.

Besides, I've grown used to the smell of the desert, to the wet fog of the mornings, the dusty fire pit of the afternoons. I like the pace of things here, the fantastic inconvenience of the time difference with London. Yes, life is good in this distant cosmos, on this planet far, far away. Perhaps I just need to take a moment—rethink, regroup, try something new.

Perhaps it's time I did something *bad* for a change.

* * *

"Aren't you feeling a bit *weird* about this?" asked Jeff, from the passenger seat of our rented cherry red Mustang convertible.

"Of course I'm feeling a bit fucking weird about this," I replied, braking for a cattle grid then stomping my foot into the deep-pile carpet, a move that produced a low, hollow rumble from the Mustang's big V8 but no discernible acceleration. We had just turned onto an unmarked road outside Carson City, Nevada. An hour earlier, we had climbed off an early-morning flight from LA.

I was ready now: ready for the Desperate Period to do its worst.

Jeff squirmed in his leather bucket seat.

"Let's stop for a drink first," he protested. "C'mon, Ayres. Let's get a *drink* somewhere."

"We've already had a drink," I said. "Two drinks. Besides, they'll give us more booze when we get there."

"I need a drink *now*."

"You didn't have to come."

With that, we fell into a fidgety silence. The road steepened, eventually flattening out as we arrived at a low, unmarked compound, guarded by an electronic gate and a steel fence decorated with razor wire. The gate rattled open automatically as the Mustang approached. I saw a surveillance camera nod and then follow our progress through the parking lot. I brought the Mustang to a halt in one of the spots near the entranceway, which was protected by yet another electronic gate, more razor wire, more cameras, and a high-tech intercom system. The temperature gauge on the dashboard read one hundred and eleven: enough to bring the devil himself out in a sweat. The long bonnet of the car seemed to bulge and ripple in the heat, its paint bleeding into the dust. We climbed out onto liquid blacktop. It was then I noticed a plaque above the spot next to us, the screws still gold and shiny. BOOT CAMP BERTHA, it read, with some pride. EMPLOYEE OF THE MONTH.

Standing side by side in a stale breeze, we looked up at the white clapboard structure ahead of us. The intercom coughed, and the gate in front of us began to grind sideways. Somewhere within the front door a heavy lock was relieved from duty. And then, through the strangled rasp of the intercom, came a giggle. "Don't just stand there, boys," said the giggle. "Come in."

We moved forward in a guilty shuffle.

Jeff pushed open the door a few inches, revealing a thin strip of blackness on the other side. We both paused. This was our last chance at redemption. "It doesn't *look* much like a brothel, does it?" said Jeff.

"No, it doesn't," I said, giving him a shove.

Beyond the threshold we blinked away desert afterburn as the door jerked closed on its springs. Christ, it was *dark*—strips of blue ultraviolet marked the outline of the room, at the far end of which was an empty bar area. It was empty because all thirty or so residents of the Twilight Kitty Lounge were lined up in front of us, each one dressed in a way that suggested she would be more comfortable, a *lot* more comfortable, out of her clothes. There was the short, busty German milkmaid; the tall, concave Russian model; the air-brushed American cheerleader; and every other combination of male fantasy profession and ethnic genre you could imagine. At the end of the line was a grinning fat man, in a supersized black T-shirt, Cuban cigar wedged between two thick fingers. "Gentlemen, welcome," he rasped. "Welcome to the Twilight Kitty Lounge. Ladies, back to your rooms. Hurry now."

With a clap of the fat man's hands, the girls hung their heads and tiptoed away, disappearing behind various black doors in the black walls of the lobby. The German milkmaid remained while another girl—not part of the lineup—emerged from what appeared to be a cashier's office and took a seat beside the bar. She was pretty, the other girl, and probably barely old enough to order a drink. She wore short-shorts in Hamptons white, jeweled flip-flops, and a skinny pink halter top. Her blonde hair was up in a ponytail.

"This is Bertha," said our host, taking the German's hand. "Our top producer this month. Bertha, these gentlemen are from London, England. They've come to write about us. I've invited them to stay the night."

This was all true—sort of. I had come to the Kitty Lounge out of curiosity, mainly. I wanted to see what it was like to opt out of dating, to meet women via credit card. I wondered if I was capable of it.

"Oh *my*," said Bertha, giggling again. She was clutching a toy rabbit to her chest and pulling on a pigtail. Bertha couldn't have been a day under forty, with eyes that expected nothing but the worst. Men always chose Bertha, we were told, because they felt intimated by the younger girls: with Bertha they had an ally, a coconspirator. Also, of course, Bertha would do *anything*.

"Jeff," I said. "Meet Bob. Bob Jones. He's the proprietor. You can talk to him about the, er . . . the photographs."

"Business, business," said Bob, shaking his cigar at us disapprovingly. "Let's sit down. Let's drink. Let's *relax*."

With that, we lowered ourselves onto a U-shaped sofa by the wall. The sofa was black. The wall was black. At that moment, Bob instructed Bertha to "give our boys a Kitty Lounge welcome." Before I could mount any serious objection, Bertha had opened her shirt, pulled aside various undergarments, and grabbed the back of my head, pushing it deep into the flesh valley within. "Oh no, please, no," I tried to say but couldn't breathe. Then I was free, free to suck in the aroma of bottled lubrication, stale tobacco, and dead romance. Now it was Jeff's turn to go under. He emerged panting and bewildered. I took a sip of my vodka and soda: the drink had strength, strength enough for courage of the most regretful kind. Bob was chuckling, causing the smoke from his cigar to plume from every orifice. For a moment I imagined he was being cremated. "Our customers pay a grand a night for that," he roared. "Not that any of 'em last that long. With Bertha, they're lucky to last a minute."

I couldn't stop looking at the other girl. Was she one of the hookers? Did she actually *work* here? And what about Bob's offer of a free night? I couldn't tell if it was genuine. Still, it was good of him to offer this manly gesture of goodwill, especially given that I had telephoned him cold from the Leisureplex after reading about the Kitty Lounge in the *Las Vegas Review Journal*. The *Journal* had reported that the state of Nevada was proposing to resolve a budget crisis with an "entertainment tax" on the handful of licensed brothels out in the desert. Bob was fighting the proposal. It was a perfect story. The Beast would love it.

"I just don't like it," Bob was complaining now, after Jeff had used the word *brothel*. "It's old-fashioned." He put down his fruit-based cocktail. "I like the term *cathouse* better. And it's not a sex act, it's a *party*. In here, when someone says the word *party,* they mean a sex act."

The drinks kept coming, unordered. Jeff began to take some photographs of Bertha, who kept pulling down her underwear. Bob found this hugely amusing. The music got louder. What was that they were playing? Jesus Christ, it was "House of the Rising Sun." Then another song came on. It took me back to London nightclubs, to student parties. At some point I stopped taking notes. My voice recorder ran out of memory. Bob kept saying he was expecting a VIP, due to land on the helipad out back at any moment. Eventually I got up to use the bathroom. I noticed a familiar numbness in my legs, a swagger in my walk. Jeff was still busy adjusting his lights. In the bathroom I stared at the wall for a long time. *We had to get out of here. We had to get back to Los Angeles.* I splashed cold water on my face and steadied my breathing as I patted myself dry. Had I had three drinks or four? *Shit*. Jeff would have to drive. After straightening my collar I pulled open the heavy door.

And there she was, the other girl, coming in the other direction. Her shorts gleamed in the UV lighting, which made her tan seem even deeper. "Hey," she said with a cool, efficient smile. "Chris, right?"

I nodded dumbly.

"I was just talking with Bob," she said.

"Ah."

"He said we should *party*."

"He did?"

"Come on," she said, taking my hand. "My room's just over here."

10

Asteroids and Neptunians

It was there in the corridor of the Twilight Kitty Lounge—tired, boozed, and close to accepting defeat—that I had a vision.

I saw my grandmother.

Now I can say with some confidence, some authority even, that if there's one place you do not want to have a vision of your grandmother, it is a brothel in the Nevada desert. At first I thought she must have died, that the vision represented some kind of telepathic ripple through space and time. Then, slowly, I realized what had happened: the juke-box had been playing "House of the Rising Sun" by the Animals, who were from Walker, the town on the River Tyne where my grandmother was born. This had somehow caused me to recall the story of how my grandparents first met, which had in turn paralyzed me with a guilt so sickening, so all-powerful, I could almost feel my soul being sucked out through my rib cage.

A soft, delicate arm curled around my back. I smelled perfume. "Chris?" said the girl in the white shorts. "Are you okay?"

"I'm fine," I managed. "I'm . . ."

I was thinking back to my first visit to Walker. It must have been—what?—mid-eighties. I can't remember why I was there. My grandparents had long since relocated farther north. But that first impression of concrete and litter has always remained. I remember thinking: if Walker wasn't the worst place in the world, then it was certainly *one* of the worst places in the world.

They used to build ships in Walker.

They don't build ships there anymore. It was 1939 when my grandfather bumped into my grandmother as she walked in the other direction through Jesmond Dene, a local park. A few weeks later he took her dancing, and the future seemed inevitable. Then my grandfather was sent off to France to fight the Germans, who killed his friends, captured him, and marched him to a forced-labor camp in Poland. A telegram announcing his presumed death was sent back to Walker. He made it home after five years—most of it spent mining granite in Czechoslovakia—just as the Americans were detonating nuclear weapons over the skies of Hiroshima and Nagasaki. The only surviving photograph of my grandparents' wedding shows my grandfather looking almost hollow, a cigarette fizzing in his hand. A year later he came down with tuberculosis, which put him in a quarantine facility —solitary confinement—for nine months. As part of the treatment, the doctors collapsed one of his lungs. Five years of mining granite and then *that*. It's fair to say that the forties weren't the greatest of decades for my grandfather. Still, it turned out well in the end. In the decades that followed came peace, wealth, leisure, technology, a daughter, and eventually a grandson—standing here now in a Nevada brothel, with a rented cherry red Mustang parked outside.

The girl in the white shorts was still beside me in the corridor. She could be mine for nothing more than the swipe of an American Express card—not even that, if the word of Bob Hoffman could be trusted, which it almost certainly couldn't. "Look," I began, unsteadily. "I'd love to, er, *party*."

"Cool."

"But I really have to go. I'm working, you see."

"Working?"

"A newspaper article."

"Poor you."

"Yeah, poor me."

In a world without disease, without fear of the Beast, without judgment, and without shame, would I have done it?

Hard to say.

Perhaps all sex will be transactional in the future. After all, we are being conditioned by TV, by advertising, by Internet porn, to have impossibly high expectations of our sexual partners.

And in an age when we take our pleasure seriously, what's wrong with that? We want the best bedsheets, the best holidays, the best spas, the best espresso machines. So why not the best sex? Why not sex with *professionals*? This goes for women as much as it does for men: the latest venture of Heidi Fleiss, the Hollywood madame, is a girls-only establishment called the the Stud Farm. And yet paying for sex seems too much like changing the rules, too much like taking a few right hooks in the first round, then coming back for the second with a machine gun. For me, it would be nothing more than a cheat, a choice made after examining a selection of nonexistent options. And when you've done it once, is there really any going back? I doubt it. If women can smell the Desperate Period, I dread to think what kind of alarm systems the new, post-brothel me would activate.

And so, as I turned away from the girl in the white shorts, I told myself that if my grandfather could still believe in my grandmother after five years in a labor camp with a Luger nine-millimeter to his head, perhaps I could believe in myself enough to hold out on the brothel, at least for now. Perhaps Los Angeles would eventually take pity on me. Perhaps somewhere out there in the dust and the heat, the dual force fields of love and chance were already hard at work.

Back in the lounge area the door buzzer rang and the strange ballet of the whorehouse began. Bras were removed, negligees flapped, and then the girls lined up as they had done before. But when the door opened a collective sigh was released. "It's Rob," said the Russian. "He's here for Calamity."

"Rob is the husband of one of the girls," explained Bob. "She's coming off a ten-day shift. He's taking her home."

"We need to get the fuck out of this place," I whispered to Jeff. "Right now." Jeff nodded robotically in agreement.

Bob lumbered over to Rob, the poor bastard, and hung a thick, gold-chained wrist over his shoulder. "She'll be out in a minute, buddy," he said. "She's just finishing up with a client." Rob gave a resigned, mournful nod. Then he shuffled over to the bar and ordered a raspberry lemonade.

I wish I could tell you that the incident at the brothel was the first in a series of redemptive experiences that ultimately resulted in my relocation to a log cabin in the mountains, where I now reside with a pigtailed girl from Utah and our five blond-haired children.

Alas, no. The lows just keep getting . . . *lower*. Today, for the first time in my life, my rent went overdue. I don't have the money. Is there any way to put rent on a credit card? If there is, I need to know.

How am I managing to *spend* so much?

Debt, I think, is my biggest problem. Debt means I'm still spending money on things I *used* to own, and couldn't afford at the time. Those loans I told you about, the ones I took out in London to buy and "restore" my MG convertable: I've barely made a mark on them. These loans extend so far into the future, the pay-off date cannot be calculated using a calendar alone—you need an astrologist and a cosmological chart. Then there are my student loans. Every month I'm spending money on cigarettes I smoked a decade ago in a dive bar on the other side of the world.

At least I still own my TV—the other contributing factor to my third world–style deficit, along with those bloody Neverland tickets. American Express seems to believe that seventeen percent is an entirely reasonable reward for having fronted me the money to buy all these things. *Seventeen percent.* Maybe the TV wasn't such a brilliant idea, after all. Maybe it's time to get one of those cheap-looking credit cards where they charge you zero interest for the first six months, then mug you with fifty percent compound daily, just when you're getting comfortable. The thing is, I *like* my AmEx card. It's the brand. It makes me feel . . . wealthy.

How do they do this? How is it possible to *control me* like this?

Also costing me money are all the addictions I seem to have picked up since moving to LA.

The LABite delivery service, for example.

Over the past year, I've been unlearning to cook. It's been hard work but I think I've just about perfected the art of not cooking now. The only upside of my takeout habit is that I must be keeping at least a dozen Chinese plastic kitchenware factories in business. With every takeout order comes a landfill of disposable knives, forks, straws, boxes, lids, pouches, bags, cups, and so on, not to mention a wedge of napkins the width of a triple-quilted toilet roll. Why do they give you so many napkins? You could eat the chicken with your hands and pour the sweet 'n' sour sauce over your head and you still wouldn't get through half of them.

Another habit I've recently taken up: electricity. Actually, it's not really a *habit,* as this suggests casual usage, and these days I'm practically a voltaholic. I need all this power not only to satisfy the cravings of my giant TV but also to feed the vintage air conditioner on my roof, which makes a noise like a jet engine filled with nails being dropped from a tall building. Thanks to the heatwave, the air conditioner has been running pretty much 24/7 since last April, when I got back from the Middle East. It can't be long now before it either implodes or blasts off into space.

Then there's all the oil I've been burning.

With depressing inevitably, my daily hike up Alta Loma Road to the Coffee Bean on Sunset has become a drive. Which wouldn't be such an issue if it wasn't for the white-painted concrete posts that block the top of the street—a rare, European-style attempt by the city of LA at traffic control. To get to the top of the hill in a car you must therefore drive down it, turn right on Holloway, head west for a few minutes in the wrong direction, swing right up to Sunset, then come back east and circle the block until you can find a parking spot. At that point, of course, you're committed: like the city itself, you're fully invested in the promise of convenience represented by the internal combustion engine. Which means no parking spot will do except for the one *directly in front* of the entrance. Which means you end up circling the block for even longer, until you finally get your spot, stand in line, buy your decaf-triple-shot-nonfat-cappuccino, then do the drive in reverse, by which time you've emptied the tank and wasted twenty dollars, not to mention an hour of your afternoon.

And gas, like every other natural resource, is getting more expensive by the minute. That's the problem with cheap money: sooner or later, everyone realizes that it's worth less than it was before. And now inflation is back. Back from a fifteen-year holiday in South America. I've been tracking the commodities indexes in the newspaper. They're going up so quickly that there soon won't be enough column inches to print them. Americans no longer have the monopoly on consumption, that's for sure. Everyone's doing it now: the Chinese, the Indians, the Russians. The Chinese are building new cities so fast that a ton of copper is now worth more than a black-market nuclear weapon. That's right: *copper.* I was under the impression that no one had needed copper since the days of underage chimney sweeps. But no, you can't build cities without copper. Or any other kind of metal, for that matter. Gangsters are moving out of narcotics and into the scrap metal trade. You read stories about them stealing parts from telephone exchanges, church gutters, shopping mall air conditioners, supermarket refrigerators, and loading them onto vast container ships bound for Beijing.

Yes, the tides of global capitalism have started to move to a new and unfamiliar moon. The kids on the street in Calcutta, they wear Rolexes now. As for the Russians, they really couldn't be happier about global warming. I suspect they keep their Ladas running overnight, just to try to speed things up a bit. Now that the icebergs have cleared from the North Pole, they can send their ships through the Arctic Circle instead of the Panama Canal. And who owns the Arctic Circle? *The Russians do*—or so they say. Yes, the Russians are excited, thrilled, absolutely overjoyed about this imminent climate catastrophe. Who can blame them? Their entire frozen continent is turning warm and green, right in front of their very eyes—while their oil reserves triple in value every other month. Russia is the future, no doubt about it. Give it twenty years and Siberian waterfront will be the new Miami beach.

"Holy macaroni," said Dr. Barry Bingblatz, as he stood behind me with a needle in his hand. "That's a *bad* boy, right there."

"Can you get rid of it?" I asked, delicately.

"I can try."

Dr. Bingblatz, Beverly Hills dermatologist and the author of *Celebrity Skincare: Dermatologist to the Stars* (out of print), lifted up his glasses and rubbed his eyes. I knew this because I could see him reflected in the mirror in front of me. There he was: fiftyish, squirrel-tail eyebrows, long white coat, black yarmulke. His face was soured with medical curiosity, as if he had just tasted a kumquat for the first time. Me and Dr. Bingblatz, we've been hanging out a lot lately. All this worry about money has been giving me acne: not the harmless, splat-your-bathroom-mirror variety, but the infected, biological-warfare-victim variety. Of course, being the author of *Celebrity Skincare: Dermatologist to the Stars,* Dr. Bingblatz doesn't accept health insurance, which means I have to add his consultation fee to my AmEx bill, which causes me to worry even more about money, which gives me more acne, which means I have to keep coming back for more . . . and so on.

The "bad boy" in question is a boil of implausible dimensions, dead center on the back of my neck. In the days before I had access to a Beverly Hills dermatologist, this was the kind of atomic walnut I might have had to live with for a couple of months before it finally went critical. Then again, two months could easily be an optimistic

estimate with a boil of this scale. It could have subsacs, secret reserves of infection, allowing it to withstand even the most violent of
hack jobs under fluorescent bathroom lighting. Back in the eighties,
back in the bad old days, I had one of these fuckers for three and a
half years.

"Been feeling any unusual stress lately?" asked Dr. Bingblatz as
he swabbed cold alcohol over the pulsating growth.

Aside from not being able to pay the rent, wondering if I should
flee the country, and living in dread that the profligate consumption
of my generation would bring about the apocalypse, I couldn't think
of anything.

"You know, it's funny. People don't think they're stressed. But even
too much pleasure can mess with your body. Too much food, too much
alcohol, too much time in the sun—it's all *stress,* in medical terms. That's
why we're seeing so many cases of obesity, diabetes, lifestyle cancers."

"Lifestyle cancers?"

"It used to be gout. The scourge of kings and the aristocracy. Back
then, of course, it took a serious amount of capital to overindulge. These
days, pretty much anyone can do it. So no stress then?"

"Not that I know of," I said, unconvincingly. "I *am* trying to sell a
lamp on Craigslist, if that counts for anything."

"Ah, *Craigslist,*" said Dr. Bingblatz, pinging the needle. "This is
cystic, by the way. The worst kind. When you've finished your course
of Tetracycline, we should probably talk again about Accutane."

Christ, *Accutane.* I recalled those luminous green pills of my teenage years, the ones that made all my skin fall off. There was no way I
could go through that again. I needed to sort out my money problems,
and fast. On the wall to the right of me I noticed a poster of a boil. It
was broken down into a diagram showing its constituent parts, with
bubbles of explanatory text. "Pus," I began to read, "is a whitish-yellow
or yellow substance produced by the body in response to inflamma-
tion. An accumulation of pus in an enclosed tissue space is known as
an *abscess.* A collection of pus within or beneath the epidermis is a
pustule or *pimp—*"

"GARGH!"

Dr. Bingblatz pulled the needle out of the boil and soaked up the blood with a tissue. "I started using Craigslist when I got bored of eBay," he said. "I collect meteorites, you know. Mini-asteroids, I call 'em. Any day now, one of those babies is gonna pop right out of the sky and send us all back to the stone age." Dr. Bingblatz giggled as he disposed of the needle. "Ever been to the NASA Web site?" he continued. "Last time I was on there it said there were *eight hundred and eighty-seven* PHAs—that's code for potentially hazardous asteroids—in a possible collision path with the earth. *Bam!* Ha-ha. You're a writer, you should write about that. Ever heard of the Torino impact scale? It's measured from one to ten, one being a smoking crater on your front lawn, ten being the annihilation of humankind. I tell my stressed-out patients, buy a meteorite, put it on your mantelpiece, get things in perspective. You'd be amazed at how many meteorites you can find on Craigslist. Buying is easy, of course. *Selling* is the tough cookie. But I've got my technique now."

"What *was* that?" I said.

"Cortisone. Anti-inflammatory. Should do the trick. But we should see you again on Thursday, just to double-check."

Another hundred dollars on the AmEx card, I thought. I began to wonder if it would be better to live in a place where it was impossible to pay a hundred dollars to lance a boil—a place like Wooler, for example. If you didn't have the option, you'd never know what you were missing. Then again, you'd have to live with the boil. And I've already done my fair share of that.

"What do you mean, *technique*?" I said, pulling my T-shirt back on.

"You don't have a technique?"

"No. I mean, I don't think so."

"Tell me," he said, making the just-tasted-a-kumquat face again. "The lamp, how long has it been up for sale now?"

"Couple of weeks."

Dr. Bingblatz winced.

"You don't have a technique," he said.

And then he told me exactly what I needed to do.

Day six of the Rent Crisis.

This morning I emptied my plastic Ikea filing cabinet and discovered that if I liquidate my company pension, I will be able to pay off (a) the MG purchase loan; (b) half of the subsequent MG "restoration" loan; (c) three-quarters of my American Express card balance; and (d) the rent.

As far as I can see, there is only one downside to this: I will die alone and broke in a crackhouse.

Does *anyone* my age have any money? Or are my financial issues generational in nature. Just think: in five months' time I will be twenty-nine years old. A year after that, I will be thirty. *Thirty*. Anywhere else in the world I probably would have been married for a decade by now. I would have kids, a house, a commute, a daily routine. I would have a useful trade. Instead I live for myself. I write stories for a living; I *e-mail* for a living. Over recent weeks I have tackled the important subjects of cappuccino cows (cows bred to produce milk with better frothing qualities); obese bears (they're getting fat on twenty-first-century human food, even though their metabolisms can burn *twenty-five thousand* calories a day); the election of an Austrian bodybuilder as governor of California; and (my personal favorite) the arrest and child molestation trial of Michael Jackson, unwitting host of the Worst Date of My Life.

Age, of course, is a subjective measurement. On the planet Neptune, for example, I wouldn't have yet celebrated my first birthday—on account of the leisurely speed at which the planet Neptune circles the sun. In many ways, I feel more like a one-year-old than I do an almost-thirty-year-old. And I'm not alone. You can see my fellow Neptunians everywhere. At the Coffee Bean, I sit and watch them with their Tonka truck SUVs, their romper-suit sportswear, their plastic beakers filled with sugary beverages. Like children, we consume and we excrete. Like children, we have no money, no possessions . . . only borrowed toys.

Another fact about Neptune: it has no gravity.

There's nothing to keep your feet on the ground.

Some good news, for a change: Dr. Bingblatz is as talented at using Craigslist as he is at lancing thermonuclear boils. His method goes as follows. You create multiple advertisements, with multiple headlines, and keep reposting them every twenty minutes or so (where does he get the *time* to do this?). It's basic marketing, basic salesmanship: you feed the design snobs one line, while trying to net the cheapskates with another, and so on, and so on. Time consuming, yes, but effective.

The first response plinked into my inbox barely an hour after taking Dr. Bingblatz's advice.

"Interested!!!" it said.

Then came another: "Love ya lamp!! :-)"

And another: "Got any pixxx!!??"

What is it with these Craigslisters and their overenthusiastic use of punctuation? If the sale of a secondhand Ikea lamp merits three exclamation marks, how does the Craigslister respond to, say, a #7 the Torino scale? How many exclamation marks does that require?

Another thing I've noticed: it's very much a female thing, buying furniture online. According to their e-mail addresses, my potential customers are named Casey, Jade, and Natalia. Unforgivably, I began to wonder if any of them were single. Appalled at the thought of becoming the kind of person who would sell furniture to meet women, I distracted myself by choreographing a *Vanity Fair*–style fashion photo shoot of the lamp. I captured it looking cool and intellectual over by the bookcase; smart and practical by the desk; warm and suggestive upstairs in the bedroom. Then I uploaded the portfolio onto my computer and e-mailed it out.

Three replies zinged back almost immediately, telephone numbers included.

As I sat there at my desk, it occurred to me that I had never before obtained three girls' telephone numbers so easily or quickly. Come to think of it, I had never before obtained three girls' telephone numbers.

Not that I cared about the girls, of course.

It was all about the money.

I needed the *money*.

I called Casey first. Her voice took me by surprise. I had been expecting a woman in her mid to late fifties, a flea-market bore, a Volvo driver. But no, she sounded young; younger than me, without question. I repeated all the things I had said in the ad. Yes, the lamp works fine; yes, the bulb is included; yes, it's a simple on/off pull mechanism, once for on, twice for off; no, there's absolutely nothing wrong with it, nothing at all. I gave the same speech to Jade and Natalia. By late morning three separate lamp-viewing appointments had been arranged.

This had been so much easier than I had imagined.

Casey was barely out of her teens and arrived wearing three-quarter-length leggings, running shoes, and a stretchy bra top, all in hot pinks and cool whites. In LA, it's automatically assumed that at any given moment you're either on your way to, or returning from, a place of exercise. Casey appeared to be actually *in the middle* of exercise. The sporting look was completed with a pair of bulbous green-tinted sunglasses and a long brown ponytail, strung through the back of her LA Dodgers baseball cap. Under any other circumstances I doubt Casey would have made eye contact with me. Yet here she was.

With an efficient, almost sarcastic smile, Casey strode through the door and immediately located the merchandise, which I had wedged against the bookshelf to help disguise its slightly damaged stand.

"This it?" she asked.

I nodded eagerly.

"It's broken," she said.

"It *is*?"

"Yeah," said Casey, flatly. "Wobbles. Look."

It was, indeed, wobbling.

"Wear and tear," I said. "I can take it down to sixty-five."

I was a grand short on the rent. A *grand*. Still, sixty-five was a start.

"It flickers, also," announced Casey. "Look."

It was, indeed, flickering.

"Probably the bulb," I said.

"Doubt it."

"Eh?"

"Looks like someone fell over it. It's scratched here on the bottom. Look."

What is this, CSI *fucking* Miami? "I can do fifty, but nothing less," I offered, now annoyed. "It's a designer lamp."

"Says here I-K-E-A," said Casey, having now unscrewed the base, which revealed the shameful black-and-white sticker.

"Ah."

"Got anything else?" asked Casey, impatiently. "Just started med school at UCLA. My room is, like, *totally* empty."

"What about this?" I said, holding up a shiny metal Ikea rack of indeterminate purpose. I gave an encouraging smile.

Casey sneered and pulled out her phone to check the time.

"Gotta fly," she said, making a big deal of leaning the lamp back against the wall. "Some guy in Westwood has a desk."

Things didn't go much better with Jade—although she too was conspicuously, almost comically, attractive. Dark, lean, with an Asian ingredient mixed somewhere within the exotic soup of her DNA, Jade entered my apartment the way a cat might enter a new room: crouched slightly, skirting the walls, and all the while subjecting me to an almost supernatural inspection with her wide, unblinking eyes. A tiny gray skirt danced up and around her thighs, which were concealed fashionably behind black rock 'n' roll leggings, giving way above the ankles to a pair of incongruously expensive heels. Her top half was wrapped in what appeared to be a white Bavarian milkmaid's blouse, secured with a wide leather belt around the stomach.

Jade was a talker. Between the door and the lamp, I learned that she was an actress, that she was unemployed, that she had just moved to town from New York, that her grandmother was sick, that her great-aunt lived in China, that she was renting, and that she was completely broke.

"It's *nice*," she said, observing the lamp from afar, as if trying to avoid emotional attachment. "Will you take five?"

"*Dollars?*" I exploded.

Jade gave a tiny nod.

"But it's *seventy*-five." With people like this as my target market, how the hell was I ever going to raise a grand?

"Five is all I've got."

Jade shrugged and smiled. It was . . . she looked good, when she smiled. I almost gave her the damn lamp for free. Then I remembered the rent, and my third and final appointment, with Natalia, later on.

"I'm sorry," I said. "It's just—"

"No problem," Jade interrupted, the smile now gone. She began to tap her way quickly back across the room, beating me to the front door and opening it for herself. She turned back to face me as she did so.

"I'm late to meet my boyfriend," she said.

Slam.

I walked back to the sofa and slumped down onto the crumpled beige fabric, wincing as my lower back connected with part of the bed frame. Perhaps this Craigslist thing wasn't so easy after all.

Still, there was always Natalia.

"Listen to this," said Jeff, reading aloud from the *Los Angeles Times*. It was the next morning, and we were gathered blearily in a tartan-patterned leather booth in Swingers, a retro American diner in the Fairfax district. "It says here that the average potato travels one thousand, two hundred miles before it reaches your plate, even though they can grow potatoes here in Southern California."

"Fascinating," I said.

Behind Jeff's head a waitress moved between the tables wearing the Swingers uniform of miniskirt, go-go boots, and fishnets. A jukebox somewhere was playing rockabilly music.

"In the state of New York," Jeff went on, "they export their apples to other countries while importing *the exact same kind of apples* from the countries they're sending their apples to in the first place." He slapped down the newspaper on the table and raised his hands in exasperation.

"Fascinating," I repeated.

"Food miles," declared Jeff. "The distance an ingredient travels from the farm to your big fat head. You should read this, Ayres, it's important. Says here that if you could convert food miles into air miles, a chicken pot pie would have enough of them for a free alarm clock and a holiday in Marbella."

"Since when have you given a shit about any of this?"

"You saw the fires, Ayres."

"And?"

"Think of the billions of tons of carbon dioxide emitted by all that unnecessary food transportation. If we're not careful, all of California is going to go up in smoke. England is going to sink underwater. It's a global disaster, Ayres. Which is why I've decided to do the right thing."

"You're having the sex change operation?"

"The One Hundred Mile Diet, Ayres. You eat food that has been produced only within a one-hundred-mile radius."

"Christ. You're serious."

"I'm a *locavore* now."

"A *locavore*?"

"Go ahead, Ayres. Mock."

"Jeff, your car is the size of the Exxon Valdez."

Jeff picked up the newspaper again and shook the creases out of it. "Actually," he announced, "it says here that mass-farming is now so energy intensive, if you're a meat eater, driving an SUV to the supermarket is better for the earth than burning the equivalent calories to walk there."

"Bullshit," I said, grabbing the newspaper from him.

I had a horrible feeling, of course, that Jeff was right. There's been a lot of news lately about the economics of food, all of it terrifying: everything is too cheap and everything *costs* to much. For years, I never gave it any thought. I remember one of my first job interviews, over at the *Financial Times*. The editor asked me what I wanted to write about and I told him: anything but agriculture. I was interested in the Internet, gadgets, "new media." The subject of agriculture, of food, seemed so nineteenth century, so Malthusian. What an idiot. And to think that I was actually worried about the millennium bug. Yes, I really thought the world was doomed, what with all those microwave ovens displaying the wrong time.

Our waiter, the only male employee in the entire establishment, approached the table. He had cartoon muscles, a tattoo that spanned his whole neck, and a facial piercing that appeared to have been made out of the tip of a Native American spear. I ordered the Argentinean corned beef hash. Jeff made a big performance of going for the Californian avocado scramble.

"Is something wrong, Ayres? You seem distracted. And what's that *thing* on the back of your head?"

"I have a dilemma," I said.

"It looks more like a boil to me."

I told him about Casey and Jade, and about my theory that I had somehow stumbled upon the most effective method of meeting girls in the history of dating. "Think about it for a second," I said. "The people browsing for furniture are almost exclusively female. And what kind of females are looking for secondhand furniture? Single girls. What's more, these girls have typically just moved into town, which makes sense, because that's what you do when you move, you buy new furniture. Being new in town, of course, means they also need friends. And boyfriends. Admit it, Jeff, it's the most genius thing you've ever heard."

"And the dilemma?"

I told him about Natalia.

She was, of course, another knockout actress: Australian, this time. I really couldn't believe it. All those hours spent negotiating with nightclub bouncers, all those bar tabs, all those hangovers, and all I ever had to do was sell furniture on Craigslist. For a while, Natalia and I seemed to really hit it off. I told her the sale of the lamp was part of an apartment makeover and asked for decorating tips. Two minutes later we were drinking orange jasmine tea and browsing Ralph Lauren paint samples online. But then came the negotiations. She worked out pretty quickly that the lamp was damaged. I insisted, perhaps too aggressively, that it could be adjusted with a screwdriver. She offered twenty-five. I stuck to seventy-five. Then it turned nasty. "The lamp is *broken*," she kept telling me. I brought it down to sixty, she countered with forty, and in the end we settled, grudgingly, on forty-eight.

And fifty cents.

Jeff starred at me blankly.

"So your dilemma—and stop me if I'm wrong, Ayres—is that you're trying to hit on these girls, but you're also trying to sell them dodgy furniture, because you can't afford the rent, because you bought a TV?"

"Yeah," I said. "That's pretty much it."

So I think about money all the time now. I think about it in bed. I think about it in the bathroom. I think about it in the office, in the car. I'm thinking about it right now. If I close my eyes this is what I see:

$$\$$$
$$\$$$
$$\$$$
$$\$$$
$$\$$$

I've started to carry a calculator around with me, in hopes that by punching in the same digits repeatedly I will find a way to reverse the laws of mathematics, thus enabling me to turn a negative number into a positive one. Money is starting to seem a lot more real, a lot more *unyielding* than it ever used to. Yes, I'm starting to think that the rules of money cannot be changed.

But there is hope.

Today a literary agent named Mark Lucas telephoned me from London to say that he thinks my book idea, *War Reporting for Cowards,* could have a future. Now I've never met this Mark Lucas, but I could spend a lot of time with his telephone voice. It reminds me of brandy, firesides, and expense-account lunches. It's a Gulfstream voice, a Monaco marina voice. The timbre suggests a fabulous yet discreet transcontinental lifestyle. Yes, I must work very hard to keep this man in my orbit. The call was all the better for being a surprise. I had almost forgotten about the messages I had left with several literary agencies (the numbers supplied by Google) back during the early days of the Desperate Period. As always, however, there is a catch: to test the market-worthiness of my manuscript, to see if it will fly with the suits, Mark says I must actually start writing it. And this, I fear, could interfere with my furniture-selling program. Nevertheless, the book represents the promise of money—serious money—which is more than can be said for anything else in my life.

In the meantime, I've found another, less legitimate solution to the Rent Crisis (now at day nine): an Internet bank in England that will allow me to take out a loan using my parents' home address. The loan should be approved by the end of the week, at which point the funds will be wired into my UK account. Three days after that, I will be able to transfer the cash to LA. In the meantime, I'm preparing for a surge in my Craigslist furniture-selling campaign.

So far, no word from the landlady on the overdue check.

It's surely only a matter of time.

It's astonishing, really, just how many things you can find to sell on Craigslist, even in a zero-capital home such as my own. So far, I've managed to get rid of an old wall mirror (not strictly mine), a couple of fold-up chairs, an outdoor barbeque, a coffee table, a rug, a mat, a stool, two other lamps, an office chair, and, most impressively, a plastic wine rack from the Dumpster in the parking lot.

Oh, yes, and the dining room table.

With all these strangers coming in and out of my apartment, my fellow residents at the Leisureplex must think I'm running a whorehouse. Or they would if they were ever at home, which they're not, which leaves me free to do pretty much what I please. Nevertheless, the building manager keeps stopping by for unannounced chats about the heat wave, while straining to see what's going on over my shoulder. But there's only an increasingly empty room.

The sales are certainly stacking up—eight hundred dollars in total, minus the two hundred I've spent on LABite deliveries—and it can't be long now before the funds from my Internet loan arrive. As for meeting women . . . this has not quite gone according to plan. All of a sudden, there seem to be a lot of *men* interested in buying secondhand furniture on Craigslist. After my initial encounters with Casey, Jade, and Natalia, not a single female has shown up to buy anything. Not one. I've thought about trying to ward off my prospective male customers, but it's impossible to determine their sex until it's too late, thanks largely to cryptic gmail addresses. And, of course, I need the money. So I've welcomed my Daves and Brians, my Marios and Sebastians, my Pierres and Armandos—I've even had a Chin-wa and a Ranja; a Kobe and a Tyreck. All have admired the size, the sheer ambition, of my plasma TV. Yes, thanks to the TV, I have discovered what it is like to experience male validation in its purest, most animalistic form. My ancestors must have felt like this when they speared a wildebeest and dragged it home to the womenfolk and the fire. To my fellow men, the TV demonstrates my stealth in the retail wilderness; my mastery of advanced financing tools; my bravery in the face of certain obsolescence.

I can't help but wonder, of course, how much further I can go with this Craigslist scheme. I need more money (and it wouldn't hurt to meet more Caseys and Jades and Natalias), but I'm running out of things to sell. I look around the room and all I see are bare floors and the ants on the skirting boards.

And yet one thing remains.

Yes, there it is: the beige carbuncle in the middle of the room, a sofa the weight of a small battleship, spiked with nails, stuffed with the feathers of a mechanical duck, catastrophically uncomfortable, and wrapped in a fabric of the most offensively poor taste. *If only it hadn't been a gift from my grandmother*. To sell this sofa would be turn my back on everything I was ever taught as a child: *Waste not, want not; I want never gets*. But I need one more chance. One more spin, one more throw. I have no choice.

The sofa must go.

11

Gone Native

So it's winter now in LA. With it comes a blizzard of warmth, a downpour of sunshine, and a breeze-force wind. People back in England ask me with genuine concern if I *miss* the seasons. I inhale thickly. I sigh. And I tell them I'm holding up. I tell them, yes, I'll be fine. I'll make it through.

And yet winter is somehow still unmistakably here. You can smell it in the air. You can see it in the fake snow sprinkled over the chandeliers that hang from the lampposts in Beverly Hills. You can even feel it in the traffic, which is lighter, slicker, more even tempered than usual. The homecoming queens, the cheerleaders, the popular girls from high school—they've all gone home for the holidays. In pickup trucks across the Midwest, corn farmers are reliving their prom nights and worrying about the price of diamond engagement rings.

I love LA when it's empty. With everyone gone, I almost feel like I *belong* here. Which isn't necessarily a good thing for someone in my precarious situation. And by that I don't just mean the Rent Crisis (now on day fifteen), which at any moment could force me to take an unscheduled holiday in Tijuana. No, there are other problems with getting too comfortable here. The Beast, for example, has an expression for the sensation I am currently feeling. "Going native," he calls it. This is regarded as a common yet fatal hazard of the foreign correspondent's trade, a signal that the sufferer should either be put on the next plane home or terminated in situ. The correspondent who goes native is a liability, an embarrassment: think Colonel Kurtz in *Apocalypse Now*. The Beast makes a sport of guessing which member of his staff will be the next to turn. *I hear Henderson in Bangkok has bought a slave boy*, he might announce one day on the telephone. It's best to reply with counter-rumor, something about Lewis in Tonga, *who has been seen with a bone in his nose*.

The Beast certainly has every reason to be concerned.

Over by the front door of my apartment there are three pairs of flip-flops lined up in a row. Not one, not two, but *three*. And these are only my winter flip-flops—to be worn with my winter T-shirts and my winter shorts. Never before have I exposed my toes to the elements. If you could see my toes, you would understand. My big toe is so white, it reflects light back up through the troposphere, beyond the atmosphere, and out into deep space, where it interferes with satellite TV programming. But I've stopped worrying about such things. Ever since my poolside encounter with Lara, I've been making an effort to assimilate. I haven't worn a suit for—what?—six months now. Ditto my elaborately ribbed socks, my lace-up shoes. After all, smart-casual is the new smart, according to the fashion magazines. CEOs wear flip-flops to board meetings. Presidents go open-toed to G8 summits. Which raises the question of how we are supposed to dress *down*. Judging by some of the people I see out at night in Hollywood, looking as though you're homeless is how you dress down. Ragged, unwashed, stripped almost naked: this is the new look for the weekend. Dumpster chic. Vagrant vogue. The homeless, for their part, appear to be rebelling against this trend. The hobo at the corner of La Cienega and Third Street, he wears a velvet trilby and tuxedo jacket. When he's not tapping on your car window, he's e-mailing on his BlackBerry. For some people, instant obsolescence has its upsides. As the world's natural resources run out, the products we're making with them are experiencing hyperdepreciation. How does this work, exactly? I have no idea.

All I know is that the homeless man on La Cienega and Third has a wireless e-mailing device.

But no food.

And nowhere to live, of course.

In many ways, being fired for going native would at least simplify my life. I would default on my American debt and return home, to my English debt, where I could beg the Beast to reassign me to somewhere at least three days away from the nearest collection agency—somewhere like the island of Fernando Póo, off the coast of Equatorial Guinea, in central Africa. Ah, yes, I can already imagine the dateline: From Chris Ayres, in Fernando Póo. Or perhaps that should be *on* Fernando Póo? I must remember to look this up.

There has to be a better way to end this crisis.

The other day I almost asked Jeff for money. But he has a girl-friend now. She's French. He calls her *Mimi*. She call him *Jeffi*. It's unbearable. From what I can tell, Mimi doesn't have a job and enjoys spending Jeffi's cash. Yes, like all French girlfriends, she's costing him a fortune, and Jeff is now complaining loudly about having no money. He's as broke as I am.

Well, *almost* as broke.

That Internet bank in England is taking an unreasonably long time to process my loan request. Due to "overwhelming volume," its two-man call center is unable to answer my queries at this time. I am advised to call back later, but I get the feeling they would rather I never called back at all. The sale of the sofabed is also taking longer than anticipated, largely because of Craigslist's new antispam software, which is making it almost impossible to use Dr. Bingblatz's multiple-posting technique. To fool the system, you now have to write a different advertisement every time you repost, which takes hours. "THE BEST SOFA BED IN THE WORLD," is my latest effort. The response has been—how to put this?—muted. And by *muted* I mean there has been no response at all. Perhaps it's the time of year.

Meanwhile, I'm working hard on the proposal for my combat memoir: my only remaining hope for a debt-free future. As much as writing a book is supposed to help a journalist's career, I'm concerned that a memoir entitled *War Reporting for Cowards* could do the exact opposite. I asked a friend in London for advice on this subject, and he said: "It might not end your career, Chris, but it could certainly *define* it." Yeah, *cheers*. What the hell is that supposed to mean? Still, I'm keeping my faith in Mark Lucas for now. With that voice of his, I'll believe anything he tells me. And he tells me that this book is going to find a publisher.

If only I could concentrate for more than three minutes at a time.

Take this morning: I woke up at seven a.m. in preparation for a full day of writing. Which meant I needed to make coffee, which meant I needed to make three separate trips to the Coffee Bean, each one lasting an hour. Naturally, it was also necessary for me to spend two hours watching CNN for research, another two hours browsing Craigslist, and finally, thirty minutes by the pool smoking cigarettes left over from a night out at the Saddle Ranch a few weeks ago.

It wasn't until early evening that I actually started to make some progress. And by that I mean I opened a Word document. I was just about to start when I heard the *plink-plink* of two e-mails arriving.

When I saw the name on the first one I froze. For a moment I felt as if my chair had been yanked from under me: I felt as if I were falling through a crack in the floor into a pit of snakes and flesh-eating beetles. As much as I had been expecting this e-mail it still came as a terrible surprise.

It was from Cali DeLongpre. Have I told you about Cali DeLongpre? Tiny, fortyish, and beautiful in a sickly kind of way, she wears below-the-knee print dresses, like she's the star of her own 1950s dish soap commercial. She reads a lot of Jane Austen. She makes me nervous.

Cali DeLongpre is my *landlady*.

"Dear Christopher," went her opening line, "I *do* hope you have been enjoying your time at the Park Wellington!"

An ominous first sentence if ever I read one.

How many days was the rent now overdue? Fifteen, sixteen? I would get paid in a couple of weeks, but by then next month's rent would be due. Presumably, this is why they call it the poverty *trap*, rather than the poverty *inconvenience*. And what about that bloody Internet loan? At least another three days before the funds would land in LA. Which left the nonexistent sofa sale.

Perhaps Cali was also broke. Perhaps she too needed the money. "After much thought," her note continued, "I have decided to sell the apartment."

There was a dull, hollow sound as I headbutted the desk.

Sell the apartment?

This was arguably worse than a demand for the rent.

How could I leave the Leisureplex? What about my mornings in the swimming pool? What about my afternoons in the hot tub?

The e-mail concluded:

I thought it best to give you as much warning as possible, so that you might go about your search for new accommodation with adequate preparation. Happy househunting!

Yours, regretfully,

Cali DeLongpre

PS: Steve and Gloria (your neighbors) are troubled by a mysterious odor. Any idea of the cause?

PPS: This month's rent check appears to have been lost in the mail. Please resend, ASAP.

This was a disaster.

How could I afford to move? Where would I *go*? Where would I find comparable leisure facilities? For a moment I was paralyzed by unanswered questions of logistics and timing. In fact, I was so shaken by the news, it took me a while to appreciate the full importance of the second e-mail.

It was the first response to my sofa advertisement.

The prospective buyer requested photographs and signed off with an intriguing "L." Could L be another young, absurdly good-looking actress? It certainly sounded promising. There was something playful, I decided, in that single, full-stopped initial. It suggested an appreciation of the tease, a mastery of suggestion. Yes, it was oddly romantic, that L. It made me forget about my imminent eviction from the Leisureplex and think instead about a long, explicit sofa bed demonstration. This L, I bet she would be a decadent creature. A wayward, foreign-born beauty, she would lie around in expensive black underwear, smoking French cigarettes and discussing Milan Kundera novels. I wondered what the L could stand for.

L for Lust.

L for Love.

L for . . . Lipstick.

Or, knowing my luck, L for Larry.

L for Leonard, Lachlan, Lancelot, Leroy, Leopold, Lesley, Lester, Lew, Lex, Liam, Lincoln, Lionel, Lloyd, Lorne, Luke, or Ludwig. Yes, that would be just perfect—wouldn't it?—a reply from a Ludwig. He would make a joke about Beethoven, and I would have to punch him in the face.

I looked again at my photographs of the sofa, which had proved to be an altogether more temperamental, less willing subject than the lamp. In vain, I had tried my best to prepare it for the camera. With kitchen tongs, I had removed a pair of boxer shorts, Neverland vintage, wedged into the far northwest quadrant by the armrest. As for the dusty sock between the center cushions—it was mysteriously heavy, as if a small farm animal had died in there—I pushed it out of sight into the black hole of the bed frame. Likewise a blue-green tortilla chip and a ringlet of old spaghetti, harder than concrete, harder possibly than space shuttle glue. Fortunately, the objectionable color of the sofa had rendered most stains invisible, aside from some remaining evidence of a recent nosebleed, which I had covered for the photograph with a copy of *Vogue*, carefully selected for my target demographic.

Please let this L be a *female,* I thought, as I loaded up the photographs as an e-mail attachment, added my name, address, and telephone number, then clicked on "send" at the precise moment another e-mail arrived. This confused the computer, which began opening and closing various windows as the hard drive clicked and whirred. After a few minutes of this, I tried rattling my mouse to no effect. By the time the machine finally regained its composure, the incoming e-mail had disappeared and my e-mail to L had been cast into the ether. To make absolutely sure, I double-checked my "sent items" folder. Yep, there it was.

The act was done.

Good riddance, sofa.

Hello L.

And then to Fat Burger on Santa Monica Boulevard. There I was, under fluorescent yellow signage (*The Day of Locust* discreetly on my lap under the counter), when L's text message arrived. I thought to myself: she sends text messages? No one in America sends text messages. Again, I pictured my foreign-born beauty: the French cigarettes, the novel, the underwear.

Her message:

Love sofa pix! R u free at six?

After considering several ways to reply in the affirmative without appearing desperate, I opted for a simple,

Yes!!!

Six o'clock. *Shit.* I had four hours. The word *wolfed* really doesn't do justice to the speed at which I finished eating that Fat Burger. I *lioned* it. I *grizzlied* it, I *pit bulled* it down. There was a lot of work ahead of me. This time, nothing could go wrong. There was no room for error. My game had to be raised. Between opening the front door and showing L my grandmother's sofa, I had, at the very most, thirty seconds. Thirty seconds to work the Ayres magic. There's only one problem, of course, with the Ayres magic: it didn't exist. So I would have to rely instead on hard work and preparation, or, failing that, outright deception.

Then out to the parking lot and into the Jeep, which carried me back to the Leisureplex on its arthritic springs. There I changed into boxer shorts and rubber gloves and cleaned with the enthusiasm of a murderer at a crime scene. Then it was time for another outing, this time for houseplants. I emerged from the Boyz Town florist with a selection of defiantly heterosexual blooms: bloody reds, military greens, police-car blues. My final assignment was a visit to a photo lab down on Hollywood and La Brea to pick up a blown-up copy of a newspaper clipping from my war reporting days. The clipping was my one and only moment of glory on the battlefield: a front-page account, in first-person detail, of how my unit had survived an ambush using only its wits, honor, and three hundred billion dollars' worth of state-of-the-art military hardware. In the byline at the top of the page, I was photographed wearing an expression that suggested gentle amusement rather than the bowel-imploding terror from which I was actually suffering. The enlarged clipping would be hung above my desk. Oh, *that,* I would laugh to visitors. *Oh, that's nothing really*.

And then home again, where I began to put together the final details of the Sofa Plan. A copy of *Being and Nothingness,* humorously annotated, was positioned next to my collection of *National Enquirer* on top of the toilet tank. Elsewhere in the apartment, I scattered Larkin, Hemingway, *The Day of the Locust,* some romantic poetry. I looked around, sweating. Were there too many books? Was there a danger of coming off as too sensitive, too insular? I wished I had some boxing gloves, a surfboard: something, *anything,* to represent my Y chromosome. Girls want the poet *and* the fighter, after all. Thinking quickly, I fought my way into the closet by the front door and emerged, triumphant, with a tennis racquet, which I leaned against the wall. That was better. Five-forty now. Twenty minutes to go.

One detail remained: the sound track to this peculiar transaction.
Music, they say, is the key to seduction. For a moment I imagined myself opening the door to L in chest wig and slippers as "Let's Get it On"
swooned in the background. No, Marvin Gaye was out of the question.
I needed something classy yet neutral. For a dizzy moment, I considered
"Ride of the Valkyries." But no, the sound track to *Apocalypse Now* was
also out of the question. In the end, I settled on Miles Davis. Surely I
couldn't go wrong with Miles. The jazz would hang there in the air, twirling
and glistening, like smoke from a cigar glimpsed through a half-open blind.

Five-fifty now: ten minutes to go.

I paced and I waited. I waited and I paced.

Five-fifty-seven.

Six.

She's late.

Then a knock at the door.

I opened it, blinked into the sunlight, and said, "Let me guess.
Larry?"

"Brian," came the surprised reply.

"Of course," I said, fighting the urge to commit a violent crime.
"*L for Brian*. Makes sense. What else could L stand for?"

Brian looked at me. I looked back at Brian. He was my height, a
bit heavier. He wore shorts, belt, polo shirt. He had good hair. I wanted
to kill him. I wanted to kill Brian more than I wanted anything.

"Uh?"

"Your signature," I said. "L for Brian. Clever. What is it, your
middle name?"

"Uh?"

"The letter L. That does it *stand* for?"

"I'm here for the sofa?"

"*Of course you are*," I said, giving up. "Come on in."

We moved into the apartment.

"Movin' out?" asked Brian, looking around at my empty living room. The Craigslist campaign had taken its toll.

"Funny you should say that," I said. "My landlady's evicting me." I thought again about the e-mail from Cali. All things considered, today hadn't gone very well. Yes, today could go straight to hell, as far as I was concerned, along with Brian. *Why would he sign his fucking e-mails with an L?*

"Sorry to hear that," said Brian, sounding about as sorry as a lottery winner at a Lamborghini dealership. "This it?"

"It certainly is."

And there it was: the sofa, oblivious to the anguish it was causing me. Brian turned away from it, as if to sit down.

"Whoa," I said, grabbing his arm. "*Slowly.*"

"Slowly?"

"Iron frame," I explained. "If you come down at the wrong angle . . . *Oof.* But please, sit. It's very comfortable."

His face now pulled tight with concentration, Brian lowered himself onto the sofa, as if he expected a landmine to go off under him. When he was finally down he released the muscles in his face and gave a relieved grin. "Comfy," he announced, wriggling from side to side. With a yawn, he picked up *Vogue* and began to flick through it. "Comfy," he said again. "And it's a bed too?"

"Yeah."

I was wondering if I should let Brian buy the sofa, or if I should try to find a way to put him off, in the hope of attracting a female buyer. The latter option now seemed more pathetic and depressing than it ever had before. Besides, perhaps Casey, Jade, and Natalia had been flukes; perhaps my Craigslist plan had been flawed all along. And I needed the money.

Yes, I *needed* the money.

"I'll take it," said Brian. "I'll give you six-fifty."

I was about to hold out my hand and offer a shake of agreement when the phone rang. I answered with a muttered "Yep?"

"Is this the owner of the Best Sofa Bed in the World?" asked the voice on the line. It was female, American.

"Say again?"

"This is *Lucie*. You e-mailed me the photograph of the sofa bed: the Best Sofa Bed in the World. Craigslist. Remember?"

I did?

This made no sense.

Was this . . . ? Could this be . . . ?

Brian was now counting out banknotes from a roll. I covered the mouthpiece of the phone. "Did the ad say it was seven hundred?" I said, with a friendly wince. "I'm sorry, it should have said three grand."

"It's *three grand*?" said Lucie.

"Noooo, no, no, no, no. That's something else." I searched the handset for the mute buttom, but couldn't find it.

"Three *grand*?" said Brian. "The ad said seven hundred!"

"Typo. Sorry."

"A *typo*?"

"Is someone shouting at you?" asked Lucie.

"Hold on," I said, clamping my hand over the microphone. *Where was the bloody mute button?* I looked up at Brian and shrugged.

"Typo my ass," he said. "You've got another buyer. Who's that on the phone? Is that the chick you copied on my e-mail?"

"What?"

"*What*?" said Lucie.

"You copied someone on my e-mail," said Brian. "I thought it was kind of a shitty thing to do, playing people off against each other like that. And now I've wasted my time coming all way over to this . . . this *freakzone* and you've already sold it to her? Couldn't you have told me? This is such bullshit, man. You're a total fuckin' douchebag." With a shake of his good hair, Brian turned and walked back to the front door, swung it open, then threw it closed behind him. A new crack appeared on the wall. It was all starting to make sense now. My reply to Lucie's e-mail must have become tangled up with the other e-mail that had dropped into my inbox at the precise moment I hit "send." I must have accidentally replied to both Brian *and* Lucie. Jesus, it was *Brian* who must have sent me the text message.

Whoops.

"The sofa's still for sale, right?" said Lucie.

"It is now."

"Can I come over at eight?"

"Let me see," I said, as if I had anything better to do. "Yes, I think eight would be good. I could make that work."

"Great, see you then."

She hung up.

I stood there for a moment, staring at the sofa in disbelief.

"L for *Lucie*," I said to myself.

12

The Best Sofa Bed in the World

Under a weary late afternoon sky, I made my way slowly around the rooftop pool of the Empire West apartment building, with its obstacle course of teak recliners and sandbox ashtrays, and came to a halt at a plastic suicide barrier. I stood there for a while, high above the parking lots and the industrial air conditioners, and listened to the drone of the city: distant, reassuring, like the engines of the starship *Enterprise*. With its crew of thirteen million, the USS *Los Angeles* was going boldly forward into an unknown future, the controls set to impulse drive.

I too am going boldly into an unknown future: a future without my apartment; a future without the Leisureplex.

Hence my fantasy apartment-hunting visit to the Empire West, located a whole one hundred yards down the street. If I could afford it (and I can't afford anything), the Empire West would be a big improvement on the Leisureplex. It has valet parking, a marble-encased lobby, and an "entertainment pavilion" on the roof, next to the pool. Then there are the more familiar amenities: the security detail, the key-coded gym, the telephone answering service, the hot tub, the tennis court. Nevertheless, I'm not so sure about the wisdom of living in a seventeen-story building in LA. According to the seismological map I downloaded from Google the other day, there are sixteen fault lines within a forty-mile radius of the Empire West. Just think: all those tectonic gearwheels, unoiled and misaligned, and ready to blow. Generally speaking, I am

not afraid of earthquakes in California. Up here, however, it's different. Up here, an earthquake would feel more like an airline disaster.

"So whaddaya think?" asked a voice behind me.

It belonged to Bernard Paxman, my new real estate broker, and
my new best friend.

"I like it," I said. "How much?"

A purely hypothetical question, this.

"Fifteen," shrugged Bernard.

Like all real estate brokers, Bernard deals only in abbreviated
numbers. As far as Bernard is concerned, zeros are a technicality.

"Per month?"

"Week."

Bernard shrugged again, this time allowing his facial muscles to
get involved. He does a lot of shrugging, Bernard. You get the impression that without the ability to shrug at insanity, in all its forms, you'd
be in a lot of trouble, generally, as an LA real estate broker. Bernard
adjusted his sunglasses and gave me the kind of squint he might once
have practiced in the mirror.

"It's a hot market," he added, flopping a mint around in his mouth.
"If they sold instead of renting, they could get two."

"Two?"

"Maybe two and half. The market's *hot,* Chris."

Bernard is at least 370 years old old. He is short, hairless on top,
and swollen with heat welts and ultraviolet blisters, as if he might once
have worked at a nuclear reactor. Today he was draped in an unbut-
toned Hawaiian shirt which exposed a truly sensational mound of chest
hair: white and gray, like chaparral after a forest fire. So far we had
looked at five apartments together: all of them total shitholes. LA is a
city of home owners, Bernard kept telling me, not renters. And as you
move up the rental price range, you just get *more* shit: more gold fixtures, more pink-veined marble staircases, more "wet bars" with knotted
wood cabinetry. The Empire West was our last, and our most promising, appointment. The apartment on offer was one of the cheapest in
the building: a second-floor unit with a view of concrete and traffic.

Bernard assured me that for at last fifteen minutes every afternoon, it got sunlight. Whoever was renting the place out considered himself a renegade talent when it came to interior decor. Three of the walls had been covered with a loose purple fabric. The remaining surfaces were mirrored, as if in homage to a bad college nightclub. "Walls of glass," Bernard had gasped, approvingly, when we first walked in.

After the tour, we had taken the elevator up to the roof to inspect the leisure facilities.

And now here we were.

"You told me two bed, one bath, in West Hollywood, with a pool and a tennis court," Bernard was complaining. "You'd be lucky to find a place like that for less than twenty, never mind *fifteen*. If fifteen's a problem, Chris, maybe we should be looking at one-bed single-families on Olympic?"

Bernard's face now illustrated the horror, the shame, of searching for one-bedroom single-families on Olympic.

"I can do fifteen," I lied.

"I'll get you an application form. They're asking for three months' deposit and two months in advance, plus bank statements, portfolio holdings, and your social security number, so they can run a credit check. Or you could just pay a year in advance. That way, you avoid the paperwork."

I fought the urge to grab Bernard by the legs and catapult him over the suicide barrier. Instead I looked northwest at Sunset Plaza Drive, which corkscrewed up like a malfunctioning rocket into the near-earth orbit of the Hollywood Hills. A truck carrying three bulldozers was coughing and grinding its way to the top. These trucks, I see them every day from outside the Coffee Bean. You wouldn't believe the stuff they carry up there: twenty-foot-high wrought-iron gates, imported from Norwegian castles; giant poolside movie screens with surround-sound PA systems; three-million-dollar supercars, boxed up in see-through, climate-controlled cases; and every kind of girder and clamp and bracket you could imagine, each one big enough to lay the foundations of a suspension bridge. Behind the trucks comes the motorcade of carpen-

ters, gardeners, plumbers, florists, postal workers, caterers, decora-
tors, architects, engineers, designers, car washers, water cooler chang-
ers, and take-out delivery people. It's a whole universe up there, a
megaleisuretropolis in the sky.

"See up there?" I said, pointing. *"That's* where I want to live."

"Hollywood Hills," shrugged Bernard. "Year on year, prices for the
Sunset Plaza Drive area are up forty-two percent. Last year, they were
up thirty-one percent. The year before that, twenty-six percent."

"It must be a hot market," I said, with as little sarcasm as I could
manage.

"You're a smart guy, Chris. The tax cuts, the rate cuts, the deficit
spending on military equipment. Every day, the Fed prints more money
and ships it out to LA. It's the perfect bubble. D'you know what caused
the last LA property crash, Chris? Nothing to do with show biz, Hollywood, all that stuff. It was the end of the cold war. The cuts in military
spending. Everyone knows they make movies here. Not so many people
know they make bombs and missiles, too."

"So the war in Iraq?"

"A goldmine—offset only by rising oil prices. But people here are
rich. They spend two hundred grand on a Mercedes convertible, they
don't care how much it costs to fill the damn thing up. Besides, you
could argue that oil prices are rising because of demand from the Chinese and the Indians, not the trouble in the Mideast. And if we *win*
the war, we protect our supply."

"Maybe they should be spending all that borrowed money on trying to make the supply obsolete instead," I said.

"Nice idea, but you're fighting entrenched interests, whereas the
military-industrial complex is all set up and ready to go. See those foundations?" Bernard pointed a withered finger halfway up the mountain
to a bluff with concrete poured over it, like poisoned icing on a granite
fruitcake. "I've been watching them go up since just before the Afghanistan campaign. You know how many engineers and inspectors and
geotechnical guys it takes to create a single viable plot of land up there,
on the edge of a cliff, in an extreme seismic hazard zone? They could

build a Home Depot on the moon in half the time. But the market can take it. The money is there. The guy who's building that place, he's in for ten years and ten million bucks, and so far he only has the goddamn foundations. Thing is, when he finally cashes out, he'll probably make ten in net profit. See those empty basins over there? Four infinity pools, side by side. The fifteen-car garage will be *inside* the bedrock."

"Jesus Christ," I said.

"Yeah, he probably wants in on the bubble, too."

I couldn't think of a reply, so I just stood there, feeling broke and useless.

"Look," said Bernard, turning to me and taking off his sunglasses. "If the rent's a problem, what about a mortgage?"

"A *mortgage*?"

"Get a loan and buy something, take out a home equity loan, remodel, sell, then buy again. That's what everyone else is doing. Interest rates are *one percent*, Chris. Money has never been so cheap."

I thought about this for a second. Back in Wooler, my parents still hadn't cleared the loan on their house, even though what they paid for it in the eighties would now barely cover the down payment on a decent SUV.

"If I can't afford the rent, how can I afford a mortgage?" I protested.

Bernard laughed, harder and with more feeling than seemed appropriate.

"I need you to call someone," he said.

I should probably update you on the Lucie situation.

Where to begin?

After that whole debacle with Brian, I just stood there in the empty apartment, thinking about the screwup with the e-mail, thinking about our phone conversation, and wondering why I wasn't already preparing for her arrival by remopping the floor, readjusting my props, and repracticing my lines. But for once I didn't feel the need. Lucie had been—well, almost *easy* to talk to. Which meant she almost certainly wasn't good-looking. The good-looking girls in my life, they have never been easy to talk to. Every time I get in the Jeep, I can still hear those silences with Lara. As for my conversations with Courage, they're on a rerun schedule inside my head, like an incriminating video clip on a cable news channel.

It wasn't like that with Lucie.

With Lucie, it was . . . *different*.

I had an hour or so to kill, so I collapsed onto the sofa and poked at the TV remote. All I could find were shows on how to make easy money from real estate: *Flip This House. Sell This House. Designed to Sell. House Hunters. What You Get for the Money. Location, Location, Location.*

In the end I settled on a different kind of property show, the one where a celebrity walks you through the rooms of his/her ecological disaster of a mansion, pointing to his/her possessions while bragging about them in a nonironic way. Today the mansion was in the Hollywood Hills. The camera was in the bathroom, and the celebrity was talking about the incredible specifications of his new superluxury toilet, a model known as the Herbeau "Dagobert" Toilet Throne (slogan: "For Your Majesty"). A voiceover interrupted to note that the superluxury celebrity toilet market is booming and that the Herbeau "Dagobert" Toilet Throne features dual armrests, a candle holder, an ashtray, and a recorded voice that recites the poetry of Alfred de Musset from within the bowl. At first I thought it was a joke, but it's true: the toilet exists. It costs twelve and a half thousand dollars.

And who knows, perhaps we should be glad. Perhaps superluxury toilet technology, like moon-mission technology, will eventually filter down to benefit the common man. Yes—I can see myself now, several decades into the future, standing in a hospital ward at a child's bedside, as a team of smiling stem-cell programmers looks on. "Just think, son," I will say, my voice thick with awe and gratitude, "if it weren't for the Herbeau 'Dagobert' Toilet Throne, we could never have made you *superhuman*."

*   *   *

A scuffle at the front door.

Then the doorbell.

I looked at the clock on the wall: Lucie was late. I muted the TV and checked myself out in the mirror: still bald, still ginger. At least the boil had gone down. Thanks to Dr. Bingblatz and his cortisone injections (latest count: three), it had been downgraded from atomic walnut to electric cashew.

With a prick of adrenaline, I wondered if Lucie would buy the sofa. Would this be my final Craigslist sale, the one that allowed me to pay the rent? And what if I liked Lucie as much as I expected to like her? Would I give the sofa away—or would I stand firm, like I had with Natalia? Adjusting my face to its best facsimile of a salesman's grin, I walked over to the door and swung it open.

Fuck, I thought, and almost blacked out.

Why was everything so difficult?

Why couldn't things go *right* for a change?

"Ah, *Chris*," said Cali DeLongpre, from beyond the threshold. "I was just passing through the neighborhood."

And then she asked for the rent.

Lucie did finally show up, a day later.

"I'm sorry," she said. "Something came up." Her smile suggested that only a miserable old bastard would get all knocked out of shape by someone turning up to a Craigslist appointment a mere day late.

Not that I was *upset,* of course.

No, upset didn't come close to describing it.

"No problem," I said. "Absolutely no problem at all." My own smile suggested that only a chronically unreliable airhead would turn up for a Craigslist appointment a day late: especially when I needed the money; especially when my landlady was making unscheduled collection visits. Speaking of which—it didn't go well, Cali DeLongpre's house-call. Not well at all.

"That it?" said Lucie, trying to get a look over my shoulder.

"Best Sofa Bed in the World," I said.

"It's *cute*. Do you mind?"

With that, Lucie powered through the front door, put down her expensively buckled pocketbook, took out a camera, and started to photograph the sofa bed as if it were a supermodel. I left the door open and joined her grudgingly in the living room, while trying not to notice just how . . . how . . . *Christ,* those jeans looked good on her. So did those low heels, with their V-shaped toes, and that neat, businesslike ponytail, and that tight sweater . . . and . . .

"Could use new covers."

"Yeah," I said, taking a deep breath. I wasn't going to argue.

"They're removable, right?"

I began to reply but quickly realized that no sound was coming out of my mouth. What the hell was going on with my throat? I badly needed a drink of water—something to help me talk, to help me swallow.

"Ooh-*eek*!!"

With a gasp and a tiny squeal, Lucie bounced down onto the cushions. "Ouch," she said, frowning. "These feathers are *sharp*." She pulled one of the razor-edged plumes from under her. "How long have you been *sitting* on this, Chris? You know you can refill sofa cushions, don't you? It costs, like, nothing. With new covers and new fill, this would be *nice*. Yeah."

I looked at her and thought: you can have the bloody sofa, I don't need the money, you can take anything you want. The other girls— Casey, Jade, Natalia—they had been good-looking, yes, but this was . . . Lucie was . . . bloody hell, my *arms* were sweating. I was starting to feel very strange indeed.

"Cash or check?" said Lucie, decisively.

"Eh?"

My throat was a hot sandpit full of broken bottles.

"I'll take it," she said. "Cash or check?"

"Oh, cash," I said, coughing again. "I need cash. I mean, cash would be great. Preferable. To a check. Thank you."

Lucie laughed unexpectedly.

"I'm a Czech, actually."

"A check is fine. Anything you want. Check, bank draft, IOU, whatever."

"No, *I'm* Czech."

"Eh?"

I really needed to stop saying "Eh?" I was beginning to sound like a Canadian bus driver.

"Born in Prague," said Lucie. "Moved to New York when I was five. Well, *escaped* to New York, technically. The communists didn't exactly know we were leaving."

Bloody hell. *She was a Bond girl*.

"Bloody hell. You're a Bond girl," I said.

"Not quite." She winked as she said this.

She *winked*.

I began to wonder: how do the Czechs do it? What is it that Czech genes know about making women that the rest of the world's genes have yet to find out? It's not as though Czech *men* are anything to look at. Christ, no. All those Vaclavs and Zdeneks, with their pilsner bellies, their eighties leatherwear, their potato dumpling complexions, they make the Russians look like a nation of *GQ* underwear models. But give them a Czech woman to breed with and, *bam,* there you have it: another masterpiece; another Eva Herzigova; another . . . Lucie. Not that Lucie was tall enough for modeling. She made me feel like a basketball player.

I *liked* feeling like a basketball player. I liked it a lot.

"Oh, before I forget," said Lucie. "It's a bed, right?"

I starred blankly.

"The sofa," she said.

"Oh, er, yeah. It folds out."

"Can I *see*?"

Another wink. Since when has anyone *winked* at me?

I showed her the bed.

Lucie stepped out of her heels and sat down on the catastrophically uncomfortable mattress, then swung up her legs so that she was lying flat. "Ha! Well, I guess this is one way to make sure your visitors don't overstay their welcome," she said. Lying there on the mattress, she looked so *small*. I had to see this girl again. I had to. I began to recite a silent prayer to Craig (*was* there a Craig?) thanking him for bringing this funny, beautiful, hugely overconfident and yet strangely anxious young woman into my apartment, so that she could try out my sofabed . . . and . . . and give me cash. Ah, yes, the cash. Could I *seriously* take this girl's money?

"Is that you?" asked Lucie, suddenly.

I tracked her gaze and found myself starring at my blown-up war clipping, now hanging immodestly above my desk.

"Oh, *that*?" I said, "Oh, that's nothing, really."

"You're a *war* reporter?"

"Used to be. Sort of."

"So—what?—you put that up there on the wall so girls ask you about it?" Lucie started to laugh. "Pretty slick, Chris."

"Actually, I was a terrible war correspondent," I blurted, trying to stop the exodus of blood to the vessels in my face.

"How come?"

"I kept running away."

"Isn't it normal to run away from bullets? The species wouldn't get very far if we kept running *toward* them, would it?"

"Editors don't care about the species. They care about the story."

"And you still . . . report?"

"Hollywood, not wars."

And that was when I did it: something inexplicable, something stupid, something I had no business whatsoever doing.

"We should go out for a drink sometime," I announced. "To celebrate the sofa purchase."

A long pause.

Too long, by any measure.

Oh, *Christ,* I thought. What have I done?

13

Giant Depressed Squid

As I might have already mentioned, my grandmother's sofa is stagger-ingly, overwhelmingly, almost impossibly heavy. There are moons or-biting Jupiter that probably weigh less than my grandmother's sofa. Once, when I was trying to move it an inch or two closer to the TV, I began to wonder if it was some kind of freak black hole, inadvertently created by a top-secret military facility out in the desert and now qui-etly sucking matter into its superdense core.

I remember the day it arrived on a truck from New York. The truck was too wide to get up the Leisureplex's driveway, so the deliv-ery men, all eight of them, had to carry the sofa up the near-vertical slope of Alta Loma Road, through the garage, up three flights of stairs, and then, finally, through the needle hole of my front door. Coun-tries have been successfully invaded in the time it took them to get that sofa into my apartment. When it was over, two men were down, the door frame was ruined, three insurance claims had been filed, and a small crowd had gathered to watch. As for the sofa: it was fine. Not a rip, not a scratch.

I'll admit it. When I first put the sofa up for sale, I allowed myself a cruel snigger at the thought of the poor bastard who would be respon-sible for having to coordinate that same operation in reverse. I imag-ined myself pouring a cold beer—stoking up a cigar, perhaps—and watching coolly from my upstairs balcony as the removal saga unfolded.

Between sips and puffs I would shout down suggestions while flipping through an old copy of *People* magazine. Ah, yes, how I was looking forward to washing my hands of the task of lugging that upholstered deadweight all the way down those stairs, through that long parking lot, down that long driveway, and then onto the inevitable truck, which would drive the sofa to its new location, where the entire excruciating procedure would have to be repeated.

So long, sofa!

Ha-ha!

You will not be missed.

"It's okay, I've got it . . . I've . . . dah . . . *oof*."

"Come on, Chris," said a young, confident male voice from somewhere in front of me. "You can get it higher than that."

"It's okay . . . it's . . . it's . . . gagh."

"Just *lift* it."

"Nneugh. Nneugh. Neughaargh."

"Chris? *Chris*? Jesus, are you *okay*?"

I was on my knees beside the waterfall in the courtyard of the Leisureplex, sweating, possibly bleeding, and very much wishing I was dead. My body was a gridlock of neurons, all of them transmitting the same five-letter message to my brain: AGONY. Resting on my flattened back was the staggering, overwhelming, almost impossible weight of my grandmother's sofa, its nail-spiked frame creating a series of deep, pulsating welts up my spine.

How had this happened?

How was this *possible*?

Lucie was how this was bloody possible.

Amazingly, my request for a drink to celebrate the sofa purchase hadn't sent her running from the apartment. Instead it prompted a long silence, during which I wanted to reach out and pull on the sound waves as they rippled out of my mouth, before they could make it to her ear canals, where I knew from a high school biology diagram they would cause a number of little bones inside her head to vibrate, which would in turn disturb the fluid in her inner ear, causing tiny hair cells to move, thus converting my words into electrical impulses that would be transmitted via the auditory nerves into her brain. But sound doesn't waste any time. No, sound knows exactly where it's going, and it gets there at approximately 769 miles per hour. It was too late. My crappy pickup line had done its worst.

"A drink to celebrate . . . *the sofa purchase*?" Lucie repeated, as if trying to make sense of the words.

I put my head in my hands and released a long, multitimbred groan. "That sounds a bit weird, doesn't it?"

"Only to a non–serial killer."

"Right. *Shit*. I'm sorry. Really, I can't believe . . . Forget I said anything."

We looked at each other. In her eyes I saw greens and browns and a million unknowable shades in between.

"Then again," she said, "this *is* the Best Sofa in the World."

I gulped. "Sofa *bed*, actually."

Lucie got up from the mattress and stepped back into her heels. "I need to go find an ATM," she announced. "I'll be back."

Yeah, right, I thought.

Back in ten thousand years.

It took her forty-eight hours to return, for a second viewing ("just to make sure"). Within those forty-eight hours we must have sent each other a dozen e-mails: silly, banterish e-mails, with nothing revealed except the time spent writing them, which revealed enough, I suppose. The second viewing went on for about an hour—I ended up telling her about a magazine piece I was working on about babies swapped at birth—after which she promised to come back with a truck.

Which is exactly what she did. But there was a problem. Lucie had brought a helper. And not a paid-by-the-day Mexican helper but a young, tall, and sharp-featured American named Jake or Jude or Josh or something similarly unbearable. Who the hell was this guy? The boyfriend? The ex-boyfriend? The *fiancé*? He had turned up in a rented U-Haul, wearing brand-new jeans, loafers, and an airy, open-collared shirt. He looked like one of those Silicon Valley guys—the ones you see on the cover of *Business Week* next to the word *billion*. Perhaps he was a fellow alumnus from Lucie's Ivy League university (she outclasses me not only in looks but also in education). Perhaps he was a relative. Perhaps he was a Ralph Lauren model with an MBA. Regardless, the presence of Mr. Rich and Handsome had left me with no choice: *I had to offer to help carry the sofa*. Not that I hadn't exhaustively considered the alternatives. I had concluded, however, that *not* offering to help to carry the sofa was essentially indistinguishable from making Lucie carry the sofa. Which would mean I would never see her again. Having said that, if this Jake or Jamie or Julian character was in fact her boyfriend, I would never see her again anyway.

"Nneugh," I said, wretchedly. "Neughaargh."

Something terrible was happening to me. I felt a warm shot of pureed lunch, spiked with acid, squirt up my esophagus. I held it down, and as I did so I felt an updraft of intense heat, as if I'd just stuck my head into a pizza oven. *Please don't vomit,* I thought. Please don't. Please. Not now, not here. And then—thank Christ—I felt a secret reserve of strength pump into my arms and I began slowly to rise to my feet, as if God himself had reached down to help me. Not bad, Ayres, I thought, not bad at all. Perhaps all those visits to the . . . perhaps that visit to the gym last week had done me some good. I began to look around for Lucie—so I could grin at her, reassuringly—and found her standing next to me, sharing the weight.

"You okay?"

"I'm actually . . . in pretty good . . . shape," I huffed. "No need to . . . *nneugh*."

"Keep going," shouted Mr. Handsome, his voice muted by the vast, abominable bulk of my grandmother's sofa. On we staggered down the stairwell, to a seventies porn sound track of grunts, shouts, and moans, as the sofa put dents in the wrought-iron railing and ripped the stucco off the walls.

Halfway down, Lucie said, "So what about eight o'clock?"

"Nneugh?"

"The drink. To celebrate."

My brief, startled pause was broken by a primitive howl of pain from somewhere below me. In my surprise I had momentarily released my grip of the sofa. Whoops. "ARE YOU TRYING TO FUCKING KILL ME?" shouted Jude or Jarrod or Jimmy or whatever the hell his name was.

"*Sorry*," I offered, without conviction.

"Try not to kill Josh," said Lucie, smiling.

"That would be fantastic," I grinned. "I mean, the drink. Not killing your . . . your *friend*. Where should we go?"

"What's that—*ouch!*—what's that place across the street?" asked Lucie, as the sofa resumed its violent descent.

No objection to the word *friend,* I noted.

"The Whiskey Bar?" I suggested, hoping this wasn't the correct answer. The Whiskey Bar is a tiny candle-lit room off the lobby of the Sunset Marquis hotel, the entrance of which is a few yards further up Alta Loma Road from the Leisureplex on the other side of the street. The Sunset Marquis isn't so much a hotel as a collection of villas, invisible behind a hedge so tall you'd need a helicopter to look over it. I know this because Jeff once rented a helicopter to look over it—a paparazzo job, way back. The hotel has its own recording studio and is popular with visiting rock stars. U2 have stayed there. So have the Rolling Stones. Personally, I've never been able to get beyond the front gate—even during the day it is guarded by a velvet rope and two earpieced and humorless bodybuilders—never mind into the bar.

"Yeah," said Lucie, decisively. "The Whiskey Bar. Let's go *there*."

A dolly was waiting for us at the bottom of the stairs. We tipped the sofa onto it, then rolled our top-heavy load slowly out of the garage and down the driveway to the truck. I was grinning so hard I feared the muscles in my face might never return to their default scowl. When the U-Haul's tailgate was closed Lucie counted out the asking price of the sofa in cash.

"Aren't you supposed to negotiate?" I said.

"I guess."

"Well?"

"Well, *what?*"

"Negotiate."

"Okay," said Lucie, slowly. "Will you take five hundred?"

"Yes."

"Aren't *you* supposed to negotiate too? You're asking for seven."

"Five will do."

I took the money.

And to be honest I didn't feel so bad about it. Because I knew then that if Lucie gave me half the chance—a quarter of chance, a *millionth* of a chance—I would give her everything. Yes, I would give her everything I ever owned, ever earned, ever wanted. And then I would try to give her more.

The situation back there with Cali DeLongpre was pretty awkward, no doubt about it. For such a tiny, prim-looking woman (tight-wrapped cardigan, long print dress), she managed to instill a terror in me that I hadn't felt since being shot at in the desert. Perhaps it was the surprise factor. Perhaps it was the rent-being-sixteen-days-overdue factor. Is there an established system of etiquette in such a renter/rentee situation? Do you offer a partial payment? Try to barter? Say you'll have the money in fourteen days, by which time the next rent check will be due? None of those options seemed viable. Besides, I had my pride. So I did the only thing I could do. I strode confidently over to the filing cabinet, took out my checkbook, wrote her a check, and handed it to her. She smiled, said thank you, and went quickly on her way.

I closed the door behind her, slumped down on the floor, and counted to one hundred. Had she put the check in her wallet or was she now sitting in her car in the underground garage, examining it under a map-reading light, just to make sure that all the details were correct? Details like the date in the top right corner, which wasn't the date at all, but a date four days into the future, thus giving the writer of the check another ninety-six hours to produce the cash.

Christ, I thought, I feel like such a *scumbag* these days.

I waited, and I counted.

I counted, and I waited.

And now to Citibank on Sunset Boulevard, where I sweat over a bleeping touch screen. It's a lot of work—isn't it?—having no money. A full-time job, practically. A career choice in its own right. All those hours, all that stress, all that *responsibility*. And there's not even any *money* in having no money.

The date on my postdated check to Cali DeLongpre passed several days ago, which means that by now it has almost certainly bounced. I can hardly bear to think of the fees this will involve and the damage it will inflict on my already fragile credit rating, never mind the next awkward situation it will force me to have with my landlady. Even with Lucie's five hundred dollars, there's a chance I still won't have enough money to clear the rent.

Maybe I'll be evicted. Maybe I'll be *arrested*.

I jab my PIN into the machine and hit ENTER.

And then something incredible: zeros fill up the screen, like soap bubbles, like beads of condensation. I can hardly believe it. Remember the five grand I spent on taking Lara to Neverland? The Beast paid it. I can't even remember filling in the claim form, it was so long ago. And yet there it is: a line item on my electronic statement, next to my three favorite words in the English language: *incoming wire transfer*. And it gets better. Next to the five grand is another, even larger sum of money, from a shady-sounding UK Internet company.

At last, my loan has arrived!

For the first time in weeks—it feels like years—I am liquid. I actually have money. Borrowed money, yes, but real, green, spendable money. I am back. I am alive again. Ladies and gentlemen, please fasten your seat belts and stow your tray tables, *we are about to reenter the economy*.

A brief victory dance in front of worried-looking bank staff. And then back to the parking lot and the waiting Jeep, where I open the glove box and take out an expensively ridged business card.

It looks like this.

Flip Jackman
Home Loan Specialist
You-Bet-You-Can Mortgage Corporation
"Dealing in Dreams since 2002!"
1-555-ARMLOAN

I pick up my phone and dial the number.

Things I have learned about Lucie: She drives a brand-new white Saab turbo with lowered suspension and body kit (she's definitely my type); her father died a few years back; her stepfather, also Czech, is a former opera singer who now builds faux castles for twenty-eight-year-old stockbrokers in upstate New York; she looks good in leather (she looks good in everything); and she has two voices: her aloof Ivy-Leaguer-in-Manhattan drawl, which she uses when she's nervous or trying to impress, and her playful, nine-year-old-at-the seaside voice, which she uses when she's not doing either of those things. Oh, and she winks a lot.

Falling is the verb most commonly associated with love. But I don't feel as though I'm falling. I feel as if I'm rising, as if I've been treated with some kind of antigravity potion. I'm listening to crap pop music. I'm even ignoring the news, with its feel-bad animal stories and emotional weather reports. Another thing about Lucie: I get the feeling she's as on the make as I am. When her parents escaped from Czechoslovakia into West Germany (a feat made possible by two travel applications to the communists, made separately by each parent from different addresses, and officials too lazy or incompetent to cross-check the names), their financial resources amounted to three airline tickets to New York. In Manhattan, Lucie's father worked as a dishwasher and a handyman. On the side he worked at being an alcoholic. From what I gather, Lucie's father wasn't a very successful dishwasher or handyman, but he was an immensely successful alcoholic. Some people just aren't cut out for America. He maxed out too soon. He miscalculated his consumption curve. America killed him—or, at the very least, it encouraged him to kill himself. A doctor's visit confirmed the worst: a tumor the size of a grapefruit inside his stomach. Lifestyle cancer, they said. Six months later, he was dead at the age of forty-six. By this time Lucie's mother had left him and fallen in love with the opera singer. They went into real estate together and now they're multimillionaires. Lessons in life, in capitalism, in the American way of things, they don't get much clearer than that.

All this I found out during our drink. Another thing I found out: getting into places like the Whiskey Bar is a lot easier when you're with a good-looking girl in tight jeans, a low-cut halter top, and a leather jacket.

For Lucie, the drink remained in the singular: a Maker's Mark on the rocks. For me, it escalated into the plural, starting with a beer and progressing to a double vodka soda, followed by three more (what was I *thinking*?), consumed over the course of two hours. I should mention that my tolerance for alcohol is right up there with the average eight-year-old schoolgirl's. All was going well—I seemed to be getting wittier and better-looking as the evening wore on—until I stood up to leave. That was when the last two vodkas kicked me in the back of the legs. It took truly heroic concentration to escort Lucie back to my apartment, where she had left behind her copy of the *Wall Street Journal* (I think she has more money than I do). I briefly considered going all in for an early lunge, but instead I offered a double-cheeker and said good night. And then I drank a pint of espresso to get my vision back.

Only one thing bothers me about the date. A moment early in the evening, when we were discussing grand life ambitions, I told her, during a pompous aside (I default to pompous when nervous), that one day I would like to own two homes. A bit rich, I agree, from someone in my situation.

"Oh, at *least*," Lucie shot back.

And now I can't help but wonder. Was she joking? Or is this the standard I've set myself up to meet?

Not a big deal, of course.

Nevertheless, I think I need to find out.

"Sally," I said, tightly. "Huge favor."

"*You* again. You only call when you want something."

"I do?"

"You do. Not that you need my help. Not after that *performance* at the Disney hall. How is Ms. Macleod, anyway?"

"Ready to have babies."

"Not yours, I presume."

"That's what I gather, yes."

"Poor you."

"Look, Sally, I need to impress someone this weekend. I need a date, a good one. Was hoping you could help."

The word *impress* didn't really come close to describing the feat I had to achieve with Lucie. Somehow, I had to persuade her that a failed war correspondent who couldn't even pay his rent without selling his grandmother's furniture might realistically provide her with the kind of transcontinental, multihome lifestyle that a twenty-six-year-old, Ivy League–educated, Czech-born knockout would naturally expect. There could be no mistakes this time. No bullshit four-hour drives into the

desert to meet crazed pop stars. No sexless, dubiously credentialed
black-tie billionaires' balls. And absolutely *nothing* for which access had
not been secured, honestly, in advance. My follow-up date had to be
spectacular, emphatic, utterly convincing—a life experience to rival
childbirth, space flight, religious conversion.

"So I'm your fairy godmother now?" said Sally, with a crack of
laughter that made me flinch.

"Sally, please. Something. Anything. What's going on this weekend? You must have some ideas."

"Aren't you supposed to be a *Hollywood* correspondent?"

"Please?" I said, with a long, desperate sigh. This was pointless.
Sally was never going to give me any leads.

"You know it's the Golden Globes this weekend, don't you?"

Of course it was the Golden Globes this weekend! How could I have
forgotten? This was exactly what I needed.

"Biggest awards ceremony in town until the Oscars," Sally went on.
"But you need to get a move on, Chris. You've already missed half the
pre-parties. Try the HBO event at Chateau Marmont. Can't get you in,
of course, but if you call the press office there shouldn't be a problem."

"What about the *ceremony*? Shouldn't I start with that?"

"Silly, it's all about the parties, not the ceremony. Not that the
HBO party is the biggest party on Saturday night."

"It's not?"

"Not by a mile."

"So what *is* the biggest party?"

Sally told me.

There was a long, thwarted silence. Then I said,

"But that's impossible."

Flip Jackman, nonconforming superjumbo Home Loan Specialist at the
You-Bet-You-Can Mortgage Corporation, is either a genius or a very
good salesman, possibly both. He understands money like a geneticist
understands DNA. He knows what it's made of, where it comes from,

how it interacts with other money: how it multiplies and mutates, to create clone money, fake money, *mortgage* money. He communicates in a language comprised only of acronyms, digits, and military metaphors. Through the metal rasp of his speakerphone, he sounds electronic, superterrestrial. When we spoke just now, he told me that he was "ready to pull the trigger on a no-documents superjumbo LIBOR-ARM at five-point-three with a nice little teaser, and move in for a simultaneous equity max out with a piggyback at eleven-point-one."

I hung up, took three maximum-strength aspirin, and called Bernard.

"He's saying that he can get you a million-dollar loan with no down payment, for about two grand a month," said Bernard.

"That can't be possible."

"You'd be surprised. Things have changed. The market is more liquid now."

"Seriously, Bernard. It can't be possible."

"It's a hot market, Chris. Rates are at one percent. *One percent*, Chris. They haven't been this low for the last forty-six years. It's thermonuclear out there. My advice to you: get in while you still can."

Can Flip's mortgage *really* be possible? Even if it is (and it can't be), I doubt it can be legal. A million dollars with no down payment, for two grand a month? It's an insult to money—an insult to the *value* of money. No wonder the LA real estate market has a problem with hyperinflation: the mortgage industry is printing its own banknotes. Like the planet itself, the LA real estate market is operating for the extreme short term, at maximum temperature. This afternoon I did some Googling and found at least a dozen blogs dedicated to guessing the precise date at which the bubble will spike itself on reality, no doubt taking the economy and the stock market with it. But it's the dollar that really worries me; it's the dollar that keeps me up at night. Where did it all go so wrong? Once proud and strong, the greenback now sits in the emergency ward, chugging its pills and wheeling its drip. If you believe the charts attached to the dollar's bedside, things are only going to get worse. Yes, if you believe the currency surgeons, the dollar doctors, it won't be long now before the dollar is dragged out of its wheelchair and thrown backward down the stairs.

And *then* what happens?

What happens when the currency of the world's largest economy is crippled for life? All I know is this: there is only one conservative, sensible, educated strategy when it comes to home ownership in LA.

I must buy immediately, while I can still make an easy profit.

I almost forgot to mention: on the way home from Citibank the other day I nearly killed the madman on the bicycle who circles the block while telling everyone the apocalypse is nigh. There he was, pedaling in a high gear down the ski-slope plunge of Alta Loma Road, just as I was swinging left into the Leisureplex. The first thing I heard was the noise: a double blast of such volume, such violence, I felt sure that I was about to collide with an eighteen-wheeler. He must have hooked up some kind of steam horn to his handlebars. And then, in a flash of purple spandex and a rush of air, his spoked missile whirred past.

"*Planet raper!*" he shouted.

"Fuck you!" I shouted back.

But why do I have a terrible feeling he's on to something? On my drive up to the Coffee Bean this morning, I listened to a news item about giant depressed squid rising from thousands of feet below the South Pacific, swimming north, then committing suicide on the beaches of Orange County. Yes, the squid are committing *suicide*. We've reached the stage in our planetary crisis, our species emergency, where you couldn't even make this stuff up anymore. As the item went on, I had to keep telling myself: *This is actually happening*. For a moment I imagined myself as a screenwriter, trapped in some neutral-toned, air-conditioned capsule in the San Fernando Valley, pitching the story to an overcaffeinated studio executive.

"Depressed squid," I would begin, anxiously. "An end-of-the-world thriller. Think Armageddon—with mollusks."

"Squid?" the executive would say, his nose encased within the cardboard beaker of his triple espresso mocha latte.

"For millions of years," I would continue, in my deepest voice, "these monsters of the sea have lived in the unexplored depths of the Pacific. Scientists have never found their eggs. But now they're starving to death because humans have overfished their ocean. What's more, the starving squid have been confused by the warming water, so they're rising from the deep and drifting north, from Chile to Southern California, where they're killing themselves on the—"

"I don't get it," the executive would say, his nose now topped with foam, like an Alpine peak from the seventies, when Alpine peaks had snow. "Is there a *plot*?"

"Humans would have to save the squid to save the world."

"Humm."

"Kind of like *Watership Down*," I would go on.

"*Watership Down*?"

"With mollusks."

A long and uncomfortable silence would follow. Eventually, the executive would cough. And then he would say, "That's the stupidest fucking thing I've ever heard."

Yet nothing seems plausible any longer.

Even in my own ecosystem, my own personal climate zone, freakish event patterns are forming. Somewhere high above the Leisureplex, Fate and Love sit at their great celestial conference table—a routine meeting—browsing documents, flipping through calendars, double-checking dates. And then, in a quickening panic, Fate notices a terrible error, a mix-up in the files.

"You mean we put Lucie, *Czech* Lucie, with *Ayres*?" he splutters, rising from his chair. "Ayres the . . . Ayres the . . ."

". . . *Craigslist* guy," moans Love.

Fate roars and punches a hole in the wall. He's been having problems with his temper recently—a result, perhaps, of all that time spent hanging around with his more successful friends Death and Weather.

"What can we do?" he asks, despair welling in his eyes.

"Don't worry, my dear," Love sniffs, dabbing at her face with a white handkerchief. "We'll think of *something*."

14

Mike's Thing

Sally was right. Getting into the HBO party was easy. All it took was a telephone call to an assistant's assistant in New York and that was that. Done. On the list, plus one. Convincing Lucie to join me had been equally stress free—almost stressfully stress free, in fact. Maybe this is how girls behave when they actually want to go out with you, I thought. Or maybe there was a catch.

There had to be a catch.

Lucie turned up at the Leisureplex just after eight o'clock on Saturday night wearing a sequined miniskirt, black stockings, black heels, and a white fur jacket, cut high above the waist. I thought to myself: if God were ever to place an ad in a glossy magazine for womankind, *this* is what it would look like. Her hair was swept upward and back in shades of chocolate and espresso and held in position with an intricate and expertly organized system of bands, needles, and clips. Oh, how I wanted to undo all those bands, needles, and clips. I began to wonder if all this was some kind of incredible hallucination. I began to wonder if I was actually blacked out on Hollywood Boulevard, moaning into a gutter full of crumpled Star Maps and used contraceptive devices. But I also felt strangely unintimidated by Lucie. She ran on a different frequency, a different energy, than the other girls I had met in LA. She ran on direct current—as direct, I imagined, as human energy comes. There was no uncertainty with her, no bullshit, no sense of a strategy evolving, of a game being played. We were on a *date,* we would test our compatibility, and that was that.

If only everything else were so straightforward.

The other party—the *real* party—was proving to be as impenetrable as an Israeli nuclear facility. By the time Lucie arrived at my apartment I had spent a good seventy-two hours trying to break the access code to this mysterious gathering. At first, I seemed to be in with a chance. Thanks to one of Sally's leads, I chased down the custodian of the guest list—a social fixer known only as Mr. X—to a dinner in Beverly Hills. As luck would have it, the dinner was hosted by a publicist friend of mine, Sarah Cairns.

Blonde, thirtyish, Sarah has a *Harper's & Queen* wardrobe and an accent to match. Our friendship would be a matter of professional convenience if it wasn't for the incredible fact that she grew a few miles north of Wooler, on the other side of the border. With her help, I invited myself to the dinner, claimed the seat next to Mr. X, and spent the evening ordering increasingly unwise combinations of booze while boasting casually about largely fictitious social connections. Whatever it was I said—the booze erased at least half of the conversation—it seemed to do the trick. Yes, I was in vintage form that night. At one point the entire table was laughing at some joke or anecdote I was telling. By the time the bill arrived (did I pick up the tab?) there was a general consensus that I should go to the party—"Mike's thing," Sarah kept calling it—and that I should bring a guest. My instructions were to await a text message from Mr. X containing both the address and the password for the gate.

There was only one rule: I couldn't write about the party. Yes, Mr X. was seriously concerned that I might actually want to turn my date with Lucie into work.

If only all rules were as easy to keep.

Twenty-four hours later and no text message. Like a Beverly Hills teenager, my phone had remained sullen and uncommunicative all day.

So I sat on a recliner out by the pool and watched as the sun performed its nightly stage-dive over Malibu, giving the horizon a bloody nose. As eight o'clock approached, I wondered if Mr. X had known all along that I was a fraud. I tried calling his cell phone but he wouldn't pick up. So I tried again, and again. And then a few times more. Under normal circumstances, I wouldn't have cared so much. Under normal circumstances, I would have been delighted with the HBO party, which, by any standard, was a respectable date in its own right. But something told me that it wouldn't be enough: no, not for a girl like Lucie. Something told me that without a double headliner all could be lost.

"I'll drive," announced Lucie as we stood in my apartment, ready to leave. Here's a girl with an exit strategy, I thought. I put up a routine protest, then quickly backed down. I was happy not to drive. It meant that Lucie didn't have to go anywhere near my joke of a car, for starters. It also meant that I could take advantage of the HBO party's inevitable free bar. On the other hand, I suspected it might not be a bad idea to go a little easier on the vodka sodas this time around.

Outside there was a black, pinholed sky and a strange warmth in the air. Typical January weather in this new, superheated century. In the Saab, Lucie buzzed open the sunroof and turned up the radio. It felt odd to be driven to a date. It felt like cheating. Still, it offered me a glimpse of Planet Lucie, with its vanilla-scented atmosphere and its strange topography of lipstick tubes, strewn cardigans, canned mints, and three-quarter-empty water bottles. Strangest of all was something wedged behind the Saab's driver's seat. It was a sports bag filled with . . . no, it couldn't be . . . *could it?* I tried to get a better look, but by then we had arrived and valets were swarming the car, opening doors, writing tickets, yelling in Spanish.

Out we climbed.

Still no text message.

Fuck.

Above us loomed the venue: Chateau Marmont, a hotel in medieval Gothic style, set into the hillside above the Sunset Strip. Built
during the glamour boom of the twenties, the Chateau scowls down at
the traffic, daring cars to get beyond the security detail at the foot of its
steep driveway. The place unnerves me—I generally try to avoid it. John
Belushi killed himself at the Chateau with a speedball overdose; Jim
Morrison *almost* killed himself at the Chateau by falling out of a window; and the members of Led Zeppelin tried their best to kill themselves at the Chateau by riding their Harley-Davidsons through the
lobby. The place has always felt to me like a holding facility, a depar-
tures lounge. At the Chateau you are not so much a guest as a passenger, booked on the overnight to hell.

In the narrow driveway we were quizzed by men with gun-shaped
lumps in their tuxedoes, then shown up to a table of clipboard holders
by the door. The Chateau seemed crueler, more menacing than I had
remembered. The turrets stood higher, narrower; the spires blacker,
sharper. For a moment I didn't realize what was wrong with the scene.
Then I saw it: a crater near the gate, and a doubled-over STOP sign, around
which was huddled a small, whispering crowd. An asteroid, I thought.
An *asteroid*. Wait until Dr. Bingblatz hears about this. But I was wrong.
We soon learned that the crater was in fact the work of the fashion photographer Helmut Newton, who had been a guest at the hotel until a
few hours earlier, when he smoked out of the underground car park in
his Cadillac SUV, veered wildly right, then tipped downhill with the
maximum velocity allowed by physics, ending his brief journey a few
seconds later in an explosion of steel and tropical landscaping.

Christ . . . the insanity of it. Out there in the driveway, no one
was sure of the details: the whats, the whys. There were hushed theories about brake failure, heart failure (Newton was eighty-three), auto-
erotic suicide. Being vaguely familiar with the themes of Newton's
work—I remember the fuss over the jewelry ad, the one where the
model was dismembering a chicken—I had my own theory: that in
death, as in life, the old man was trying to tell us something.

Something about death, perhaps.

Death and cars.

Beyond the crater was a line of paparazzi, like glass-faced cyborgs, visiting earth from the planet Nikon. I blinked into the white light and
for a second imagined Hiroshima before the firestorm. One by one,
limos pulled up to the cyborgs and tipped out more celebrities—like
human specimens, presented for examination. I wished I was better
with names. There was that guy from that show, that Movie Director,
that Actress I Liked. What were they all *doing* here? Didn't they have
better things to do on a Saturday night? Then I reminded myself: for
them, this was work. These days in Hollywood, parties aren't social
occasions, they're marketing opportunities. They're all about the spectacle of extreme consumption, designed to encourage the rest of us to
follow suit. The irony, of course, is that the celebrities don't pay for
any of it. The dresses, the cars, the gadgets, the booze—it's all free. At
the Golden Globes, the celebrities who hand out the awards are given
a gift bag of products worth twenty-six grand. At the Oscars, the gift
bag is worth four times as much. They even have "gifting suites" now:
mini–department stores of free merchandise, set up backstage. Why?
So the organizers can itemize the free products and hand the list out to
people like me, who report it as news, even though it's advertising.

It's happening in every industry now, not just show business: the
one-upmanship of profligacy, for the sake of a free headline. Down in
Palm Springs, it is now possible to buy a thousand-dollar omelet. When
I first heard about it I almost rushed down there with my AmEx card.
But the omelet's old news now. In Lancashire, England, a chef has re-
taliated with a sixteen-grand pie, made with two bottles of 1982 Château
Mouton Rothschild. And now the Japanese are having a go. They've
baked a fruitcake and sprinkled it with diamonds and put it up for
sale for $1.5 million. I can only imagine what the Russians are plan-
ning. Yes, I can see it now: an Olympic-sized swimming pool filled

with caviar, in which the diner is submerged, naked except from edible blini underwear. . . .

After checking our names against the list—no drama this time—we were escorted to an unmarked double doorway, through which was an antique elevator. On dusty gearwheels it hauled us up to a dark, pulsating lobby. The place was a cauldron of body heat, but I got the sense that the guests were passing through, that they were en route to somewhere else, somewhere better, somewhere they could settle down for the night. In LA you don't just go to *one* party for the evening: like a hedge fund manager, you distribute your capital between a portfolio of events. I was beginning to recognize the faces now. That was Al Pacino, standing over by . . . yes, that was Jude Law. And that was Quentin Tarantino . . . and that was Uma Thurman . . . and that was . . . who *was* that? I checked my phone again: no message.

Everyone seemed to be leaving.

Two girls in high boots and short skirts hustled past. "Going to Mike's?" said the first one.

"You kidding me?" snorted the other. "This is the warm-up crowd."

I pretended not to hear.

So there we stood in the Chateau's lobby, me and the girl who bought my sofa, on a date that was about as probable as Helmut Newton's death in a freak driveway accident. The crowd swilled around us toward the elevators, like the contents of an unplugged sink. Perhaps we were too late. Perhaps we were too early.

"Who's *Mike*?" asked Lucie, suddenly. "Everyone's talking about *Mike*."

I looked at my phone again. Was it even getting a signal in here?

Bloody Mr. X.

Say nothing, I thought. Say nothing at all. Don't overpromise. Don't put yourself through that again. But I couldn't help it. Why can't I *ever* help it? "Mike's throwing a party tonight," I announced, conspiratorially. "A big one. Even bigger than this. Sponsored by *Vanity Fair* magazine."

"But who *is* he?" Lucie asked.

I shrugged and said, "Let's get some drinks and check out the garden. And then we should probably get going, too."

"But we've only been here *two minutes*."

I knew then that what I was about to say was unnecessary, that it was reckless, that it could ruin everything. All this I knew, yet the words had already gathered their momentum. They wanted out. And there's nothing you can do, really, to stop the words when they need their freedom like that.

"Wouldn't you rather hang out at Mike's?" I said.

"We're *invited*?"

I laughed, and in the laughter there was despair: despair at never knowing when is enough; of never knowing when to give up. One day, one day soon perhaps, I think I would like to know when to give up.

"Of course we are," I grinned.

Twenty minutes later found me inside a locked stall in the Chateau's bathroom, standing over the toilet, my head against the wall. "Fuck," I hissed. "Fuck. Fuck. Oh, *fuck*." I looked at my phone for the eight millionth time: nothing. Tomorrow I would hunt down and kill Mr. X.

How could I get myself out of this? Why had I been so ridiculously certain that a man I had met *once in my life* would make good on a drunken promise to put me on the list for the world's most impossible-to-gatecrash party? *Wouldn't you rather hang out at Mike's?* I mouthed to myself, with childish sarcasm, as I kicked the flush lever by the gaping ceramic. The thought of my overblown promise to Lucie was enough to induce a spasm of fury, and before I could control it I had punched the wall, realizing too late that the wall was covered with ridged art deco tiles. I stuffed my shredded knuckles into my mouth to silence the cry.

"*Idiot*," I whimpered.

Moments later, I emerged somewhat sheepishly from the bathroom with an excruciating pain in my hand and the pattern of a tile embedded in a red welt on my forehead—an unintended consequence

of having rested my head against the wall. Yes, I had really underesti-
mated the hardness of that wall. The population of the party had halved
during my bathroom exile. I peered through the gloom, trying to blink
some moisture into my contact lenses. Where was Lucie? What the
hell was I going to tell her? Maybe I could stall, maybe I could—

"Chr-*is*?" said a familiar voice from behind me. It was a delicate
sound, pure . . . intimately close.

Was it . . . ?

No, it couldn't be.

"Courage!" I yelped, as I turned around.

"Hey," she said, coolly. "Thought you were back in Baghdad."

Yes, this was just what I needed, just what I wanted, at this particular moment in time: Courage supermodel Macleod.

"That's n-n-next week," I said, clasping my bloodied hand behind
my back and hoping it was too dark to make out the imprint on my
forehead. "The ticket's booked. Al Qaeda Air: safest way to fly."

I laughed weakly. Courage offered a tolerant smile.

She was wearing a black dress with her hair down, but her
schoolmarm glasses—her supermodel invisibility cloak—remained in
place. Beside her was one of her music industry friends. In snakeskin
boots, skinny jeans, and tapered jacket, he hung back moodily, with an
expression that suggested he would rather be out in the garden, smoking something illegal. Under white cuffs I saw tattoos. A tough guy.
Courage liked the tough guys. I almost wanted to laugh—at our night
at the Disney hall, at our Beverly Hills lunch, at those ridiculous battle
stories I told her. Meeting Lucie had made me realize how off target I
had been with Courage Macleod. Yes, with Lucie, everything had come
into focus. Where *was* she, anyhow?

I was trying to look around the room without looking as though I
was looking around the room, when Courage said, "Oh, how rude of
me, have you met Dickie?"

"*Dickie?*" I coughed, inhaling an ice cube. Suddenly I was a
beached fish, separated from my oxygen supply.

"Richard," said Dickie, reaching out with a cold, bored palm.

This was Dickie?

"Hi," I managed, through what turned out to be the first of a series of violent windpipe contractions. "I had no idea . . ."

"Uh?" said Dickie. His face registered limited interest. Expressed as a percentage, his interest would have been in the low single digits.

"I mean, I thought you would be—"

"Didn't Sally tell you?" Courage interrupted, linking arms with the man I had never wanted to meet. "We're getting—"

There was a buzz in my pocket.

My phone.

It was my *phone*.

"We're getting—" Courage paused for a second time as she watched me now struggle desperately to prize the phone from my jeans pocket, a task made exponentially more difficult by my injured hand.

"Excuse me," I gasped, as I finally pulled it free. I looked down at the words flickering on the tiny, glowing screen.

"We're getting *married*," said Courage, finally.

But I wasn't listening.

I was too busy looking at the screen.

"Follow Sunset west to Bev Hills, turn right up Benedict Canyon, right again on San Ysidro, then keep going until you reach the top," read the message. "Shouldn't need p/word, just give your name. Good luck!'

Shouldn't?

Good *luck*?

The message was from Sarah—my publicist friend—not Mr. X. Was this a good sign or a bad one?

It was better than nothing, that was for sure.

After escaping from Courage and Dickie—their engagement hardly came as a surprise, yet it still somehow came as a *surprise*—I found Lucie under the heat lamps in the garden, where she too had bumped into an old friend. "What's wrong with your *face*?" she asked as I approached. I told her I had bumped into a wall and that the redness would soon disappear. In fact, the redness seemed to be reddening. Stress, probably. Stress and the booze.

And of course the whole tile/head thing.

Soon enough we were back in the Saab, speeding into Beverly Hills. As we tumbled west on Sunset Boulevard—Lucie is a girl who likes to use her turbochargers when exiting a corner—I tried to get another look at the bag behind the driver's seat, but its mouth had folded in on itself, leaving only a thin glimpse of something black and shiny within. What was she *hiding* in there? Finally we turned up into the hills and then right up San Ysidro Drive. I had never driven this way before. I was beginning to realize that the parts of Beverly Hills I knew were actually the *cheap* parts of Beverly Hills. The higher we went, the bigger the houses became, until they weren't houses so much as ranches, set far back from the street behind ten-story hedges and manned sentry boxes with ARMED RESPONSE signs.

As we corkscrewed higher, a pressure began to thicken in my head, a force so intense I feared my brain might burst and leak out through my ears. And then, finally, as the Saab leveled out onto a pristine two-lane street at the top of the mountain, I swallowed hard, my ears turned inside out, and my hearing suddenly sharpened, as if someone had switched to a high-definition broadcast. I exhaled. This was where Sarah's directions ran out.

Which way now?

"Oh my *God*," said Lucie.

"What?"

"This is Beverly Park."

"Beverly *Hills*," I corrected.

"Chris, you don't understand. This is Beverly *Park*. This is what real estate people dream about when they go to bed at night. I've read about this place in magazines. It's the wealthiest gated community in America. The world, probably. The houses are forty, sixty thousand square feet each. *Everyone* lives here: the CEO of Google, Barry Bonds, a couple of Saudi royals, Eddie Murphy, Rod Stewart. The Homeowner Association is like the Gestapo, only with better lawyers."

"Wow," I said, staring at the words *good luck* on my phone. Sarah's message was beginning to make more sense.

Lucie seemed troubled.

"Chris, is this party at someone's *house*? Are you sure we're invited? I feel like they might shoot gatecrashers here."

"Everything's fine," I said, without conviction. I reached for the air-conditioning. It was getting hot. "Look—over there."

To the right of us were gates. More specifically: a gatehouse, stacked with cameras and capitalized warning signs, behind which stood two latticed-iron barriers, each one the height of an office building, secured on either side by giant motorized hinges. The U.S. Marines would have a hard job getting in here, I thought. These people probably had snipers, grenade launchers, Howitzers. Lucie pulled up slowly. There were no other cars anywhere. We were alone on this private road, in this billionaire's Legoland, somewhere above cloud level in Beverly Hills. Now the boiled and plucked face of a security guard was framed within the Saab's window. He took a long look at us, then stood back to inspect the car.

Perhaps *he* knew what was inside Lucie's sports bag.

"Name?" he asked.

"CHRIS AYRES," I boomed, leaning over the handbrake and being careful to pronounce the "r," like Americans do.

Barely a second passed before the gate began to open. This didn't make any sense. Had he memorized the guest list? Was he *sure* we were invited? I almost wanted to ask him to double-check, but Lucie was again exercising the Saab's turbochargers. "Oh my God, Beverly Park," she giggled. "This is going to be *wild*."

We continued up the empty street, which was lit immaculately from above, as if by our own personal director of photography. I cracked open my window. The air somehow smelled of money. That, and vast desert lawns, generously watered. All you could see from the street were more gates and more gatehouses, each one rigged with the same military-grade surveillance technology. The people who lived in this place were clearly scared of something. Come to think of it, they were probably scared of people like us: civilians, nonbillionaires. We drove on. And then suddenly there were floodlights and limos and valets and publicists and an outdoor table stacked with bags emblazoned with the logo of *Vanity Fair* magazine.

"Gift bags," said Lucie, quietly. "*Nice.*"

The valets took the Saab and up we walked through a white gate to a long, wide parking area, to the right of which was Mike's place— modest, it seemed, by Beverly Park standards. Lucie—apparently an expert on real estate—guessed its size at ten thousand square feet, which would make it worth twenty to thirty million dollars. The mansion had been built in conservative East Coast style, with stone walls on the first floor giving way to white clapboard on the upper level. Black shutters made the windows look like they had eyelashes. On we walked to a raised and covered porch, held up by four Roman pillars, and then on through the front door and into the high-ceilinged inner chamber, with its vast and intricate chandelier, its curved stairway, its hanging tapestries, its polished Steinway.

I briefly considered over-riding the authority of the guest list and asking myself to leave.

We didn't belong here. This must have been some kind of mistake. *How could we ever have made it onto this list?* Directly in front of me, for example, was a man I recognized as The Proprietor of the newspaper that employs me: the Beast's boss, one hundred times removed. I felt a new heat now in my forehead. Behind The Proprietor was— Christ!—it was Clint Eastwood. And that was Sir Elton John, huddled under what looked like a Picasso with Barbra Streisand. And over there was Sharon Stone: tall, imperious, scowling.

I tried to move on quickly, but our progress through the pillars at the far end of the entryway was slowed by a formation of waiters, their silver trays raised like medieval shields. I scooped two cocktails from one of them, emptying the first and holding on to the other. Lucie did the same. The weight of the power in the room was crushing me. Gravity had thickened. One mistake in here—in this crowd—and my life, my career, my everything, it could all be over. I waited for the cocktail to do its work, to perform its blood-sugar magic.

It didn't take long to find out who Mike was. There were photographs of him everywhere: Mike with presidents. Mike with movie stars. Mike with Extremely Beautiful Young Women. Mike with God. Mike was a big-time movie producer. As I looked at one of the photographs I suddenly knew his last name: Medavoy. Yes, Mike *Medavoy*. Now it all made sense. Medavoy was a former studio boss, the ex-head of TriStar Pictures. He was responsible, or at least partly responsible, for *One Flew Over the Cuckoo's Nest, Rocky, The Terminator, Platoon,* and *The Silence of the Lambs.* Yes, Mike was as big as they came in Hollywood —and not much of a looker, judging by the photographs. This is how it is with men. The good-looking ones get a lot, and they get it early. The short ones, the fat ones, the bald and ginger ones—they're the ones to watch. They play the long game. And in the end they clean up. For two decades now, I have taken great comfort in this. On the piano was a photograph of Medavoy and a woman several decades his junior.

"His wife," I whispered to Lucie, as the details of a long-forgotten gossip column came back to me. "Irena."

"Wow."

"Yeah."

We broke through the waiters and into a long corridor. "I've read about this place," said Lucie. "If you push a button in the living room, a twenty-foot movie screen drops from the ceiling, speakers rise from the floor, and the bookshelf sinks down behind you to make way for a projectionist."

"If you push a button in *my* living room," I said, "the lights come on. It's incredible. I'll show you sometime."

Lucie laughed. She looked beautiful when she laughed. She looked beautiful when she didn't laugh, too. I tried not to think about how emphatically, how irreversibly, I was falling for her.

It took us a good five minutes to get to the other side of the mansion, where patio doors opened up to a garden, in which a huge, climate-controlled marquee had been erected next to a swimming pool. The pool glowed from within, like a gateway to a small blue universe. Medavoy must rent a power station to keep all this stuff up and running, I thought. If he turned off the electricity for a minute, a coal mine somewhere in Pennsylvania would go bust. I began to wonder about his neighbors' houses, the ones that were six times the size. What do you *put* in a house that measures sixty thousand square feet? What do you *do* in it?

I wish I could report that the spectacle of so much wealth, of so much consumption, was somehow offensive to me. But it wasn't. Medavoy's house was paradise. Still, I couldn't help but wonder at what point material accumulation becomes meaningless. Perhaps it never does. Perhaps the need for more, for better, can never be satisfied, only managed. Look at Paul Allen, the Microsoft cofounder. He owns everything you could ever imagine owning: houses, cars, sports teams, a four-hundred-foot yacht. And now he's launched his own space program. What next after that? A private moon? A custom planet?

Then again, perhaps we're all different. Perhaps we all max out at different rates—with Mahatma Gandhi at one end of the scale and Paul Allen at the other. Unfortunately, I fear I'm closer to Allen than Gandhi. But I've been thinking lately that I would like to change. Yes, for the sake of my sanity, my bank account, my *health,* I would like very much to change.

From the marquee emerged Sarah Cairns, her blonde hair made blonder by a winter tan. She looked at ease. This was her territory, her habitat. It was a relief to see a human being amid the walking movie trailers.

"Ah, Chris," she said, smiling. "You finally made it."

We exchanged kisses.

"Sarah, Lucie," I said, "Lucie, Sarah. Thanks for the text message, by the way. Mr. X had me worried for a while."

I hadn't told Lucie about Mr. X. There seemed no harm in it now.

"Worried?" laughed Sarah. "You charmed the pants off him at dinner the other night. He thought you were hilarious."

"Drunk would be a better word," I said, pleased with this report. I grinned at Lucie, as if to prove the alleged charm.

"You had us *all* in stitches," Sarah continued. "That story about selling furniture on Craigslist to meet girls. *Brilliant.*"

Sarah's grin widened.

My heart stopped. It actually *stopped*. For how long I can't remember. But there was definitely a pause—a long one, too. By the time the valves had resumed their important work it was too late.

"How did the date with sofagirl go?" Sarah went on, oblivious to the unfolding catastrophe. "Tell me, was she better-looking than lampgirl? Oh—but there were *three* lampgirls, weren't there? *Hih-hee!*"

This is how Sarah laughs: *hih-hee!*

What the hell was wrong with her? Couldn't she see that . . . ah, *shit*, now I remembered. I had told Sarah that my date tonight was a colleague, flying in from the East Coast. And now Sarah was asking me about deskgirl, coffeetablegirl, *bedgirl*. Oh, Jesus. The horror, the horror.

When she was done there was a pause—a pause long enough to hold its own among the major units of the geological timescale. Sarah's smile flickered, then dimmed, and then lost power completely.

Even the bloody music stopped.

"Sarah," I said, eventually. "This is Lucie, *the girl who bought my sofa.*"

Another terrible pause.

Did Medavoy have a gun I could borrow? A sword, perhaps? I needed to get this over with as quickly as possible.

At all three points of our awkward triangle, uncomfortable thoughts were now forming. Skin prickled and crawled. Meanwhile, on the stage at the back of the marquee, someone had started to sing: a sad song, a song about losing everything. Was this *it*? Was it all over now? Was this how my mission would end? I imagined Lucie turning and walking stiffly away, and my inevitable pleas and apologies by the door, as Clint and Sharon and Elton looked on.

"Just kidding, darling," said Sarah, with a flawless counterfeit laugh. I reminded myself what Sarah did for a living: yes, she was a publicist. She was a *professional*. "You have to get used to the British sense of humor," she giggled. "We like to tease, don't we, Chris? We like to tease people."

Lucie said nothing.

"*Hih-hee!*"

The muscles in my face were tent poles, propping up a ragged smile. But it was windy out there, and with every new gust the poles bucked and groaned, as they were slowly worked free from the ground.

"Sofagirl, huh?" said Lucie, beginning to laugh.

15

When Piggybacks Don't Fly

Well, it's been five months now.

Five months since the party.

Or maybe it's six. It's getting hard—isn't it?—to look at calendars, when you know where they will eventually lead.

Time has certainly sped up lately.

The clocks are spinning faster—as they always do when a countdown is under way. Readouts are flashing. Somewhere, a Klaxon is sounding. If scientists are responsible for inventing this planetary crisis, their acting is from the Method school. Yes, they're good, these eggheads—they deserve Academy Awards. Did you hear the latest? Out in the dead zone of the Pacific, they're dumping iron from a boat called *Weatherbird II,* in the hope that iron will help the plankton grow. I didn't even know we were out of plankton. Come to think of it, what *is* plankton? Can't we do without it? After all, we seem to be getting along fine without plenty of other things: forests, ice caps, animals. Yes, the animals are checking out at a rate of 150 species per day. So much for two-by-two. They've had enough, apparently. It's just no *fun,* sharing a planet with human beings.

* * *

Meanwhile, the weather has become almost a bore, almost a cliché. Mention the hail showers, the frog storms, the reverse cyclones, the summer downpours, the winter droughts and people just roll their eyes at you. Every day, a new weather record is broken, a new antinorm is normalized. If it's hot, it's global warming. If it's cold, it's global warming. We know. *We get it.*

Having concluded that reversing human consumption is impossible—it's just not in our DNA, not in our evolutionary software—the world's governments are now looking at other ways to cool down the earth: mirrors in space, giant air conditioners, fake volcanoes that spew out cooling sulfur into the atmosphere. They've even come up with a man-made tree that can suck carbon dioxide from the air and turn it into liquid, which can then be pumped underground into all those empty oil wells we now have. The Chinese, meanwhile, are way ahead of the game. They're firing rockets filled with silver iodide into the Beijing sky to make it rain. Cloud seeding, they call it. There's only one tiny problem: the rain belongs somewhere else. It's *stolen* rain. Perhaps that's why the Gobi Desert keeps getting bigger every year. Desertification, they call it. Or maybe there's another explanation; maybe the plants, like the animals, have also had enough of sharing a planet with human beings.

By all accounts the apocalypse is standing in the wings, waiting for its cue. Nothing escapes blame for this impending catastrophe: our cars, our houses, our food . . . *us*. Children are the latest culprits. If only it weren't for *children,* everything would be fine. When the Reverend Thomas Malthus published his "Essay on the Principle of Population" in 1798, the world's head count stood at a laughable one billion. (Malthus cheerfully recommended "misery"—in the readily available forms of war, pestilence, plague, and famine—as good ways to stop the poor from ruining the lifestyles of the leisure class.) If only Malthus could see us now: seven billion earthlings wedged onto this same circling rock, all of us dreaming of bigger homes and bigger cars. I fear it is only a matter of time before the neo-Malthusians have their day. I fear it is only a matter of time before they start asking us to make the ultimate carbon reduction: the one that involves not exhaling anymore.

In case you're wondering: nothing happened with Lucie.

Not at the party, at least.

At about two-thirty in the morning we left Medavoy's faux Cape Cod mansion, collected our gift bags—no eighty-inch plasma TV or first-class Tasmanian cruise tickets, just a scented candle, a bottled hangover cure, and the latest copy of *Vanity Fair*—and went to stand outside on the street with the scurrying valets. Soon enough we were back on San Ysidro Drive, descending fast through the clouds into the ten-million-dollar slums of lower Beverly Hills. Then came the Sunset Strip, which shook and grumbled to an artillery barrage of modified exhausts and industrial subwoofers. For two miles we barely talked amid the pressure waves. I knew then that the night was over, that my opportunity had been lost. Still, it could have been worse. It could have been so much *worse*.

Christ, what a week.

What a year.

And then—finally—back to the Leisureplex, where the Saab banked into the steep U-turn of the driveway, coming to a halt under the atrium walkway with its gold railings and gold doors and gold "Park Wellington" plaque. I was trying to think of how to say good night when Lucie unclipped her seat belt and turned to me. The engine was still running.

She smiled.

What *now*? I thought.

And that was when I lunged.

I just did it, without even thinking.

Now I have since come to realize that there are several important elements that make up a successful lunge, chief among them being practice, of which I did not have the benefit. It was therefore only in mid-lunge that I realized the ambition, the logistical complexity, of the task at hand. Having originated the lunge in the passenger seat of the vehicle, for example, I was required to perform a flawless ninety-degree turn before reaching my target. Compounding the difficulty was my state of cocktail-induced vertigo and a persistently dry left contact lens, which had further degraded my judgment of space and distance.

First obstacle: the gear shifter. Yes, a gear shifter can really get in the way of a journey from passenger seat to driver's seat, especially when the journey is performed at speed, and with romantic intent. Same goes for the armrest, and the handbrake, and—this one really took me by surprise—the steering wheel. By the time I had made it over to Lucie's side of the vehicle, my advance had encountered so much physical resistance that my open mouth was headed not for her mouth but for the area directly below her neck. This caused me to instigate an urgent last-minute diversion upward, which in my enthusiasm I overshot, slamming hard into the sun visor, which in turn caused me to slump down with a yelp of surprise and horror until finally, with great relief and no small amount of luck, my lips located hers.

We kissed. We *kissed*.

And that was when the car began to roll downhill.

"*Fuck!*" I said.

"Whoa there, Chris," giggled Lucie, reaching around me to shift the transmission into park. This time, our encounter was interrupted by the horn of a car behind us. We were blocking the driveway. I invited Lucie back to my apartment, but she declined politely, and I was glad. The lunge had really taken it out of me. The lunge had been enough for one night. Untangling myself, I backed slowly out of the car, shutting the heavy door behind me. Lucie waved and the Saab pulled away. Shaking my head in disbelief, I climbed the steps to the marble foyer, where Steve, the security guard, was sitting alone at the front desk.

"Good night, Steve," I said.

"Better luck next time, Chris," he replied.

The next morning I awoke with a cringe. What the hell had I *done*? Had my lunge been too quick, too forced? I busied myself with the usual hangover routines—making espresso, checking e-mails, browsing the news channels on my giant TV, configuring an Aston Martin on the Internet (onyx black or meteorite silver? contrast stitching or embossed monotone?)—until the realization came: something was different. Something was *very* different. It was . . . it was the smell. For a few minutes I thought I must have become trapped in a freak transapartment jet stream, a rare microclimate between the open door and the air conditioner. I froze on the spot. Nose quivering with anticipation, I moved my head *ever so slightly* to the left. Nope, nothing. Could it be? Surely not. I shuffled to the east, sniffing all the while. Still nothing. Gaining confidence, I paced west. Still no smell. I jogged south, then north, then widened my probe into a broad circular pattern, eventually branching off into the downstairs bathroom, the kitchen, and then, finally, the upstairs bedroom. The smell had vanished. Gone! Disappeared! Thank *Christ*. After a five-month siege I had been liberated.

Could this mean . . . ?

I think it could.

I think this could mean the end of the Desperate Period.

Still, the lunge was a semidisaster, no doubt about it. In fact, I couldn't get it out of my head. My brain kept replaying it, over and like, like a World Cup goal: a goal scored and celebrated and then disallowed. Accompanying the footage was the voice of a demented 1970s football commentator: *And he's gonna go for it, he's created the chance, he*

could capitalize, he could put this one away, and, YES, he's moving in,
HE'S MOVING IN FOR THE LUNGE, and . . . and . . . ooomph . . .
well, ugh, that wasn't pretty, Tony, that wasn't pretty at all, but still, he
got the result, and that's what matters at the end of the day. Still, Tony,
I bet he'll be asking himself in the morning: after that performance, will
she be back for more?

Of course she wouldn't be back for more. I wondered if I should call her to apologize. But aren't there rules, strict rules, involved in this kind of thing? How long are you supposed to wait before the call? One day—two, three? The thought of waiting until Wednesday was excruciating. And so I settled in for the evening on an inflatable camping mattress in the living room (the sofa was gone, it was *gone*), with only my headache and my worsening mood for company.

Then the phone rang.

The Beast, probably, I thought. A celebrity must have died or gone to jail. A dull pain now in my head. Misery, misery.

"*Yeah?*" I said, picking up.

"Wow," came the startled reply. "Sounds like a bad one."

Then I remembered: Lucie doesn't play by the rules. With Lucie, there is no game, no strategy, no bullshit. And so we talked. Ten minutes into the conversation I also decided to abandon the rules.

"Why don't you come over?" I asked. "We can go for a swim."

"Cool," she replied.

An hour later, at dusk, we crept out to the swimming pool, which glowed turquoise from within. We dived in and floated there for a while, cutting patterns in the mist created by heated water hitting cooler air. Above, the palm trees waved at me in celebration, in congratulation. From the pool we moved to the hot tub, which swirled and burbled on its tiled pedestal. Don't stare at the bikini, I kept thinking to myself. *Don't stare at the bikini.*

I stared at the bikini.

Later, we called out for sushi, which we ate with disposable chopsticks while sitting on cushions on the floor. I kept looking around, waiting for Lucie to say something, waiting for her to notice.

My apartment was *empty*.

Yes, all of my furniture was gone.

"Bad news, Chris. The lenders are uncomfortable. We're cool on the adjustable and the teaser, but we're meeting some resistance on the piggyback. They want us to submit documents, Chris. Proof of income, bank statements, wage slips, tax returns, the whole deal. We might have to rethink."

Flip Jackman never sleeps. At night he downloads, he resets, he upgrades. Flip Jackman is a cyborg, a brokinator.

"Uh?" I said from under a mound of bedsheets. It was early, and I had expected the Beast when I reached for the phone.

"We have to ditch the piggyback, Chris." Flip's breathing was quicker than usual, and in the background I could hear a steady, muffled beat. Was he *jogging*? Did Flip make calls on his morning run? I imagined him in laundered vest and aerodynamic shorts, head back, earpiece dangling.

"Piggyback?" I repeated, dumbly.

"The second loan. Remember?"

Ah . . . yes. Now it was coming back to me. While planning my highly leveraged home purchase, Flip and I had discussed applying for a second mortgage using the down payment on the first mortgage as collateral. Only there wouldn't technically *be* a down payment, because we would be using the second mortgage to pay the down payment on the first mortgage. This was the whole point, and the reason the second mortgage was known as a "piggyback." The key was to close the two loans simultaneously, before anyone noticed that I was buying a house with nothing but my signature. I remembered chuckling in admiration as this strategy was outlined to me. Completely legal, too. In the time it would take to close the deal, the market would almost certainly be up again, I could cash out the new equity—through a third loan, perhaps—spend the profit on some new appliances, advertise the house as having an upgraded "chef's kitchen," then sell for an even

bigger profit. On a million-dollar property, I could expect to make eighty
grand in six months, if all went well.

Some of Flip's better clients have apparently done this a dozen
times or more since Greenspan urged Americans to do their bit for the
war on terror by taking out cheap home-equity loans. One of them
retired to his ranch out in Utah last month. He's twenty-two.

The plan was brilliant. It was everything I needed.

"So what's the problem?" I said, reaching blearily for the aspirin
by my bed. The bottle rattled like a children's toy.

Flip coughed. "It's your FICO score, Chris," he said.

"My *what*?"

"Your credit rating. It's . . ."

"Yes?"

"It's not good, Chris."

Flip explained. My credit rating is apparently represented by something called a FICO score. And there's a small problem with my FICO
score. On a scale of zero to eight hundred, my FICO score is practically a negative number. Turns out that the people at FICO keep track
of AmEx balances and dodgy internet loans. The people at FICO are
better informed than the CIA. They know things about me that even I
don't know. Still, there's one upside: borrowers with FICO scores as
low as mine are usually either in the late stages of bankruptcy or in
minimum-security prison. By the standards of my FICO demographic
I'm an overachiever.

"With your FICO where it is now, the piggyback isn't viable," said
Flip, sharply. "We should focus on the ARM."

"The ARM?"

"The adjustable-rate mortgage, Chris. The original loan. I have
a great product lined up for you with a great introductory rate.
After that, it resets to LIBOR plus two percent, with a prepayment
penalty."

The aspirin wasn't working. My headache was getting worse. And
Flip wasn't making any sense.

"LIBOR?" I said.

"It's an index, Chris. It stands for the London Interbank Offered Rate. Catchy, huh? All loans are based on an index, Chris. And remember, you can always refi later if you have to."

He meant *refinance*.

"But what about the down payment, Flip? Where do I get the down payment if I can't get the piggyback loan?"

"You're gonna have to use your own cash, Chris. You're gonna have to liquidate. Sucks, but you don't have a choice."

"Liquidate?"

"Cash in some life insurance, sell some Google, dip into your rainy day money-market funds. Do what you've gotta do."

"I don't *have* any Google."

"Look, take your time," said Flip, impatiently. "Think it through. You're gonna need a couple of hundred grand."

"A couple of hundred grand," I croaked.

"Make it a great day," said Flip, and hung up.

A couple of hundred grand. Jesus *Christ*.

In Flip Jackman's world, of course, everyone has a spare two hundred grand. Not me. Not even if I liquidate my company pension, which I have thought about doing every single day since moving to LA.

I suppose I should be grateful. I should be grateful that Cali DeLongpre took my apartment off the market only a week after she put it up for sale, thus buying me all this time to prepare my LA housing bubble debut. The reason for Cali's change of mind? Her boyfriend was hit by a car. There he was, ill-advisedly walking—on a sidewalk, no less—when an SUV jumped the curb and threw itself at him at twenty miles per hour. It's conceivable, I suppose, that the motorist had never seen a pedestrian before and simply didn't know what to do with one. Regardless, Cali's boyfriend was thrown sixty feet into a neighbor's cactus garden. He is now encased in plaster and connected via tubes to a series of plastic bags. He'll be fine, eventually —although never again will he be able to go near magnets, or walk through an airport X-ray machine. Now Cali says that instead of selling the apartment she wants to move back in. Something to do with tax, she claims, although I suspect it has more to do with my consistently overdue rent payments.

I have six weeks to leave.

Lucie is particularly excited about the long-awaited move. And I am particularly excited that Lucie is particularly excited about the move. For five months now, I have tried to work out what it is about me that she finds attractive. I have concluded that she is under the impression I can *provide*. By talking often and loudly about buying a house, this is a conclusion I hope to reinforce.

How much longer can the illusion be maintained? I have nothing left to sell and, as Flip said, my credit rating is *done*—it's junk. My only hope is the proposal for *War Reporting for Cowards,* which I finally completed and FedEx'd to Mark Lucas in London. In the end, it weighed in at a surprisingly convincing twenty thousand words. Perhaps I really *can* sell this book. In a voice as hushed and reassuring as the interior of the Bentley he undoubtedly owns, Mark tells me he is optimistic. He tells me that we could be looking at a "rather fun little auction" between the publishing houses, which could have a positive impact on our bottom line. Or, rather, that's what he *told* me. All this happened a few weeks ago. Since then: silence. My e-mails never get replies. My calls go straight to voice-mail. Perhaps he's on holiday. Yes, Mark Lucas is almost certainly on holiday, stretched out on the bleached shore of a private island somewhere, oiled beauties seeing to his every need, as his Gulfstream IV idles in the distance, ready to cast him through space and time to unmissable money meetings in Tokyo, Paris, London, and New York.

Hurry home, Mark Lucas.

Hurry home, *please*.

*   *   *

Meanwhile, the zeros are disappearing from my bank balance faster than the ice is disappearing from the North Pole.

For five months my borderline-fraudulent Internet loan has been keeping me in the kind of lifestyle to which I am pretending to be accustomed. My gym visits are now followed by eighty-dollar tennis lessons; my Dr. Bingblatz sessions are now followed by one-hundred-dollar facial sessions, administered by a masked woman with a steam wand and a tweezer, who removes my blackheads, one by one. This was Lucie's idea. It's certainly doing wonders for my complexion. I'm beginning to age in human years, not dog years. If I keep up this regime, perhaps some day I might be able to pull off that time reverse trick that so many British celebrities perform when they make it big in America: the advancing hairline, inverting belly, the whitening teeth. Nevertheless, a hundred dollars (not including tax or tip) is an awful lot of money, especially when the appointments come twice a week. In fact, it works out at about one dollar per blackhead. (I counted.) Still, I'm impressed that this service even exists. How do these leisure economy capitalists do it? How do they calculate the *exact moment* at which people are suddenly prepared to pay a hundred dollars for an hourlong blackhead-squeezing session? They certainly don't come along too often, these Cleopatra phases, these Marie Antoinette moments. They don't tend to end very well, either. They end with barbarians and guillotines, with dark ages and reigns of terror.

As for my take-out habit, it has escalated, perhaps inevitably, into a restaurant habit. It's astonishing—isn't it?—just how much it is possible to spend on three meals per day. Last week I outdid myself and took Lucie to a new, wildly nouveau canteen on Melrose Place called Bastide. The meal began with a foie gras piña colada and ended with a desert of french fries and brown butter ice cream—the fries were made of pineapple and arrived with a pot of strawberry ketchup. And the bill? It was certainly an event, I'll give it that much. Overall, I think it was the sheer quantity of digits that most impressed me. At least the valet parking was free. Still, I slipped the guy a ten on the way out. It made me feel important, like I deserved to be there, like I wasn't charging the meal to a credit card that I would be paying off with a loan I applied for on the Internet using a semiphony address.

Even staying in is expensive these days. Last week I drove the Jeep over to my local supermarket and bought two precooked almond-encrusted chicken breasts with precooked carrots and two individually shrink-wrapped potatoes, then drove home again. What is it that makes us buy individually shrink-wrapped vegetables? What is it about the thought of actually *picking up a vegetable and putting in a plastic bag* that seems so impossible? Nevertheless, staying in felt good. It felt practically monklike, in its abstemiousness. Jeff later informed me that between the farm and the Leisureplex, the ingredients of my meal had traveled a combined sixty-eight thousand miles. Jeff can be annoying like that sometimes.

And just how serious are things with Lucie? Pretty serious, I would say. Aside from the nights when she disappears to spend time with "the girls," we are inseparable. Mind you, I still haven't figured out what exactly it is she *does* for a living. Something to do with music, she keeps telling me. It pays well, apparently. As for the mystery of the gym bag in her Saab, I finally solved it. Inside was a pair of boots, high and shiny, with tall heels and metal buckles. They had me worried, those boots. Turns out they were a prop for a music video that Lucie was producing.

I think Lucie is more successful than I am.

There's no doubt about it. I have fallen for this girl, and fallen hard. And against all odds—against all the evidence of the Desperate Period— the elation and light-headedness appear to be mutual.

Sometimes I wonder what forces must have been at work in bringing us together under such *unusual* circumstances. It terrifies me to think of how close we came to not meeting at all. What if I had sold the sofa to that idiot Brian? What if I had missed her call? Likewise, it terrifies me to think of all the hundreds of ways I could still find to mess this up.

Which is why I have asked Lucie to move in with me. The plan is to consolidate our possessions before relocating to the house I am supposed to be buying with Flip Jackman's piggyback loan. Jeff asks me how I can be so sure that I'm in love. I tell him that when you know, you *know*.

Take yesterday, for example.

Yesterday I drove a rented U-Haul truck to Lucie's apartment over in Little Russia. In a state of almost transcendental calm, I left the truck outside and made my way upstairs (three flights), then let myself in with the spare key. I shut the door quietly behind me and exhaled noisily. Sitting there in front of me was my nemesis turned savior.

"Greetings, friend," I said.

In silence, my grandmother's sofa stared back at me.

I have come to believe that this sofa has magical properties, that my grandmother knew what she was doing all along.

I won't have a word said against it.

Not a *word*.

In the end, it took a good six hours to get it back to the Leisureplex, with the help of a one-toothed Mexican I picked up in the parking lot of the Home Depot out by the 101. And guess what? I didn't mind. I really didn't. I barely raised my voice when my fingers got caught in the bed mechanism causing them to ache and bleed. I didn't so much as curse when my back gave out halfway across the Leisureplex parking lot, causing me to roll and gasp on the concrete floor. Likewise, I maintained an almost superhuman composure when a missed step near the fountain caused three leg muscles to cramp simultaneously, prompting another bout of rolling and gasping on the concrete floor. Indeed, it was only an hour or so later, as I convulsed for a third time over the bleached abyss of the toilet bowl, that I finally allowed myself to observe what some might regard as the irony of my having to carry the sofa all the way back to the Leisureplex, only five months after having hauled it out.

And now my apartment is full again. Atop the sofa are piled boxes and hangers and lamps and side tables and framed pictures, all of them imported from Lucie's rented apartment in Little Russia, the short-term lease on which helpfully expires on the same date Cali DeLongpre throws me out. We are consolidated. We are a unit. We are ready now, ready for the move.

The move that I was going to finance with Flip Jackman's piggy-back loan.

The move that I can no longer afford.

16

Walls of Glass

"I've found it," said Lucie, her face emerging triumphantly from behind the real estate section of the *Los Angeles Times*.

"Found what?"

"Your house. Your clifftop bachelor palace."

It was Sunday, and we were having a late breakfast at the rooftop café of the Barney's New York department store, high above the toytown intersection of Wilshire Boulevard and Rodeo Drive. Ahead of us, the Hollywood Hills were framed against the blue halo of the desert. The quality of the light was such that it was possible to imagine the mountain as a giant piece of theater scenery, mounted on casters and ready to be rolled aside at the next intermission.

Not that there are any intermissions left, as far as my own personal script is concerned. Since Flip Jackman broke the news about the piggyback loan, another two weeks have passed. That's the thing about time: it doesn't waste any *time*. It doesn't ever cut you any slack.

In one month, Cali DeLongpre will move back into the Leisureplex and I will become homeless—as will Lucie, now that she is sharing my apartment. In one month, my inability to qualify for the most freely available debt in the history of American capitalism will be exposed, and Lucie will finally discover that I am broke, that I am done, that I am *junk*.

Yes, this is my final act. After this, it's curtains and house lights.

Leaning over, I took the newspaper from Lucie, being careful not to spill my seven-dollar cappuccino into my thirty-five-dollar bagel. At Barney's, they fly the bagels in daily from Manhattan. As much as I admire the spirit of profligacy, I can't help but think they would be better off getting them from the Jewish bakery down the street. The bagel might well be a versatile food, but it is not designed to be pressurized and flown cross-country at three-quarters the speed of sound. Not even the people who *eat* the bagels are designed for that.

In furrowed concentration I studied the listing Lucie had circled. It showed a flat-roofed box, about the size of a suburban garage, located in what appeared to be the direct path of a rockslide. "AFFORD-ABLE CHIC IN CELEBRITY NEIGHBORHOOD," read the headline. The house had beige stucco walls and a concrete planter of bamboo instead of a front garden. On the upper level were two bug-eyed windows: the photographer had made them glow from within to accentuate the retro-futuristic look. At the bottom of the listing was the asking price—a series of digits so long I almost expected them to be continued on the next page. I thought to myself: two years ago this house would have cost half as much.

Not that it mattered. Not that I would be buying it anyway.

"It's a bit *small*," I said. My eyes were beginning to sting.

"It's the Hollywood Hills," said Lucie.

"I guess."

"We should go see it, anyhow. Research."

I exhaled and nodded. Must be the sun, I thought. Must be the sun causing the problem with my eyes.

Don't get me wrong. I'm a big fan of bubbles. Blips, booms, rushes, rallies, spikes, swings, swells—whatever it is you want to call them, they're my idea of a good time.

I've long believed that bubbles capture what it is to be human. Here we are, with our measly double-digit life spans, in a universe that is almost fourteen billion years old. How can we consider ourselves anything other than creatures of the extreme short term? Besides, the long term is overrated. In the long term, the sun implodes; an asteroid hits; time runs out and goes into reverse while the universe contracts to the width of a peanut. In the long term, *there is no long term*.

My fellow bubble lovers understand this. We accept it. We are only too happy to celebrate the fleetingness of things.

I was—what?—fifteen years old when I first rented a copy of *Wall Street* and watched it over and over again (I had to borrow the VHS player, because my dad had refused to buy one), always stopping the tape at the moment when Bud Fox's exploitation of the Reagan-era stock market bubble is paying off and he has just moved into his Upper East Side penthouse. In my own personal cut of the film, the final scene is the sequence with the Talking Heads sound track, when we see Bud playing with his high-tech kitchen appliances at his first dinner party, just before he stumbles off to the master suite with a brooding Daryl Hannah.

Ah, yes, the Daryl Hannah scene.

I let it play to the real ending only once. Disappointed? I almost put my foot through the TV screen. During the fight scene in Central Park, I was completely on Gordon Gecko's side. Bud had let everyone down. He should never have betrayed his short-termist ideals. He should never have been corrupted by his father's blue-collar decency.

He should never have sold out to the long term.

Thanks to *Wall Street*, the bubble of the eighties made a big impression on me. And by the time the next one came along I was ready. By then I was a financial reporter, assigned to cover those empty shells of dot-com companies that kept going public, making their founders rich on other people's retirement money. Every week, another twenty-six-year-old would retire when another pension fund manager liquidated his position in General Electric and moved deeper into the online pet retailing sector. On the day America Online bought Time Warner for two hundred billion dollars of nothing but its bullshit stock certificates,

I almost threw up with excitement. It validated everything I had ever thought about money: it's all just a game; it's all just a code that you can manipulate, break, rewrite. You just have to be smart enough, ballsy enough. You just have to be willing to take a *risk*.

My first ever visit to LA came during that transatlantic dot-com gang bang. Back then, the first-class junkets came biweekly, like the pay raises. I stayed at the Belage Hotel on the Sunset Strip, in a room with a balcony and a view of the hills. It was February: eighty degrees, with a transparent sky. I was twenty-two. Everything was paid for, even the fifty-dollar room service burger. I knew then that I had to live on the West Coast of America. And now *here I am,* in another decade, another life, another universe—with a brand-new bubble to call my own.

By all rights I should be having the time of my life. With house prices in LA rising faster than they can rewrite the newspaper listings— and with Flip Jackman's money factory handing out mortgages like gift bags at a *Vanity Fair* party—I should be laughing myself to sleep at night. But of course I'm not. I'm benched, hobbled, neutralized. And all because of my credit score, all because of a number issued by a Minnesota company called FICO, or the Fair Isaac Corporation.

Fair? I've waited almost a decade for this housing bubble and now I can't take part. That doesn't seem very fair to me.

Sundays are the worst.

Sundays are the day when the OPEN HOUSE signs appear on every street corner in blooms of corrugated plastic. Sundays are the day when all of LA becomes a real estate showroom: when home owners from Pasadena to Bel Air throw open their doors, put out flyers and buffet food, and invite complete strangers to walk in off the street and make them an offer. Could you imagine this happening in London? Within the first ten minutes of an open house in Notting Hill there would be no house left to sell: it would be stripped down to the fuse box and the bathroom tiles. In LA, the inaccessibility of the homes—not to mention the private security militias—keep the opportunists away. Yes, the system works exactly as it should, except for those rare occasions when a quiet type turns up to an open house during a slow period and leaves with the real estate broker in a selection of heavy-duty plastic bags. But there are always hazards when engaging in risky, high-cost transactions with the general public—just ask the boulevard walkers down by the rent-by-the-hour Hollywood motels.

For the most part, however, the worst the brokers have to put up with are the fantasists and the voyeurs. People like me, in other words. But as long as the mortgage industry keeps printing its own money, no one is complaining. Back in the old days, people came to LA to make it big in the movies. Now they come here to make it big in single-family homes. People are *leaving* Hollywood to go into real estate. The actors, the stuntmen, the directors, the writers: they all have their spec houses in Mar Vista, their upscale condo units in Culver City.

Perhaps I too should give up my job and move into real estate. Perhaps I too should become a broker. They certainly seem to be enjoying themselves. You can't go anywhere in this city without avoiding their grins. Billboards, bus stops, coffee cups, newspaper vending machines—any surface you can buy, there they are, beaming out at you. Ah, those brokers' grins: as airbrushed as they are unreliable. Aside from acting and professional boxing it's hard to think of any other field of human activity in which clinical narcissism is a prerequisite for taking part. In the *Los Angeles Times* real estate section, the brokers' headshots are bigger than the photographs of the houses they are selling. I get the feeling I would feel right at home with these people, what with their reflexive exaggeration, their reality phobia, their relentless aspiration. Lucie tells me that anyone who sells a property in LA has to give six percent of the price to the brokers involved in the transaction: three percent to their own broker and three percent to the broker negotiating on behalf of the buyer. That means the commission on a ten-million-dollar home is three hundred grand. Sell a couple of those every year, spend the rest of the time shifting properties in the mid-seven-digits range, and pretty soon you're clearing a million or two a year. And if you actually *invest* in the property you sell you can double your takings again. Ten years ago, of course, you needed some collateral to do this— you needed some *down payments*. But then came the Flip Jackmans and the piggyback loans and now the property market is a zero-capital democracy. Anyone can play, and everyone does.

With one notable, maddening exception: me.

Yet I persevere with the open houses. I go through the motions, in hopes that something, anything, will change. Not that I have much choice, given my promises to Lucie. Until I can think of a backup plan, or a way to come up with two hundred grand, I must keep going as if everything is in place.

Fortunately, even with my fantasy budget of a million dollars, it's surprisingly hard to find anything to buy in the Hollywood Hills. In Wooler, you couldn't even spend that kind of money on a house: you'd have to buy a street. It's the same out in the desert boomburbs—home of LA's supercommuters—although even the properties there are getting more expensive by the minute.

For the time being, however, the impossibility of finding an affordable house in LA's most unaffordable neighborhood suits me perfectly: it buys me time. And so every Sunday I take Lucie to open houses at some of LA's most hyperinflated addresses. We've toured eight-bedroom clifftop palaces with circular driveways, eight-car garages, and subterranean home theaters. One place we saw had a dozen sixty-inch plasma TVs in waterproof casings, mounted on poles around an Olympic-sized infinity pool. Another featured a tennis court that hung off the side of the mountain, like a Manhattan window cleaner's cage.

With a budget of, say, twenty million, these homes would be entirely within reach. As it is, my single, lonely, malnourished, and largely imaginary million will buy me what the brokers like to call "teardowns": rotting cabins on wonky stilts with no parking and sandbags in the living room. Yes, for my utterly insignificant seven figures, I am relegated to write-offs, ruins, "unpermitted additions." By those standards, the house that Lucie had found in the real estate section of the *Los Angeles Times* looked almost robust. However, it was also priced at *one and a quarter* million dollars, a full two hundred and fifty grand over the ceiling I had set for myself, back in the days when I thought I could get a piggyback loan.

It was unequivocally beyond my means.

Still, as Lucie said, it was research.

Research of the most pointless and demoralizing kind.

"I should call Bernard," I said, signing the triple-digit bill for our Barney's breakfast. If I was going to keep up this Sunday morning home-searching charade, I might as well try to make it look official.

Lucie made a face. "The sleazy guy?" she said. "The one with the Hawaiian shirt and the chest wig?"

"Yeah, him," I said.

"Urgh."

"What d'you mean, *urgh*?"

"I think you should fire Bernard, Chris."

"You can't fire someone for having a chest wig."

"Not for *that*."

Lucie explained. If I called Bernard and ended up buying the house, he would probaly want to claim a commission, even though we had found the place ourselves in the newspaper. If I didn't call Bernard and used whichever broker was representing the seller of the house, the broker in question would get *two* commissions: six percent, not three. On a one-and-a-quarter-million-dollar property, that would add up to seventy-five grand. In return for keeping Bernard out of the transaction, I could expect a kickback from the seller's broker of at least ten grand. A win-win for everyone—apart from Bernard—and the kickback could pay my property tax for the first year. (Property tax? There was *property tax* to pay?)

"How do you *know* all this?" I asked.

"I told you. My mom's a real estate developer. You've got to be smart about this, Chris."

"So if I fire Bernard . . ."

"You save ten grand. At least."

At the word *save,* I flinched. Still, Lucie's strategy made a lot of sense, there was no denying it.

"You know what?" I said, getting up to leave.

"What?"

"I never liked Bernard much anyway."

"Walls of glass," said the man in the loose-fitting suit, thirty minutes later. "Jetliner views. Celebrity neighbors. Did you see the backyard? Outstanding indoor-outdoor flow. This house is an entertainer's dream."

Now I'm getting used to this kind of bullshit. "Walls of glass" means the house has windows. "Indoor-outdoor flow" means it has doors. An entertainer's dream? It means the house is small (sorry, "cozy") and that there are no walls that separate the kitchen from the living room. As for being a celebrity neighborhood: LA is a celebrity neighborhood. We had been told that this particular house was three doors up from Ryan Seacrest's place—Seacrest being the DJ and host of *American Idol*. I had tried hard, very hard, not to find this exciting.

"It's . . . *nice,*" I said.

Unfortunately, I meant it. It was more than nice. It was the ultimate clifftop bachelor palace. We had entered from the street through glass-paneled doors into a long and narrow TV room, at the end of which was a laundry room and bathroom. The house had probably once been held up from the front by stilts—the rear of the building was on higher ground—with an off-street parking space beneath the overhang. But now the parking space was the TV room, which was fine by me. Whoever had remodeled the place had done it on a miser's budget but with the taste of a style magazine editor. The hardwood floors had been stained a dark chocolate color, as had the door and window frames. The fixtures were all stainless steel. There was no gold, no pink, no knotted wood cabinetry. As for the upper level—the upper level was a double-page spread in its own right. The living room, kitchen, and dining room were open plan and lit by two giant floor-to-ceiling windows that displayed a widescreen view of the LA grid, as clear and symmetrical as the illuminated map on a car navigation screen. The spectacle was framed by the walls of the canyon, to which several dozen mansions, tennis courts, and infinity pools clung, like flotsam after a high tide. To the west, over Malibu, I could make out the impatient blinks of the jumbos arriving from London, incinerating jet fuel in the airborne gridlock over LAX.

This was exactly what I had imagined when I first arrived in LA. This was the mission, right here. This was the mission *accomplished*. I had to call Flip again. I had to get that loan.

The man in the floppy suit smiled.

His name was Brett Minsky, the seller's real estate broker. Not that he looked old enough for the job. He looked like he needed a note from his mother to be left unsupervised. Even his pants and shirt were too baggy for him, as if he expected to eventually grow into them, like a new school uniform. And his voice . . . what the hell was wrong with his voice? It sounded like someone had methodically punctured his windpipe with a fork until it buzzed like a kazoo.

Still, like all real estate brokers, Brett seemed to be doing well for himself. His blacked-out Jaguar was parked outside by the bamboo planter. It was the biggest, most expensive Jaguar of the range.

"And check out the chef's kitchen," said Brett. "Granite countertops. Top-of-the-line stainless steel appliances."

"Impressive," I said, my throat now hot and tight.

Brett grinned.

"So," he announced. "You like it?"

Like it?

I wanted to cry. I wanted to lick the walls.

"What do *you* think?" I asked Lucie.

"I love it," she said. "Oh, Chris, I *really* love it."

I wiped my eyes—they were stinging again—and looked around. The style of these midcentury houses is known as "post and beam." This essentially means that they are held up by nothing more than vertical posts and horizontal beams, balanced on top of each other as

if in a late-night dare with gravity. Back home in Wooler, such architecture would be classified using a different term: "shed." Yes, the
house was a shed, in a location that had become exponentially fashionable over the years, meaning it was now a shed worth one and a
quarter million dollars. And it really *did* appear to be in the path of a
rockslide. One little seismic yawn or shudder from any of the sixteen
fault lines in the vicinity and there would be a mountain in the living
room. Still, the place had survived this long. And Ryan Seacrest's
house looked even more precarious: it dangled from the decomposing granite like a stockbroker after a two-thousand-point Dow Jones
correction.

"I'll take it," I declared, before I could stop myself.

"You will?" said Lucie.

"You mean you'll make an offer," said Brett.

"No. I'll take it."

"There are *three* other offers," said Brett.

"That's *so* great," said Lucie, reaching out to hug me.

"So then I'll make an offer," I said. "Where do I sign?"

"Who's your broker?" said Brett.

"You are," I replied.

After leaving Flip Jackman my twenty-fifth voice message of the day—
they started out relatively calm and became progressively more demented as the afternoon wore on—I decided to take a walk up to
Sunset.

I needed some fresh air.

I needed some time to think, to plan.

What a day. Even by my own recent standards I had really done a
number on myself today. Lucie seemed to be oblivious, or perhaps she
just had rationalized my stress as a natural by-product of offering one
and a quarter million dollars for an eighteen-hundred-square-foot shed
with a backyard barely large enough for a table and chairs and a garage
barely large enough for a bicycle. Besides, no sooner had we returned

from the open house than she had disappeared on one of her mysterious nights out with the girls. What does Lucie *do* on these nights out?
Whatever it is, it certainly takes it out of her. She returns long after
midnight, red-eyed and with a strange metallic smell to her, and goes
straight to bed. One day I'll ask her. But I don't want to intrude. There's
nothing less attractive than paranoia, after all. Not that I suffer much
from paranoia these days. To be paranoid, the fear has to come without reason. I think it's safe to say that there is no lack of reason for
my fear.

I emerged from the Leisureplex at a pace almost approaching a
jog and took a sharp left up Alta Loma Road, toward the concrete posts
that turn the street into a cul-de-sac. As I passed the Sunset Marquis
Hotel—venue of my first date with Lucie—I noticed a familiar car
parked outside: a black SUV with no plates and blacked-out windows.
Its engine was running. Strange, I thought. I stared at the car for a while,
my pace slowing. Then, as I passed, the driver's-side window slid discreetly into the door frame. Sitting behind it was Jeff.

"Get in," he said. "Hurry."

"Eh?"

"*Hurry.*"

I did as he said.

"What the bloody hell are you doing?" I gasped, closing the door
behind me. The cabin smelled of boredom and leather. On the dash
was a miniature, battery-powered TV. Jeff had been in here for a while.

"I'm waiting for someone," he said, glumly.

Jeff looked almost yellow with worry.

"Who?"

"Long story," he said. "What's up with you, anyhow? You look like
you just dropped your candyfloss in a dog turd."

"You look like you just *ate* a dog turd."

Jeff closed his eyes and shook his head. "Problems with Mimi,"
he said heavily. "Remember? The French girl."

"Yeah? Well at least you didn't just offer one and a quarter million
dollars for a house when you don't have a mortgage."

Before Jeff could respond there was a commotion by the hotel entrance. Men in black suits jostled. A velvet rope was unchinked. And then a young man emerged with a baby in his arms, followed by what appeared to be a delegation of South American nannies. In the instant this began to happen, Jeff reached across to the backseat and pulled out a camera with the lens the size of a Soviet-era nuclear warhead, almost knocking me unconscious as he did so.

Never before had I seen Jeff this alert, this hyperconcentrated. I looked ahead of me, imagining the windshield as my own viewfinder. With a jolt of anxiety I realized that the man with the baby was a celebrity: a big celebrity. As big as they come. He was holding up the baby and smiling and making goo-goo noises. Jesus *Christ. Jeff was on a stakeout.* Hadn't he given up being a paparazzo? Hadn't he gone legit? I reached for the door handle but realized there was no way I could get out. The celebrity had seen us now. He was staring. He wasn't physically big, this celebrity, but he was a sportsman, a drinker, and probably a brawler. He certainly wasn't beyond assaulting a photographer, or a photographer's friend—and I wouldn't necessarily blame him, either. He was with his *son,* for Christ's sake.

Now Jeff was gunning the shutter, taking shot after shot. This was insane. I wanted no part of this. Now the celebrity was holding up the baby again, directly in front of Jeff's camera. It was almost as if he *wanted* to be photographed, as if he was pretending we weren't here.

"What the *bloody hell,* Jeff," I said, when I found enough breath.

"These are the first pictures," he said. "They'll love this in England and Australia. Maybe they'll syndicate to Japan, too."

"I thought you'd given up being a paparazzo?"

"It's the French girl, Ayres. She's costing me a bloody fortune. And I'm freelance. I don't have a *salary* like you."

"Stop giving her money then."

"I'm *not* giving her any money, that's the bloody problem. Anyway, I got her a job as a receptionist at the hotel. She gives me tips and I get the photos. Ten grand, Ayres. Ten grand for a set like this. With syndication, it could be more."

"But he's with his son, for Christ's sake."

"And what makes you think he doesn't *want* his picture taken? He wasn't born yesterday, Ayres. Why is he standing here in the street, bouncing his son around like this? This is a lovely picture, look." Jeff showed me the glowing postage-stamp screen on the back of his camera. It was, indeed, a beautiful father-and-son photograph. It looked almost posed. Perhaps Jeff had a point. Perhaps the celebrity was trying to prove something to the boy's supermodel mother—from whom he was separated, if I remembered my gossip correctly. As I was thinking this, the celebrity handed the baby to one of the nannies and they both climbed into the back of a waiting SUV. As it pulled away a hand waved from the window.

"See?" said Jeff.

"There has to be a better way to make money," I said.

"Nothing legal," said Jeff.

It was at that maoment I realized exactly what we had to do. "Hold on a second," I said. "You've just given me an idea."

17

Hitting Nineteen

With a bang and a terrible rumble, my seat fell away from me like a trapdoor, and I felt a sudden icy wetness in my lap. It was my vodka soda. Somewhere below us, Death Valley had thrown up another heat bolt, catching the half-empty Southwest Airlines jet smack on the jaw. That was pretty much the last thing we needed, up there in the cheap seats at twenty-nine thousand feet, heading northeast at four hundred and twenty miles per hour.

"Thermal pockets," said Jeff, stiffly, as he tightened his seat belt.

"Pain in the arse, more like," I muttered, trying to steady my breathing while soaking up my drink with pages torn from the in-flight SkyMall catalogue. I read the sales pitches as I mopped: "Children's touchscreen ATM bank: includes junior card and PIN to withdraw funds; polar fleece footed pajamas: keep your feet happy and warm in fleecy soft comfort, now in adult sizes."

I often wonder if the products in these catalogues are real or if they are planted there for reassurance, to let us know that somewhere out there other people are doing even *worse* things with their money.

"Animatronic Elvis robot," I continued reading, "talks and sings, just like the real King."

Another bang, another rumble.

The plane shook as it rode the next thermal swell. Even by the standards of the recently departed Desperate Period it was hot outside. Or, rather, it was hot twenty-nine thousand feet below, on the desert floor.

I looked out of the window at the sand and the rocks below. The drought in the West could be the worst in five hundred years, say the scientists. I didn't even know that deserts could *have* droughts. Apparently so. Apparently even deserts get heat fatigue. The Colorado River, which is made of melted snow from the Rocky Mountains and provides water to seven western states—including California—is at its lowest level in eighty-five years. And now the scientists predict that by 2020 the drought will have become permanent, with the snow disappearing and the globally warmed air carrying away moisture before it has even arrived. Soon the entire American West will be a dust bowl: like Okalahoma in the thirties, or like Owens Lake a decade earlier, when the Owens River—also made of melted snow—was diverted to the swimming pools of Beverly Hills. Soon even the Death Valley cockroaches will be scouring the Internet for cheap Arctic getaways to get a break from the heat and the gathering dust. Not that the Arctic will give them much refuge—not now that it's full of Russian cargo ships carrying plasma TVs through what's left of the ice.

Jeff tipped the last of his complimentary dry-roasted peanuts into his hand and stuffed the wrapper into his seat-back pocket.

"Ayres," he said, "are you *sure* this is a good idea?"

"Probably not," I murmured, remembering our last trip to Nevada, to the Twilight Kitty Lounge. "But it's worth a try."

The pitch of the plane's engines rose an octave as they continued to incinerate a gallon of jet fuel every eleven hundred yards. We banked left, hit another heat welt in the troposphere, then leveled off again. I thought for a moment about how glamorous air travel had once been. I grew up believing that, in the future, we would cruise between cities in sleek white leisure pods at hypersonic speed. Instead this: a ninety-eight-dollar supersaver round trip on a plane that could pass for a Greyhound bus. Sometimes I wonder if we should be glad that travel is so cheap. Then again, maybe it's *not* cheap. Maybe we're just racking up a tab somewhere else.

Now I felt a familiar pressure behind my ears. Our descent had begun. The view through the window turned from yellow to green as desert gave way to golf courses and swimming pools. Then came the undulating blue of Lake Mead—I could almost make out the chalky tide line where the water used to be, before the drought started emptying the reservoir faster than the Colorado River could refill it. Then the Egyptian Pyramids, the Eiffel Tower, the Rialto Bridge, and the Empire State Building: side by side, like a dying architect's final dream. We had arrived. Yes, here we were. Las Vegas. Fastest-growing metropolis in the Western world. Capital of consumption. Home of the seven-day weekend, and the Imminent End of the Universe.

Christ, just look at it.

Every month, another six thousand people move to Vegas—ready for the leisure-industry opportunities, ready for the zero-percent income taxes. They can't build the power stations fast enough. They can't fly in the frozen seafood fast enough. And they can't build the *houses* fast enough.

Yes, the housing bubble in Las Vegas makes the real estate market in LA look almost laid back, almost conservative in its optimism. According to an article I read the other day in the *Las Vegas Review Journal,* house prices in Las Vegas have been rising by forty, fifty percent every three months. In some areas, empty plots are *tripling* in value every year. They don't have open houses in Las Vegas: they couldn't manage the crowds. Every time a property goes up for sale the brokers get ten, twenty bids. Yes, LA might have its problems, its vices, its guilty quirks. But at least it goes to the recovery meetings. At least LA knows what's wrong and wants to get better. Not Las Vegas. Las Vegas wants to get *bigger.* It wants more.

"Remind me," said Jeff as the landing gear fell with a clunk and a whine. "What's the *official* reason for this trip?"

"Officially," I announced, "we are here for the grand opening of the Las Vegas Monorail."

"Didn't that happen last week?"

"No one wrote about it."

"Maybe there's also a paint-drying facility we could visit, while we're covering the World's Most Boring Stories."

"I don't remember you having a better idea."

Thirty minutes later we had been fired like pinballs into a jangling box of one-armed bandits, flashing pixels, and buzzing carousels. And this was only the arrivals hall. We found our baggage and made our way outside, beyond the life-support system of the air-conditioning, to the outdoor taxi stand.

If the heat was a joke it wasn't funny.

After an excruciating wait, we dove into the back of a white SUV limo, which was soon idling all eight of its cylinders in choked and angry traffic just south of Las Vegas Boulevard—aka the Strip. To the left of us was a truck pulling a pyramid-shaped billboard featuring a giant airbrushed photograph of a hooker, naked except for bra and G-string. "HOT GIRLS WHO WANT TO MEET YOU," read the heavy breath of the caption. Underneath it was a toll-free telephone number. To the other side of us was the scorched insanity of the sidewalk, where a fat man stood wearing a lime-green "Strippers Direct" T-shirt, the cotton under his armpits turned heavy and black. He was handing out shopping catalogues of girls, who apparently could be at our hotel room within fifteen minutes. The photographs in the catalogue no doubt bore little resemblance to the middle-aged cocktail waitresses actually on offer.

WHAT HAPPENS HERE, STAYS HERE, read the sign on the concrete underpass ahead of us. Next to it were more enticements: WELCOME TO PLEASURE CENTRAL, SIN CITY: THE WORLD'S ENTERTAINMENT CAPITAL.

I was wondering how Las Vegas was possible, how it was *legal,* when I felt a vibration from above, accompanied by a hollow groan. I looked up to see a white suppository-shaped pod slide along an elevated rail.

"Fuckin' monorail," announced our cabbie, who until now had maintained a respectful silence, aside from the occasions when he had felt it necessary to point out the road conditions, the behavior of other drivers, the heat wave, the situation in the Middle East, and his martial problems—in particular, his wife's decision to abandon him for a French-Canadian animal handler.

"What's wrong with it?" I asked, reaching for my notepad. Might as well get the interviews over with now, I thought. From the glass that enclosed the driver's cage I took down his name: Vincent Santino.

"It's for cheap people," said Vincent. "And it's not even convenient. You have to *walk* to get to the goddamn stations."

"So you haven't used it, then?"

Vincent turned heavily in his seat and I saw now that he was young, or at least younger than I had expected. Late thirties, probably. He was big, too: big and hot and caged and pissed off. My question had offended him. "Have I *used* it? I haven't used public transportation in thirty years," he said, battering his fist into the horn. "You know something funny? A lot of the people think the monorail is free. They think this is fuckin' Disneyland. I tell them: *This ain't fuckin' Disneyland.* This is Las Vegas, take a cab, you're on vacation, you cheap fuck."

"Some people, eh?" I said.

"IT'S FUCKIN' GREEN YOU ASSHOLE," said Vincent, assaulting the horn for a second time. "Where you headed, anyhow?"

"Over there," I replied, pointing.

"Uh?"

"*There,*" I said. "The monorail station."

It took a while to convince Vincent I wasn't joking. And then, after establishing that I wasn't joking, it took a while to calm Vincent down. For a moment, in fact, I thought we might be in trouble. But Vincent was just worried about his livelihood. He was worried about losing his fares to monorail. After getting as close as possible to the station—Vincent was right, you did have to walk—I dropped off Jeff with instructions to get some pictures and meet me later at the hotel. He exited the taxi, hauling behind him a roller bag of cameras and cables and lighting equipment. As he moved away I watched the asphalt as it shimmered around him.

We were booked at the Venetian—a $1.5 billion dollar replica of Venice, complete with permanent-twilight trompe l'oeil skyline, Grand Canal, singing gondoliers, three-acre casino, and celebrity-grade shopping mall (the place where Michael Jackson allegedly spent a million dollars in a single blowout). There are no rooms in the Venetian's thirty-five-story accommodation tower, only suites. But instead of telling Vincent to drive me there I told him to take me to another hotel, the Bellagio, on the other side of the Strip.

There was something I needed to see. Something I needed to do.

Ten minutes later found me standing at a glass counter in a glass-fronted store, under the glass-paneled roof of the Bellagio's tropically landscaped retail bubble. On the way in I had passed a man-made ocean in which twelve hundred electric nozzles were firing up jets of water in synch to the tune "Hey, Big Spender." In the store, the sound track was Mozart. I watched as overtanned men with no socks and tasseled loafers browsed. In here was the real reason we had come to Las Vegas. In here was the real reaon why Jeff was by now lying by the side of a concrete overpass in the triple-digit inferno of a Nevada afternoon, trying to get an artistic long shot of a monorail. He was a good friend, Jeff. A very good friend. I took a long gulp of the cool, hyperoxygenated air. It was as brisk as a Wooler winter under the air-conditioning, but I could still feel the heat of the desert behind my face.

A sales assistant moved efficiently toward me.

"Can I help you, sir?" she asked, her voice almost a whisper.

She was tall, this assistant, tall and slim and expensively perfumed. She could have been twenty or she could have been forty; it was impossible to tell. In Las Vegas they wouldn't have it any other way.

"How much is it?" I replied, looking down.

"This?"

"Yeah. That."

She told me, and I frowned and nodded as if her answer was entirely acceptable, entirely within expectations.

"And do you offer . . . financing?"

Her expression changed.

"That depends," she said.

"On what?"

"On whether you qualify."

"My credit rating?"

"We have our own criteria. Do you want me to call the finance manager? He can help you with any further questions."

I smiled and felt my forehead prickle.

"That won't be necessary," I said.

I suppose I should tell you exactly what happened back at the open house, just before this emergency trip to the desert was conceived. After declaring that I wanted to make an offer for the property—I could always back out, I figured, as long as I did it before the two-week deadline when the deal became unconditional—I drove with Lucie to Brett Minsky's office to write up the paperwork. That was when Brett informed me that the seller required every bidder to write an essay: one thousand words of embellished sycophancy, to help persuade him to accept my offer. The essay could be "creative" if I wanted it to be, explained Brett.

I almost walked out, but Lucie stopped me. Sellers have egos, she said. And in a hot market egos must be flattered.

So there I sat, at Brett's computer, writing my ode to an overpriced Hollywood Hills shed and wondering how I could hack into FICO's servers to manipulate my credit score. I was also beginning to wonder if the momentum of a pending transaction might actually tempt Flip Jackman into a finding a more creative solution to my down payment crisis. Perhaps Flip knew a way to tweak my credit score but just wasn't telling me. *Why wouldn't he answer his goddamn phone?* Perhaps I should adopt the same technique with Flip as I had with Brett and offer him a kickback. Maybe ten grand would do it. Maybe it would take twenty, *thirty* . . .

Was it legal to bribe a mortgage broker?

At some point Brett left the room to make a personal call to his boyfriend in Paris. My essay wasn't going well: "I have just returned from viewing your magnificent home in the Hollywood Hills." It sounded like one of Cali DeLongpre's Jane Austen–inspired e-mails. Directly above my head, a fan spun faster and faster, winding my head-ache tighter. I began to wonder how old Brett was, how much *money* he made. Lucie was sitting on the table next to me, kicking her feet.

Brett had been gone for perhaps five minutes when she said, "You aren't still thinking about getting that piggyback loan, are you?"

I looked up from the computer. I had just used the words "exquisite taste." Christ, I thought, and I write for a *living*.

Lucie looked back at me.

Had she just said what I thought she just said?

"Eh?"

"*You* know. The shady loan you keep talking about with that guy you keep calling. Whatsisname—Blip, Dip, Ship?"

"Flip," I said.

"*Well?*"

"How do you know about the loan?" I said, trying not to look as guilty as I sounded.

"Chris, you leave voice-mails for him eight times a day. Besides, the other night you were saying 'piggyback' in your sleep. I thought it must have been a pet name for your ex-girlfriend. Then I Googled it."

"There's nothing shady about it. Mortgages have changed, Lucie. Globalization. Liquidity. We have more options now."

Did she know that I hadn't qualified for the piggyback loan?

"Those loans are insane, Chris. I asked my mom about them. She says it's like buying a house with a credit card."

But that's what I *like* about it, I thought.

"But that's what I *like* about it," I said.

Lucie exhaled and shook her head.

"Bubbles don't last forever, Chris."

"But house prices *never* fall," I protested. "Besides, why not let the market do all the work for me?" I wished that Flip Jackson's words could sound more a bit more convincing when I said them.

"I want to buy the house with you," said Lucie, suddenly. "Seriously. I'll make the down payment, you pay the monthly and the tax. We can draw up an agreement, in case . . . in case things don't work out."

I paused, unable to process the incoming data.

"Deal?" said Lucie.

The data still weren't processing.

"*Chris?*"

"The down payment is *two hundred grand*," I managed.

"My dad left me some money."

"He did?"

"He saved, Chris. That's what people used to do."

"He saved *two hundred grand*?"

"Not exactly."

"Then where the hell did he get it all from?"

"I invested it after he died."

"In *what*?"

She told me.

"Jesus *Christ!*" I said, rising from Brett's thousand-dollar office chair. On the screen next to me my essay flickered.

"I got lucky."

"And you're *serious* about this?"

"Totally. As long as you can pay the monthly. You can pay the monthly, right?"

Thanks to Flip Jackman's creativity, the monthly payment on his proposed adjustable-rate mortgage was impossibly low, lower even than the rent that I had been regularly failing to pay to Cali DeLongpre.

"Oh, *please*," I said.

* * *

The casino floor of the Venetian Hotel twinkled and bleeped like the control room of some vast intergalactic starcruiser. Hunched creatures sat at the gurgling slots, gray-faced and hollow-eyed, watching the fruit symbols twirl and stop, twirl and stop. They take their work seriously, these creatures. That's why they eat and smoke and drink right where they sit. Every so often, a riot of sound and a chug of coins, but no celebration. If you sit for as long as these people do, there is never any celebration. Back in LA the leisure industries seem like a natural by-product of life extension: a way to fill all the extra time we have, now that we live forever, now that we don't *make* anything anymore. In Las Vegas, the leisure industries seem more traditional, more destructive in nature, a way to distract from the shortness and cruelness of things while conspiring to make things that little bit shorter and crueler.

The tables, at least, were less depressing.

Roulette, craps, poker, blackjack: all were on offer. The demographic of the tables was younger, less prone to dressing in ankle socks, plus-size shorts, and tucked-in corporate-logoed polo shirts. Even the waitresses assigned to the tables seemed marginally less close to retirement than the others. They were friendlier, too, and more generous in their servings of the free casino-floor booze. There at the tables it was possible to believe that skill might affect outcome, that the rules of money could be cheated with green felt, colored discs, and triple-deck cards. And it was there at the tables that I met Jeff, just before midnight, after the words and pictures of the monorail story had been filed back to London. Our job was done now, our expenses were covered. Now it was time for the real work.

"Did you find the ring?" asked Jeff.

"Oh yes."

"Where?"

"Tiffany's, at the Bellagio."

"How big?"

I told him.

Jeff laughed. "Do they come any smaller?"

"Not at Tiffany's."

"Did you speak to Lucie tonight? You didn't *tell* her, did you?"

"She's out."

"Out with the girls?"

"Yeah."

"She goes out a lot."

"I know. Anyway, I'm ready now."

"Then let's go."

So I'm going to propose to Lucie.

I've known this from the very beginning, of course. People tell you that marriage is a big decision, but in my case it feels as if there is really no decision to make at all. In terms of difficulty, the decision to ask Lucie to marry me ranks up there with the kind of decision you have to make before calling the lottery company with your winning number to claim the half-a-billion-dollar jackpot. Now let me see . . . should I call, or should I *not* call . . . ? To be honest, within a minute of Lucie's first visit to the Leisureplex for that sofa bed demonstration (you've got to wonder how this story will go down at the wedding) I could have told you exactly how things would end up, if she ever agreed to go out with me.

Not that I expected things to happen so fast. It's been—what?—seven months now, almost eight. A year would have felt a little more grown-up, a little more *considered*. Then again, why mess around? Why wait? Why not enroll in the Courage Macleod school of thinking and just do it, just do what you know you're going to do anyway so you can get on with all those other things you know you're going to do anyway? (Did I mention that Courage is pregnant? I think I might have forgotten to mention that Courage is pregnant.)

The mortgage, of course, has forced the issue.

If I buy a house with Lucie as a bachelor, then the loan will become our sole legal bond—aside, that is, from the agreement we've drawn up to sell the house and refund her down payment if things go horribly wrong. Not exactly romantic, is it? Which is why we must get married immediately. Or rather, why I must buy a ring, and then propose, and then hope I get the right answer.

Ah, yes. The ring.

The ring is . . . the ring is a problem.

Not long ago, I would have bought the ring with my American Express card and never given it another thought. But my AmEx card is as maxed-out as an alcoholic's liver. Which leaves me, yet again, with a problem. I've spent so much money convincing Lucie to marry me that I have no money left with which to ask her to marry me. Of course, I could always buy her a *fake* diamond. Or a diamond from somewhere other than the Most Expensive Jewelry Store on the Planet. But that doesn't exactly seem in the spirit of things, now does it?

I realized what I had to do as I was sitting in Jeff's car after the paparazzi incident. Whenever things get tense or dull in LA, Jeff and I always try to find a reason to get out of town and do a story somewhere. Hence our visit to the brothel. Hence last month's croquet tournament up in Napa Valley ("Croquet is the new golf"), which I don't think I mentioned at the time. And then there was our trip last year to Vegas, to cover the World Series of Poker. This is held every summer at Binion's Horseshoe Casino, in the older part of the city, the part where you can't find hot-pebble spa treatments or forty-dollar Caesar salads. It's Vegas as it used to be: dirty and hot and creepy and founded by genuine criminals—the criminal in this case being the late Benny Binion, he of the white Stetson and white buffalo coat.

I like Binion's more than I should. It still has those leather seats that vibrate for a dollar. It still has men with wet-perm mullets who try to feel up the elderly waitresses. And it used to have a million dollars on display in a plastic case (the bills were in ten-thousand-dollar denominations) until it was sold by Binion's daughter to save on insurance. Ah, the Binion family. The silver buried in the desert. The murder trial with the stripper. The jail time for tax evasion. The alleged heroin overdose. All that nasty business with "Fat Herbie"

Blitzstein over there in Chicago. Entire books have been written about the Binion family.

Anyway, before that trip to Las Vegas for the World Series of Poker I had never been interested in gambling. I just don't have the brain for it. When it comes to money, I'm good with abstraction, with *economics,* but give me some actual numbers and I'm a mess. Still, we ended up staying for three days to cover the tournament. Early on, I interviewed some of the players. One of them was a twenty-seven-year-old accountant from Tennessee named Chris Moneymaker, who had qualified for his seat at the table with a single forty-dollar bet on the Internet. Another was Scotty Nguyen, who told me he was a "poker professional." I'll always remember Nguyen, with his gold chains, his blue shell suit, and his ominously bandaged middle finger. I asked him what he'd do with the money if he won. He rubbed his finger and said, "Pay off debts." In the end, it was Moneymaker who took the $2.5 million grand prize. For the first time in my life, I thought it might be worth learning how to play cards. I never did, of course, and a few months later Binion's Horseshow Casino was raided by U.S. marshals and shut down for short-changing its pension funds. I never gave the subject another thought, until I was sitting there in Jeff's car, listening to him tell me that there was no better legal way to make ten grand in a few minutes than to be a paparazzo. That was when I told him that he had just given me an idea.

"The last time you had an idea you ended up in Neverland," he said.

"This is different," I said.

"That's what you always say."

"You play poker, right?"

"Blackjack."

"The last time we were in Vegas how much did you win?"

"Couple of grand. Maybe three."

"That's *it,*" I said.

"That's what?"

"We're going to Vegas."

*   *   *

So there I was, on a tall stool beside a ten-dollar-minimum blackjack table, surrounded by men who might once have been big in concrete before they retired to Boulder City with their third wives. Why is Las Vegas never as glamorous as you want it to be? Why does no one ever wear a tuxedo or drink martinis with a twist? In front of me was my croupier—my pimp of the chips. She was Asian, fortyish, and bored to the point of French existentialism. She performed her job as if her brain were a circuit board and her heart a lithium-ion battery.

"A ten and a nine," I declared, looking down at the two cards I had been dealt. "What should I do? Hit or stand?"

"Stand," said Jeff, from my right. By his elbow was a free vodka soda and a stack of multicolored chips. His stack of chips was much larger than my stack of chips, which was already almost half gone.

"Bugger it," I said, tapping the felt. "I'll hit."

Without altering the lines of her frown, the croupier pulled out a card and lay it faceup in front of me. It was a king.

Shit.

"You're bust," said Jeff. "You had *nineteen,* Ayres. You have to be a vegetable to hit a nineteen. The idea is to get as close to twenty-one as possible, without going over. *You have to start listening to me.*"

At blackjack I was turning out to be a slow learner. A slow learner and a somewhat reluctant learner, much to the annoyance of my tutor. So far, I had lost twenty of my fifty ten-dollar chips—purchased with the last meaningful sum I could take from my Citibank account without sacrificing rent or food. As much as I had never seriously expected the Vegas plan to work, I was nevertheless disappointed at how quickly, how emphatically, it was failing. Luck was definitely not with me tonight. No, luck was back at its hotel room, watching a *Girls Gone Wild* video.

I watched as the other players hit or stood and then as the croupier pulled out an ace to join her king. Blackjack. *She had a blackjack.* I would have gone bust anyway. So much for Jeff's brilliant advice.

The croupier swept up the chips. For a moment they looked like toy soldiers, victims of a toy ambush in a toy war.

"Unlucky table," Jeff announced, draining his vodka. "We should move."

"No," I said. "Let's stay."

"So you can hit a *twenty* this time?"

"Seriously. I can feel a roll coming on."

Now another hand. This time an eight and a nine. I struggled to add the two numbers together: seventeen, yes, I had *seventeen*. If I hit and got a four I would have a winning twenty-one, and I would double the ten chips, worth a hundred dollars, that I had pushed out into the dealer's no-man's-land. If I hit and got a five or higher I would go bust. If I hit and got under a four, and the dealer had a blackjack (so far she had a queen, which Jeff said was worth the same as a ten), I would be spared from going bust, but I would still lose. The rules of blackjack were beginning to make sense to me now. And I didn't like them very much.

"You've got seventeen," said Jeff. "Stand. Just bloody *stand*."

"Why?"

"Basic strategy, Ayres. You *always* stand if you get a seventeen, no matter what the dealer's got. If you stick to basic strategy, then in the long run the dealer has only a one percent advantage. Which means that if you hit the right table at the right time of night, then *bam*—viva Las Vegas."

Jeff sang the word *viva* as if he were Elvis, and the men who had probably once been big in concrete looked over at him like he was from another planet, which, in a way, I suppose he was.

"But if you're guaranteed to always lose in the long run," I said, "why not take a risk? Why not have some *fun*?"

"There's a difference between risk and stupidity. Besides, you have *more fun* if the game lasts longer—and you might actually win something. If you keep hitting nineteens, you'll have fun for three seconds, then you'll be wiped out. It's the Armageddon strategy. It's insane."

The dealer was looking at me, awaiting a decision.

I looked down at my two cards.

"Bugger it," I said. "Hit."

Jeff put his head in his hands as the croupier dealt me a king.

Shit.

Now I was down to my last hundred.

The other players made their moves. The dealer drew a five, hit it, then went bust with a ten. Winnings were dispensed. Jeff was up again. Then it was time for more bets to be placed. I ordered a whiskey from a passing waitress and imagined a Tiffany's diamond engagement ring hanging from a thread above the table. "Bugger it," I muttered, pushing out all twenty of my remaining chips.

Seven o'clock, the next morning. My suite at the Venetian whinnies and grumbles as the air-conditioning struggles to maintain the temperature at sixty-nine degrees. My head feels like a medium-sized rodent died in it overnight. I open my eyes, fearing damage. I can smell the free casino whiskey on my skin. Urgh. What did I *do* last night? Ah, now I remember: the ring.

The *ring.*

Here's a funny thing. That stupid bet I made, the one where I put down my final twenty chips? I won. A blackjack, straight out of the deck. Doubled my money. And then I went all in with my original bet and my winnings and hit another nineteen. Yes, I know, I *know.* I did it mainly to prove Jeff wrong. A shame, because instead I proved him right. I think my days of hitting nineteens are over now. I think it's finally out of my system. The card I was dealt was a five, and it was over, over in one cruel turn of the croupier's cruel wrist. Armageddon. All hope of the ring was lost. By the time I left Jeff he had been upgraded to a high roller's table and was surrounded by bunny girls. The entire casino was cheering him on. I was glad for him: he needed the money to maintain his French girlfriend habit. *Basic strategy,* he told me as I left the casino. Always basic strategy. Never hit a nineteen.

And now I must get out of bed and face the desert. Guess which floor I'm on, by the way? That's right: nineteen. From now on, me and nineteen have officially fallen out. Me and nineteen are done.

My cell phone rang.

I groaned.

Almost certainly the Beast. Maybe he was having second thoughts about the monorail story, now that he had read it. I didn't blame him. To be honest with you it had been a struggle to make an electric train sound interesting. I suspect this might have had something to do with the fact that electric trains aren't interesting.

I let it ring.

Ring, ring . . . even the phone was taunting me about the *ring*.

With a grunt of frustration I picked it up. If it was the Beast he would just end up calling the hotel—I had stupidly given him the switchboard number—and then he would be in a shitty mood because someone would have put him on hold and forced him to listen to Celine Dion for fifteen minutes.

"Good news," said the telephone.

"Uh?"

"Sorry I've been a little hard to pin down. But you'll be delighted to hear that the auction's closed. The bids are all in."

"Mark?"

"None other."

Mark Lucas, my literary agent.

"Chris," he said. "Where *are* you?"

"Vegas," I coughed.

"Is it too early? Should I call back?"

"Noooo. No. What's going on? What's the news?"

"We sold it. We sold *War Reporting for Cowards*. You're about to become a published author, Mr. Ayres."

"That's fantastic. That's *incredible*. That's . . . that's . . . How much?"

He told me.

"Are you *sure*?"

"Paid in four installments, of course. The wire transfer is all ready to go, as soon as you can sign the paperwork. But yes, it's all very agreeable, isn't it? Now all you've got to do is write the bloody thing."

Not exactly, I thought.

Now all I had to do was go back to Tiffany's and buy a ring.

18

Reverse Millionaire

"This is a big moment for you, huh?" said the man with the handkerchief in his blazer pocket. He patted me on the shoulder. Behind him I could see white walls and glass merging into a polished marble floor.

"Huge," I said.

"You must be pretty excited."

"Oh, very."

"And a little bit nervous, I imagine."

"Not so much, actually."

"A man who knows what he wants, huh? I bet you've been waiting for this moment for a long time."

"All my life," I said, and I meant it.

"Well, you chose wisely, my friend. You chose wisely. These moments don't come along very often, after all."

"It's a big commitment, that's for sure."

"Oh, I wouldn't go that far."

"You wouldn't?"

"This is Los Angeles, Mr. Ayres. Typically, we give it two years. Then most people trade."

"They do?"

"Oh yeah. Anyway, let's finish up the paperwork. You're going for the nineteen-inch alloys and the upgraded luxury interior package, which includes satellite navigation, parking sensors, heated leather-

covered steering wheel, dual-level heated front and rear seats, adjustable air suspension, eight airbags, ambient interior lighting, triple-zone
climate control, and integrated ski bag. Would you also be interested
in the rear seat entertainment package? That's two TV screens, embedded in the back of the headrests, hooked up to a DVD in the trunk."

We turned now to admire the almost three-ton vehicle parked on
the showroom floor: a brand-new Range Rover, the very latest in carbon-
emitting technology, fresh off an oil-burning container ship from
Southampton. Through the tinted windows I could see that the stainless steel air vents in the cabin were still covered in protective film. I
wanted to climb inside and breathe in the aroma of glue and plastic
and hug the fourteen-way adjustable leather armchairs. As a boy in
Wooler I had spent entire weekends studying Range Rover brochures.
And now here I was, all these years later, about to actually buy one. Or
lease one, to be more accurate.

"How much are the TVs?" I asked.

"Two and half grand. It's an aftermarket package."

"Christ. Okay, I'll take them."

"And would you like to upgrade the TVs? The standard size is five
inches. But we can do seven inches. Or nine."

"How much extra are the nines?"

"Two and a half grand."

"Forget the TVs. I'll take the car as it is."

"So you don't want the rear seat PlayStation?"

Of course I wanted the rear seat PlayStation. "I think I'll have to
pass on that," I said. "It's all getting a bit . . . expensive."

"You're the boss."

"One last thing," I said.

"Yes, boss?"

"What does this thing do, fuel-economywise?"

"Oh, you know, it's not *that* bad."

"How bad?"

"Ten. Maybe eleven. Ten, mostly."

"Ten?"

"Mostly."

"*Ten miles per gallon?* But it says sixteen on the sticker."

"That's freeway driving, not city. Besides, sixteen is the number from the Environmental Protection Agency. As a rule, the numbers from the EPA are, well, they're usually on the optimistic side."

"The unprotective side?"

"We subtract twenty percent, as a general rule. Not that the people who buy our cars worry much about the price of gas."

"It's not the *price* I'm worried about. It's the cost."

"Say again?"

"What about a diesel engine? Can't I get one with a diesel engine?"

"We don't sell those in California."

"Why not?"

"They cause smog."

The man with the handkerchief shrugged, and I felt my eyes begin to sting again. They've been doing a lot of that lately.

"Where do I sign?" I asked.

Las Vegas seems like a long time ago now.

In the end, it took me about a month to get the first installment of my advance from the publisher. I have been sworn to secrecy on the exact details—suffice it to say that each installment is worth about a quarter of what the Beast pays me in a year. All that money, and for *words*. For an entire seventy-two-hour period after the wire transfer I actually had more assets than liabilities. What an unfamiliar feeling *that* was. It felt wrong, as if I wasn't fulfilling my consumer duty, as if at any second an auditor from the Internal Revenue Service would seize the funds as punishment for my lack of commitment to the national debt. And now the first installment is gone. Spent. Done. To be honest, it never even felt like my money. When you've never had any money, I think this is how money feels.

It actually *wasn't* my money, mind you. It was an advance. As Mark Lucas keeps pointing out to me, it was conditional on the delivery of a completed manuscript of *War Reporting for Cowards*.

A delivery that hasn't yet been made.

But the Jeep couldn't wait. It had to go immediately. There was never any serious question. The day the advance landed I made the call, and a man arrived with a tow truck to take it away—the end of my loan from corporate HQ. It would have been natural to feel a slight tug of melancholy over its departure, we've been through a lot together, after all. But I honestly couldn't have been happier. "Where's the switch for the windows?" the driver asked me, after a long fumble inside the car. I told him it had a winder, not a switch. At first he didn't believe me. And then the winder came off in his hand. "Even my seventy-eight Chevy had goddamn electric windows," he kept saying, over and over. Then he tried to find the switch for the locks. I told him that the doors had to be locked manually, one by one.

He went quiet after that.

Everything on the Range Rover is electric, and it's all controlled by a touch-screen computer on the dash. If I ask it to, the computer will even display my speed and fuel-consumption averages. Fifteen miles per hour and nine miles per gallon is what the display last showed, before I switched it off and vowed never to look at it again. *Nine miles per gallon*. You know many miles per gallon the Model T Ford could do, a century ago? Twenty-five.

I never *meant* to buy such a big car. I was going to go for something sportier, but the hypothetical requirements of work, of carrying Jeff and his twenty-foot lenses around, ruled out anything with two seats. And somehow I ended up with the Palace of Versailles on wheels.

Did I mentioned that I'm *leasing* the Range Rover? This means that I'm paying the difference between the price of the vehicle and it's predicted value in three years' time, plus sales tax and interest. At no point does ownership ever come into the equation. I was thinking about this the other day and realized that I'm actually paying a bank to *borrow depreciation*. Brilliant, isn't it? Brilliant apart from the suspicion that the person who was clever enough to invent the concept of borrowing depreciation almost certainly never borrows any depreciation.

Yes, you can bet he owns *his* car.

The guilt of SUV ownership comes in aftershocks of varying magnitude. I should have bought a hybrid, I keep telling myself. But then I get angry. For as long as I can remember I've believed—been conditioned to believe—that it is a man's purpose on earth to work hard to earn money to buy a decent car. And now that I've finally worked hard enough to qualify for a lease that allows me to borrow the depreciation on a decent car, why shouldn't I be allowed to enjoy it for a while? Why must I feel as if the one thing from which I derive relatively uncomplicated pleasure is not only obsolete but also proactively hastening the apocalypse? I drive around in the Range Rover and feel as though I might as well be selling crack pipes to one-year-olds or dumping plutonium into the water supply. And then I get stuck in traffic and in front of me is one of those snail-shaped Toyotas with the IMPEACH BUSH sticker on the sloped rear window. I want to climb out and tell the driver that the battery strapped to the engine of his Japanese smugbox was hauled around the world in oil-burning ships and made using nickel deposited in Canada nearly two billion years ago by a meteorite impact (this is actually true), proving that we're buggered *no matter what we do*. Even if you plugged the damn hybrid in to the grid at night and ran it on battery power alone, the car would still be fueled ultimately by coal, because that's what the Los Angeles Department of Water and Power burns to keep our electrical outlets working, even though we live in the solar reactor of the Mojave Desert.

Ah, my head hurts.

The more you think about this stuff, the more overwhelmed you become. Take biofuels. Turns out that you have to burn an awful lot of oil to farm crops for biofuels and along the way you make corn more expensive, which causes riots in Mexico over the price of tortillas. Then there's hydrogen. There are several ways to make hydrogen, the most popular of which involves natural gas, which is no better than oil. You can also make hydrogen using electricity, but the electricity comes from coal. What are we supposed to do about all this? Buy a car that sounds like a good idea but achieves nothing? Or go on as before, only with less enthusiasm. Clearly, I've chosen the latter option, but I can't say I feel good about it.

And I'm not alone, I suspect.

These days, everyone's a hypocrite, and everyone's defensive. Take Lucie's friend Rob. He came over for Thanksgiving this year, took one look at the turkey, winced, and told us he was a vegetarian because the rearing of animals is too energy-inefficient. When it was time for him leave—he barely touched his food—he went downstairs and climbed into his new car, which was parked outside. It was a Hummer. "There goes the Hummertarian," I said, as he pulled away.

I fear this is our future.

I fear we all will be Hummertarians soon.

In case you're wondering, I did buy the ring—*of course* I bought the ring. I got it from the Beverly Hills branch of Tiffany's, having selected the style from the store at the Bellagio. They even financed part of it after I showed them my publishing contract. The plan was all set: I would propose to Lucie in Prague, on a long-scheduled trip to visit her grandmother on her dad's side.

I had the whole thing worked out.

After visiting Prague we would travel north to Lucie's stepfather's hometown of Humpolec—official slogan, "The Town by the Freeway"—for a family celebration. My parents were going to fly over from Wooler, although I didn't tell them the reason. Yes, I had it all worked out, right down to the last detail. I even bought a special Lloyd's of London insurance policy to cover the ring while we traveled.

It was going to be *perfect*.

And it might have been, if Lucie's grandmother hadn't died before we got there. A heart attack in the bath, said the coroner.

The trip went ahead, regardless.

Most of our time in Prague was spent excavating a dusty apartment for mementos and haggling with lawyers and distant, non–English speaking family members over the terms of the inheritance. Turned out there was a lot of bad feeling over the escape of Lucie's dad to America. Escapes to America can do that to a family. I wonder how my great-great uncle Tom's move to Pennsylvania back in the twenties went down at the time. Only marginally worse, I imagine, than my own announcement that I was crossing the Atlantic. In Prague, as in Wooler, there's a sense that going to America is like taking the easy life, the easy money.

But money's easy only for a while. It's easy only until it gets harder than it was before.

I almost didn't propose.

Bugger it, I thought, I'll wait for a better time.

Then I went ahead and did it anyway.

There was a certain poetry to it, after all. We had met because of my grandmother, and there we were in Prague with an engagement ring because of hers. Besides, I got the feeling that Lucie's grandmother would have approved. Apparently she had a "typically Czech" sense of humor—which I suspect is a lot like having a typically British sense of humor, in that you spend a lot of time laughing at things that aren't funny at all.

Lucie cried for quite a long time when I finally did the kneework. So did I, in fact. To think how close we came to never having this future. To think how it all came down to a caption on a Craigslist furniture ad. Amid the tissues and disbelief, I didn't quite hear the word *yes*. But I assumed it had been said, and Lucie didn't contradict me, so now we're getting married in July.

Lucie wants to have the ceremony in Scotland, at a nineteenth-century country house just over the border from Wooler, in the town where I took my driving test. The location means that all the relatives can attend. Perfect—aside from the fact that the pound is on a rocket-

powered trip to the moon, while the dollar is crashing without a parachute into the sea. In terms of expense, this wedding is going to be right
up there with a royal coronation. At the current exchange rate you could
buy a vineyard in Napa Valley for the price of the flowers. Per hour,
the registrar, who officiates the ceremony, will cost more than an investment banker on weekend overtime. As for the food and the booze,
it's not even worth thinking about. Neither, for that matter, is the conversation that Lucie will soon have to have with my future in-laws.

She hasn't told them about the venue yet.

So tomorrow at noon we will own the house.

Or at least we will own twenty percent of it, with the rest of it
belonging to our bank, IndyMac, based over in Pasadena. What kind
of name for a bank is *IndyMac*? Shouldn't banks have pompous names—
or at the very least names with the word *bank* in them? The deal was
finalized when a notary came over to the Leisureplex with a fingerprint
set to go over the terms and stamp the forms. In spite of the three other
bids for the house we ended up paying less than the asking price—about
a hundred grand less, in fact—perhaps because it was gratuitously
overpriced to begin with. We also had Brett Minsky on our side, thanks
to our kickback arrangement (he doesn't call it a kickback, he calls it a
rebate).

Still, I couldn't help but wonder if it was really such a good idea
to have the same person representing both the seller and the buyer.
Surely there was a conflict of interest there somewhere?

But who cares when the repayments are a truly laughable two
grand a month for the first six months—the so-called teaser period—
after which they reset to the LIBOR index, plus two percent. Oh, and
we pay only interest—no principal. Lucie made the mistake of asking the notary how we could ever pay off the loan if all we were paying was the interest. The notary replied that our loan was relatively
conventional by California standards, in that we were paying *all* the
interest, as opposed to paying *less than* the interest and having the

unpaid balance added every month to our principal, like the world's scariest AmEx card.

"Tell me," said Lucie to the notary, "how many people *have* these kind of loans anyway?"

The notary shuffled her files.

"Adjustable rate mortgages?"

"Yeah."

"Nationally, about forty percent of all new applications are for ARMs. And just about all of them come with some kind of other loan, like a piggyback. With houses being so expensive now a lot of people tack on a second mortgage to the first, otherwise they can't afford the down payment."

I looked at the floor.

"But what if we *never* pay off the loan?" asked Lucie,

"Then we can get a reverse mortgage," I interrupted. "I've seen them on TV. You give your house back to the bank and they give you a check for whatever equity you have left."

"A *reverse* mortgage?" said Lucie, now sounding annoyed. "And what happens when you run out of equity?"

"You rent," I said with a shrug. "Or you move in with your kids. Or you get your kids to pay the rent."

"What's the point of buying in the first place?"

To make an easy profit, I thought, while the market's still good.

"To make an easy profit," I said. "While the market's still good."

"I don't know, Chris. Shouldn't we just get a fixed-rate loan?"

We can't *afford* a fixed-rate loan, I wanted to shout, not if we wanted to buy a house in the Hollywood Hills.

"Relax," I said. "It's all perfectly safe. A house is the safest investment you can make. Safe as houses, right?" As I said this I turned and smiled at the notary, who offered me a sympathetic look in return.

Lucie sighed and said, "The appropriate cliché is *betting* the house, Chris."

I smiled again at the notary.

"Where do we sign?" I asked.

*　*　*

I should have listened to Lucie, of course. After all, she is clearly talented when it comes to money. Guess where she invested her dad's
inheritance? Apple stock, pre-iPod. That and a down payment on a shoe
box on the Upper West Side of Manhattan (a thirty-year-fixed mortgage, because in New York co-op buildings you're not allowed to buy
with anything else). She made double her money on the New York apartment and the Apple stock is up 300 percent.

But for some reason I just wasn't worried about the mortgage as
we sat there with the notary, signing and thumb-printing the documents. Perhaps it was because I was so used to living day to day, fi-
nancially, that even the six-month certainty of the teaser rate seemed
like overplanning. If I was worried about anything, it was the filing
cabinet of documents—entitled "geological report"—that Brett Minsky
had couriered over to us earlier in the day. This turned out to be a
molecule-by-molecule analysis of the ground upon which our new
house was built.

I read it over lunch. Page one:

The granite bedrock is generally massive.

And then:

*The steep-cut slopes present on the site are considered to be grossly stable,
however the cuts are susceptible to erosion and block failures.*

I wondered if "block failures" were bad. They certainly sounded
bad. And what if the block failures were *generally massive?*

Next to all this was a map showing the fault lines crisscrossing the
foundations of the house, like expertly placed dynamite. "The potential
seismic events postulated to most likely affect the site," read the text,

*are a magnitude six to seven earthquake on the Newport-Inglewood Fault,
located approximately three miles southwest; and a magnitude eight or*

greater earthquake on the San Andreas Fault, located approximately thirty-three miles northwest.

I looked up "magnitude eight." According to Wikipedia, a magnitude eight earthquake produces the same amount of energy as a one-gigaton nuclear weapon. Generally speaking, I am not afraid of earthquakes in California. I am, however, afraid of one-gigaton nuclear weapons. Two levels up on the Richter scale and the energy released would be the equivalent of a mile-wide asteroid landing on the Coffee Bean down on the Sunset Strip.

The report concluded:

Hillside properties are especially subject to hazards which include, but are not limited to, seepage, erosion, concentrated drainage, flooding, landslides, mudflows, differential settlement, high groundwater, and expansive earth materials. The subject property is situated in a Landslide Hazard Zone and a Very High Fire Hazard Severity Zone.

And now, finally, we're in. We've moved.

The house is great.

The house really couldn't be better.

I look out the window and feel like I'm in a tugboat that's washed up on a volcano somewhere. To either side of us are the bigger vessels: the beached cruise liners, abandoned by the same long-retreated tide. Every night, they glitter and pound to wild deck parties, the guests finally calling and giggling their farewells at daybreak the next morning.

The biggest of all our neighbors' properties teeters on a bluff to the east—a glass-walled pleasure temple with an infinity pool out front and a diving board that ramps out over the horizon, as though you would need a parachute to use it. The day after the move I noticed a pulse of light coming from one of the balconies—a strobe, perhaps, or a flashbulb. I borrowed Lucie's opera glasses to take a closer look, and guess what I saw? *Pornography*, midshoot.

So this is it, I thought.

This is the Hollywood Hills.

We never really see the neighbors.

We just see their cars. Range Rovers, mostly, with chrome-plated rims and blacked-out windows, ferrying back and forth between the hillside and the shoreline of the Sunset Strip. As for Ryan Seacrest— he drives by every day, but he never makes eye contact. Neither does the fashion designer who lives across the street (the house used to belong to Fawn Hall, former secretary to Oliver North and noted document shredder during the contraband-weapons-to-Iran affair).

Meanwhile, someone just bought the property two doors up, on our side of the street, for nearly four million dollars. You can't even see the place from the street. There's a garage drilled into the rock and above it a walled compound, hidden behind five stories of jungle foliage. The house itself is somewhere to the back of the property, visible only from the air. I knew that it had been sold when I saw a double-decker truck edging its way up Sunset Plaza Drive, delivering what appeared to be the new owner's collection of Ferraris. Every day something new arrives. The place is a riot of activity. Whatever it is they're doing up there, it's taking a lot of manpower. There are so many workers hanging around that our street now has its own Mexican lunch truck—or 'maggot wagon,' as Jeff calls it around here—which announces its presence at noon every day with a blast from a horn that sounds like it was stolen from a Mississippi riverboat.

Then, a couple of weeks ago, came the heavy envelope on my windshield, tucked under the wiper overnight. In it was a typewritten message on embossed notepaper. "Dear Neighbor," it began,

My name is Laurence Hallier, and I just purchased the house two doors up from yours. I am a developer in Las Vegas and have built many homes, condos and apartments. I am going to have a party on Tuesday beginning at 9 pm for friends and family. We have hired a professional staff includ-

ing security to handle all aspects and have requested that all the guests park at the Hyatt Hotel on Sunset. There will be four limos bringing people up. I am sorry for this late notice but wanted to inform you. Anytime you need tickets to the Cirque du Soleil show at the Bellagio, let me know, as I have allocations sometimes.

There was no signature.

"Is it me," asked Lucie as we studied the letter over the kitchen counter, "or does it sound as though we're not invited?" She read aloud from the notepaper, which I noticed had the texture and consistency of hardened double-fat cream: "*We have hired a professional staff including security.*"

"Perhaps it's a noninvitation invitation," I said. "Or perhaps it's a reverse invitation. An *anti*-invitation."

"That does it," said Lucie.

"Does what?"

"We're going."

At eleven o'clock the following night we were standing outside our neighbor's four-million-dollar estate. In front of us was a velvet rope and a three-hundred-pound black elf, wearing a Christmas hat. He was holding a clipboard. Yes, there was a velvet rope and a clipboard holder *on our own street*. Not to mention a three-hundred-pound black elf, wearing a Christmas hat.

Limos came and went.

The TV host Bill Maher strolled past us, arm in arm with a girl half his age and twice his height.

"Name?" asked the elf.

I knew this had been a bad idea.

It's one thing to be turned away from a nightclub; it's another to be turned away from your neighbor's house and then have to perform the world's cruelest walk of shame back to your own front door.

"We're the neighbors," said Lucie, arms folded.

"Then welcome," said the elf.

Clearly, Laurence Hallier didn't want any trouble.

The rope was unhooked and we were in. As easy as that. I won-dered what we would *say* to Hallier—and then I realized that neither of us had any idea what he looked like. I knew about his business, however, because I had Googled it. Hallier was building one of the world's most expensive apartment buildings in Las Vegas. Panorama Towers, it was called. Leonardo DiCaprio and Tobey Maguire had bought places there. While browsing property Web sites I had come across an ad for the three-level "chairman's suite": the balcony alone was bigger than our house, with a glass-bottomed Jacuzzi on the main floor that served as a light fixture for the game room below. The win-dows in the living room were twenty-two feet high.

"Walls of glass," I remember saying to myself.

Beyond the elf was a door that led into the bedrock of the moun-tain. We walked through it and found ourselves funneled into a nar-row passageway, the left wall of which had been constructed entirely of glass, presumably so guests could admire the Ferraris parked on the other side. Then came a glass staircase. We climbed it and the air pressure seemed to change. Finally we emerged from the granite into a high-altitude breeze. We turned to see a lawn wrapping around us in a U shape, like a viewing platform or the bridge of a ship. I could see now that the property was built on its own promontory like an an-cient fort. Beyond the curved wall of the lawn was a 180-degree view of LA, glittering and silent, as if it had been put there for no other purpose than Hallier's viewing pleasure.

From across the lawn a fire-eating waitress approached, wearing a Santa bikini. In her free hand was a tray of martinis.

"Thank you," I said, and took one.

Lucie did the same.

There was nothing else to say.

Behind us was the house, a two-story affair, straight-angled, mod-ern, balconied, almost Japanese in character. At the entrance was a porch where a sushi chef worked. Next to him was a barbeque pit and, next to that, more fire-eating waitresses in Santa bikinis. Beyond the porch was a curved stone platform with a pool sunk into it in which floated what could only be described as great balls of fire. They bobbed and flickered as a DJ played Brazilian lounge music. Our fellow guests were older, male, with leather jackets and pocked faces. It was the kind of crowd that made you think of lawsuits and offshore bank accounts. We circled, like neighborly apparitions. At midnight, a troupe of break dancers arrived. So too did Paris Hilton and Luke and Owen Wilson and some other people I recognized. This Laurence Hallier, I thought, he knows how to throw a party. If only we knew who he *was*. Maybe he wasn't even here. Maybe he was rich enough to avoid his own social events.

"Who *is* this guy?" I said.

"I keep expecting someone to tell me he's an 'oggsford' man," said Lucie, laughing.

We drank more, ate the sushi, consulted one of the roaming Tarot readers, then decided to call it a night.

On the way out I thought of something.

"Do you think he has an adjustable rate mortgage?" I said.

By two o'clock we were lying in bed in our hut down the street. The walls shook to the music from Hallier's mansion. Outside on the street, I could hear limo doors slam, men shout, girls whisper, phones trill.

"Chri-*is*," said Lucie, in the darkness.

"Yes?"

"There's something I should tell you."

"You work for the CIA."

"No."

"You're imaginary and I'm hallucinating."

"Not exactly."

"What then?"

"I have . . . I have a hobby."

"A hobby?"

"Yes."

"Don't tell me. You collect stamps."

"I *dance*, Chris."

"Dance?"

"Yeah."

"I was with you all evening, Lucie. I know."

"No, Chris. I *dance*."

"I don't follow."

"On a pole, Chris. I dance on a pole."

"*Eh?*"

"Those nights out with the girls. The bag in the back of my car, with the boots. That's . . . that's what I do."

"You're a *pole* dancer?" I spluttered, sitting upright and spilling the water next to the bed as I reached for the light.

"Do you think less of me?"

"I thought you worked in *marketing*."

"I do, I do. It's just . . ."

"Jesus *Christ*, Lucie."

"I was going to tell you before."

"Before I asked you to *marry* me?"

"Do you take it back?"

And now the deluge.

All of a sudden everything is going wrong.

It's raining, for a start. Now, I know what you're thinking: this should be a *good* thing, given the drought and the dust bowl predictions. But this isn't good rain. This isn't the kind of rain that nourishes the plants and fills up the reservoirs. Oh no. This is the kind of rain that drowns the plants and bursts the reservoirs. This is the kind of rain that falls in miles, not inches.

So far, we've had more rain in the past two weeks than has ever been recorded in a single two-week period since the days when LA was run by Spaniards. It's as though the author of that geological report I was given by Brett Minsky has decided to give us a practical demonstration: seepage, erosion, concentrated drainage, flooding, landslides, mudflows, differential settlement, high groundwater, expansive earth materials—all are on display outside in the Hollywood Hills. The only thing we're missing are some block failures, of the generally massive variety.

The fires—hard to believe they were fifteen months ago—have made everything so much worse. Out in the LA boomburbs, the trees destroyed by the blaze used to hold the earth together. Now there's only mud. And mud doesn't do very well in rain. The other day in La Conchita, rain turned an entire mountain into brown liquid, burying ten people alive as they sat at home. You can see the footage of it on the news. They're playing it over and over. It's carnage out there.

The traffic lights are out all along Sunset. At every intersection, dented cars and scattered plastic. The street itself is like an underwater obstacle course, what with the palm tree logjams, the trash can flotillas, and the drowned coyotes bobbing along in the gutter. All of which are washing down the sheer cliff face at the back of our house, along with just about everything else you can image: bricks, paint cans, children's toys, Big Mac wrappers. If there are waterfalls in hell, this is what they look like. Clearly, when they built the houses up here, the contractors spent more time looking at the view than they did thinking about drainage. Every day I buy more sandbags and place them strategically around the house. And then I just stand there and watch it all coming down while counting to a million dollars.

Did I mention that our insurance doesn't cover floods? That's right. I was given a flood option when I bought the policy—I laughed in the agent's face. "Flood insurance, in LA?" I chortled, with all the confidence of a man who knows when he's being taken for a ride. Instead I went for the earthquake option. Christ, what a tourist. I called the agent back yesterday and guess what? They don't let you buy flood insurance when it's raining. They make you wait.

I can only imagine the scene at the beach, where all these rivers of shit in the hills presumably end up. Down there at the beach it must look like the twenty-first century had diarrhea and threw up, both at the same time. In some cases, the shit is *literally* shit.

Over in Eagle Rock, a sewage plant just burst a tank and spilled two and a half million gallons of untreated human waste into the LA River. Yes, the LA River, that concrete drain with its poisoned trickle. I used to think that the LA River was an exercise in civic irony. Now I have a new respect. If it wasn't for the LA River half the city would be underwater by now.

At least this isn't our fault.

At least this isn't more evidence that every single thing we do these days somehow fucks up the weather.

Right?

Wrong, of course.

According to the weather people, the rain has been caused by a tropical disturbance called the Madden-Julian oscillation. That's what globally warmed weather systems do, apparently: they disturb, they oscillate. All that water being evaporated from the oceans has to end up somewhere. And as the temperatures rise further, we can expect the oscillations to get even more disturbing. They'll come along more often, too, gathering more power every time. Which means this drought-stricken city can expect to be periodically drowned. Hilarious, isn't it? I always suspected that the planet had an ironic sense of humor. Meanwhile, they're calling this particular weather event a Pineapple Express, on account of the rogue jet stream that is carrying up rain from the tropics and over Hawaii—trashing the bars and harassing the hula-girls en route—then dumping it all down on LA.

The name was a joke by a weatherman back in the eighties—back when people could still make jokes about the weather.

Maybe the weather people have got it all wrong. We worry about our effect on the planet, but maybe we should be worrying about the planet's effect on *us*. Look what happened over in Indonesia: one earthquake in the Indian Ocean and a quarter of a million people drown. A quarter of a million people, gone in minutes. The scientists are still trying to work out exactly what happened. I can tell them one thing: earthquakes aren't caused by global warming.

Driving east in the Range Rover now, to buy more sandbags. The electricity is out all over the city and the rain clouds have fallen so low and so heavy you can barely see the STOP signs as they emerge out of the gloom. I brake to avoid a fallen tree and almost hit an abandoned car facing the wrong direction. Not even Britain could match this weather. If Britain had this weather the entire island would sink.

But I'm not thinking about the rain any more. There is another crisis—a more personal crisis—that I must deal with.

It seems I made a big mistake. It seems I rushed into something I didn't fully understand. And now I must decide what to do. I must decide how to resolve this problem, how to save everything from ruin.

It's the mortgage.

In sixty days my teaser rate ends, and with it my laughably low two-grand-a-month payments. Which wouldn't be a problem, if Alan Greenspan hadn't raised interest rates six times—*six fucking times*—since we bought the house. It would be fair to say that I have feelings of deep personal animosity toward the chairman of the Federal Reserve. This is the problem with adjustable rate mortgages: they adjust. In sixty days my payments will become the LIBOR rate—which has risen in line with the Federal Reserve's—plus a margin of two percent. In other words, my payments will double. I expected them to increase, of course. But at no point did I expect Greenspan to raise interest rates *six* times.

The problem isn't just the doubling payment. The problem is that Greenspan still thinks rates are too low. Maybe someone finally told him about the three hundred percent land appreciation out in Las Vegas. And now every time Greenspan blinks, he raises interest rates. Every time he farts, he raises interest rates. And if he keeps on going like this, as everyone is certain he will, my payments will be squared, not doubled.

Flip Jackman is working on it. Through the death rattle of his speakerphone he tells me I can refinance with a new product that will keep my payments nice and low for three years. It's a *creative* product, he says, from one of the more forward-thinking lenders around. But there's a catch: to refinance I must pay a twenty-grand penalty to my old lender, IndyMac. Relax, says Flip, the penalty is tax deductible, and I can add it to the principal of my refinanced loan, which will officially make me a reverse millionaire.

According to Flip it's all fine, it's all okay. And when he signs off on the speakerphone he advises me to make it a great day.

At least I'm not alone. Thanks to the hyperinflation of the housing bubble, America is now a nation of reverse millionaires. Even the U.S. government itself is up to its neck. The tax cuts, the war, social security, the fact that we live forever and don't *make* anything anymore— it all adds up. Thanks to the national debt, the U.S. government is eight trillion dollars in the hole, and sinking further by one and a half billion dollars every day. They used to keep track of the debt with a clock in New York's Bryant Park, but the clock is no longer there. It had to be moved to make way for the headquarters of a mortgage company.

Where does all this money *come* from, anyway? Who is the global economy's equivalent of the man at the back of the bar with the gold watch, the roll of banknotes, and the unclear repayment terms?

The Chinese, apparently. Now that the Chinese sell the Americans everything that the Americans used to make for themselves, they have more dollars than they know what to do with. So they loan it all back to the U.S. government in the form of treasury bonds. All of which suited both sides fine—it helped keep money cheap—until the rest of the world noticed what was going on. Then came the sirens and the flashing lights and the dollar's high-speed journey to the emergency ward, where it is now visited every day by men with baseball bats, not flowers.

The Chinese can't be too happy about this either. Their surplus is invested in a currency on its way to the morgue. They're so invested, they can't sell. If they sell, they could start an even bigger panic—they could push America into the abyss, dragging themselves in at the same time.

Relax, say the economists. It's all fine, it's all okay.

Yes, the economists tell us that it would take a truly extraordinary crisis to make the Chinese sell, a crisis as truly extraordinary, perhaps, as a nationwide housing crash and a simultaneous run on the banks.

I come to with a jolt and steady the car. I must stop thinking about the mortgage. I must stop listening to the news.

On the passenger seat my phone is ringing.

I pick it up.

"Ayres?"

"Yeah."

"You'll never guess."

"Never guess what?"

"Something terrible."

19

And the Lion Opens its Jaws

So now I'm lying faceup and shirtless on a massage table in a Beverly Hills hotel while a woman in a white laboratory coat smoothes caviar over my forehead with a spatula. Outside, the world is about to end but I'm trying not to think about that. "Caviar is nature's beauty cream," the woman with the spatula is telling me. "It shares an almost identical cell structure with human collagen."

I close my eyes and focus on the piped-in sound track of whale song and plinking synthesizer noises and imagine myself on a beach in the South Pacific, white shirt billowing against a turquoise horizon.

"This is the ideal preevent facial," says the woman, as more caviar is applied. "There's no picking or extraction."

Perhaps she's right, I think: perhaps this *is* the ideal preevent facial.

Perhaps this is what everyone should be doing on the day before the end of the world.

I still can't believe what happened to Jeff.

I always knew there was something up with that French girl. Never trust anyone with a name like *Mimi,* that's what I say.

And to think it took him so long to notice. She must have pulled her stunt pretty early on in the relationship, probably when she was keeping him company during one of his stakeouts. It must have been pretty easy for her to wait until Jeff got out of the car, then reach down into the storage pocket of the driver's-side door and take out his checkbook—even easier for her to fake Jeff's signature, over and over. She was paying herself about a grand a week at one point. And Jeff never noticed, because he never checked the credit and debit accounts on his bank statements. It was the win in Las Vegas that did it. He deposited it and within a week it had gone. That was when he went to the bank, where the teller remembered the nice French girl who had been in a few times. Because the fraud went on for so long undetected, and because Mimi was Jeff's girlfriend, there wasn't much he could do—apart from break up with her and ask for the money back. But she doesn't *have* any money. That was the point.

"I've been robbed," said Jeff, when he called me to break the news on that godawful afternoon, six months ago now.

"We've *all* been robbed," I told him.

I've started to say things like that lately. There's something wrong with me, I swear. When I first moved to LA, my internal monologue was that of a middle-aged American woman, soothing and breathless, adopted from some high-definition TV travel channel. Where did this woman go? I need her; I want her back. *Rich in antioxidant vitamins and botanicals,* she would be whispering to me now, *the caviar facial is specially formulated to firm, tone, and hydrate the skin.*

Yes, I miss my friend from the travel channel. These days, the narration in my head is provided by some cardigan-wearing loser from National Public Radio. His voice is nasal and saturnine and accompanied by soft-jazz intermission music. I *hate* the guy from National Public Radio. He points out things like the citywide outbreak of fungus that is killing the palm trees along Beverly Boulevard; things like the color of the sky today, which looks like it has been violently ill over the San Fernando Valley. He moans about the stolen water used to irrigate my bamboo, the air conditioner in Lucie's new convertible, the coal-fired power plants in Utah that illuminate my landscaping. He scolds me for having inefficient lightbulbs, for melting ice shelves by leaving my TV on standby. Given half the chance, he would probably tell me that the caviar in my facial comes from an endangered species of sturgeon in the Russian waters of the Caspian Sea, before giving me a lecture on California's own indigenous sturgeon, which were fished out of existence a century ago. Scientists now breed the fish in tanks out by Sacramento airport—even though no one wants to buy fake sturgeon from tanks, especially when they actually plan to *eat* the caviar instead of just having it smeared over their faces at a hotel in Beverly Hills.

He's certainly up on the news, the guy from National Public Radio. And not the kind of news I still find myself writing and e-mailing back to the Beast in London. ("'I will not sleep with boys again. I will change my life,' vows Michael Jackson.") No, he likes only the bad news, the very worst kind of news: a hurricane so intense that with every second it can scoop up a million cubic miles of sky and throw it at the state of Mississippi; an area the size of England being turned to mud and rubble; an unstoppable tide that can drown a city of half a million people. All of which is *actually happening* beyond the walls of this room, with its sound track of whale song and plinking synthesizer noises.

But, like I said, I'm trying not to think about that.

The weather never really recovered after the rain. For six months now the sky has seemed on the verge of some kind of breakdown. It blows and it snivels, it moans and it bawls. Over at the National Weather Center, they've counted twelve tropical depressions and five hurricanes this year, and there are still another three months to go before the end of the season. They're going to run out of storm names pretty soon. They're going to have to go around the alphabet twice.

The news says it's all the fault of the unusually warm water in the Atlantic ocean. And we all know whose fault *that* is.

The rain hasn't done anything for the drought, of course. "WATER SUPPLIES STILL NOT NORMAL," declared the headline in the *Los Angles Times* a few days ago. No, there's just no stopping this drought. This drought is working nights and weekends to keep up with its rivals in the new and fast-growing apocalypse sector. It's even doing overtime out in the Amazon, where the river is disappearing so quickly, entire towns have been left stranded in the mud (along with all the boats and the fish and the people). This drought has a big future, no doubt about it. Over at the Chicago Mercantile Exchange, there's talk of setting up a "water futures" market so brokers can trade the drought like they trade crude oil. I should tell Lucie. There could be money in it.

This drought could be the next Apple.

Lucie isn't a pole dancer, by the way.

Not *technically,* anyway, even though she does in fact spend two nights a week dancing on a pole. It's a new women's fitness class, and her fellow pole dancers have all become friends. I should have known. In the old days we made movies about other people's lives. Now we re-create those lives and sell them as leisure experiences. After pole dancing, Lucie wants to enroll in boot camp, then spy school. It can't be long now before the Equinox gym down on Sunset starts offering Stalinist forced-labor camp classes, complete with beatings and executions. Not that anyone's going to need this kind of distraction for much longer.

Oh no.

Soon our own lives will be interesting enough.

As for the wedding—what can I say? It was expensive. Right before the ceremony the dollar fell out of bed so hard it went clean through the floorboards. An historical all-time low, said the news. The exchange rate loss on the hotel bill alone could have brought down a small hedge fund. But they handled it well, my new in-laws. They're troupers. And Lucie looked incredible. The next morning, every male guest at the wedding must have put up a furniture ad on Craigslist. The whole story came out during the speeches, of course. I had prepared for this by positioning my grandmother at the back of the room and asking the kitchen staff to switch on the microwave, in hopes it would interfere with her hearing aid frequency. But she found out anyway, and she seemed pleased. Everything's so *interconnected* these days, she said. She's right: this is the defining fact of the twenty-first century.

It will be either our salvation or the end of us.

We flew to Hawaii for the honeymoon. The hotel was great, perfect: a Four Seasons resort with a pool right next to the beach. When they invented pools, I don't think they meant them to be right next to beaches. But whatever. The service was impeccable, especially by the pool. The Four Seasons employs a person whose only job it is to spray your face with a mist of chilled water whenever it becomes mildly flushed. In my case, this meant every fifteen seconds. Another person brings you cool lavender-scented towelettes, while another keeps your glass of iced water at a constant 95 percent fullness. There's even an employee tasked with the immediate removal of fingerprint smears from your sunglasses.

It's almost too much.

Almost, but not quite.

Then I made the mistake of reading the guidebook, which Lucie had warned me about. You don't need a guidebook at a grand-a-night resort, she said; it could give you dangerous thoughts about leaving the compound, where you might have more fun for less money. I ignored her and soon discovered that the name of the place—Hualalai—was also the name of a volcano. Interesting, I thought. And then I realized that the hotel was *on* the volcano. The book said that the last time Hualalai went off was in the 1800s. The date was vague, it added, because the witnesses had all been encased in burning lava before they could take notes. I wondered when it was expected to go off again. Any day now, said the book.

I told Lucie we had to leave. "Chris," she said without looking up from *Italian Vogue*. "We bought a house with an adjustable rate mortgage located on top of sixteen fault lines in a landslide area and an extreme fire hazard zone. And you're worried about a volcano? Life involves risk. Relax."

I lay back in my recliner and an attendant began pumping my face with cold water. I looked up and saw what I had earlier mistaken for an ocean mist. It was steam—steam from a vent in the hillside.

A man brought me a fruit kebab.

"Does it always do that?" I asked him, pointing.

"It's a volcano," he replied.

Like the weather, my finances never really recovered after the rain. On the surface, of course, everything is fine. The house is great. The car is great. *War Reporting for Cowards* was released in Britain two months ago and will be launched in America soon. On the surface, I am on the move, I am upwardly mobile, I am doing all right. The book advance cleared my student loan, my two MG loans, my sketchy Internet loan, and my AmEx card and paid for the engagement ring, the car down payment, and the honeymoon. Or at least it paid for *most* of all that. Yet one man is doing his very best to wreck it all. One man is trying extremely hard to turn me into a cautionary tale. His name is Alan Greenspan, and he is the chairman of the Federal Reserve. Since my last update he has raised interest rates another four times. *Four times*. This makes a total of ten interest rate hikes since we bought the house. *Ten*.

They say that Greenspan is trying to slow down the economy. They say he's worried about the bubble. He should try having an adjustable rate mortgage—*then* he'd be worried about the bubble.

We got rid of the old loan, of course. Flip Jackman refinanced it in less time than it takes most people to brush their teeth. I don't know how he does it. It's not human. I had barely put down the phone with him when a courier arrived from Santa Monica with the documents. The new loan is with a company called Countrywide Financial, which is apparently America's largest mortgage lender. For a while I couldn't figure out why the name sounded familiar, and then it came to me: Countrywide's headquarters are out by Calabasas, where I had picked up those Neverland tickets. God, that seems like a long time ago now.

I remember driving past the building: the black-mirrored walls, the rose garden, the sprinklers, the country club, the Ferrari dealership next door. Yes, they print their own money over there in Calabasas.

And now we have a new loan.

The payments are fixed at a low rate for three years, which I suppose is a relief. But the loan is all wrong. There are Mafia captains in federal prison who could learn from this loan. When we first bought the house, the notary warned us about mortgages like this: the payments are low and fixed only because we're paying *less* than the interest, with the balance being added to our principal every month. They call it a "negative amortization" loan—*negative* being the predominant word. But the market is still going up, which means that, in theory, we're still getting richer. We're letting the market do the heavy lifting, as Flip Jackman says.

Why does everything he tells me sound so much like bullshit these days?

When the caviar treatment was over, I added the two-hundred-dollar charge to my AmEx card, tipped forty, then crossed a thick carpet to the hotel's gold-plated elevator, which I rode in silence to the lobby while searching for evidence of caviar enhancement in the mirror. Out in the hotel driveway, by the statues and the floral displays (the hydrangeas are flown in every morning from South America), a valet retrieved the Range Rover from one of the more prominent parking spots. I love it when they leave the Range Rover in one of the more prominent spots: it makes my balls feel as big as artillery shells. It makes me feel like a player. It makes me want to use jargon from *Daily Variety* —*I hear Peterson has been ankled from the Mouse after Johnson nixed his yawner*—and say "fuckin-A" into my cell phone. On a bench in the waiting area I noticed an early edition of the weekend *New York Times*.

I picked it up and read.

Jackson Hole, Wyo.—In a generally sanguine outlook at a Fed sympo-
sium here this weekend, Mr. Greenspan said that both the excesses of the
housing market and the nation's unprecedented dependence on foreign
borrowing were likely to correct themselves through the normal function
of market forces.

The phrase "unprecedented dependence on foreign borrowing"
stayed with me as I climbed into the car, and I began to wonder if the
funds for my negative-amortization mortgage had come from the Chinese. Maybe the funds for the Range Rover had come from the Chinese, too. *Maybe I was borrowing depreciation from the Chinese.* Soon I
was cruising north on Doheny Boulevard in my soundproof and hand-
stitched leather universe. Deep within the engine bay, a gallon of the
finest Saudi petroleum was being consumed every nine miles. The
Range Rover will drink only the expensive stuff—it has a sensitive pal-
ette. While other, lesser vehicles are happy to guzzle anything pungent
and flammable, my car demands a ninety-one octane vintage, which it
swills around in its stainless steel tank, analyzing the bouquet and *terroir:*
Ah yes, I can hear it moan, *I'm getting the cologne of a nuclear-armed*
dictator . . . sandstorms and blood . . . an unusually warm ocean breeze.
If the woman from the travel channel were still around she would love
my car: *Unequaled and uncompromised,* she would declare in her ex-
alted whisper, *the Range Rover is the ultimate benchmark of luxury and*
refinement. But she's gone, and all I have for company is the guy from
National Public Radio. He hates my car. Of course he does. He can't
fucking stand it.

As Doheny dead-ended, I swung a hard right onto the billboard
gauntlet of Sunset Boulevard, rumbling east between the giant air-
brushed breasts of a new cast of TV starlets. Above, a newscopter was
being serenaded by a police siren. Then came a steep left onto Sunset
Plaza Drive, which lifted me up in its familiar corkscrew motion until
I could see the city's electric horizon in my rearview mirror. It throbbed
and hummed as the Los Angeles Department of Water and Power

pumped three thousand megawatts of electricity through its super-heated core. Up I went. Up and up. NO SMOKING IN THE HILLS, warned a signpost, on which was drawn a cheerful diagram of a blazing man-sion and a screaming figure inside.

I pulled up beside the bamboo planter and made my way inside the house. The front door had swollen because of the rain and I had to kick it to get it open, then kick it again to get it closed behind me. Finally I climbed the stairs to the living room, where I looked out at the flat circuitboard of the city, above which blinked at least a dozen helicop-ters and jets. I tossed my jacket over the new white Eames lounge chair—one of Lucie's recent purchases—and strolled into the spare-room-cum-office, where I hit PLAY on the answering machine.

The Beast awoke.

"Chris, where *are* you? I've been trying your mobile for hours. We need you to fly to the Gulf coast, as close as you can get. Drive if you can't fly. That tropical depression we've been keeping an eye on is going to make landfall as a category-five hurricane, as I'm sure you've already seen. That makes it the second category five of the season, with two more on the way. It's Armageddon down there. Call me as soon as you get this. And pick up your *phone* . . ."

There was a long pause, during which I could hear the din of the newsroom and the Beast fumbling with the receiver while he told some-one to hurry up with the graphic of New Orleans.

"There was something else I meant to tell you," he resumed. "Ah, yes, *right,* your caviar facial idea. This isn't a ploy to put your beauty regime on expenses is it, Chris? Not exactly the best of timing, either, as I'm sure you can appreciate. But write it anyway. We'll see if it works."

Beep.

Another message. This time, the publicist for my American publisher.

"We're *so* excited about the launch of *War Reporting for Cowards.* We're booking all the press for next week, to coincide with the *Times* review. Letterman's interested, and you're all set for CNN's *American Morning*. We need you in New York ASAP. Call me when you get this."

Beep.

And another message.

The Beast, again.

"Oh, Chris, forgot to mention. Remember the global warming angle. People are asking if this is all our own fault."

Beep.

I swore quietly to myself, collected something important from the bathroom, then set about preparing an overnight bag.

So this is it, I thought.

This is the end of the world.

Midnight at LAX.

I was halfway down the Jetway when the second pill kicked in. Here we go, I thought, as my legs buckled under me and I found myself swinging like an orangutan from the metal railing. Insane grogginess. And then I was looking into a female face, a face worn thin by long-haul shifts and cosmic radiation. It was saying something about Sarah and the UK. *Just let me get on the plane,* I thought. Again, Sarah and the UK. I tried to turn away but my shoulders weren't cooperating. Now another face loomed. This one belonged to a man wearing a blue hat. He also seemed to have some kind of problem with Sarah and the UK.

Then my ears popped and my head cleared.

"Sir, are you okay?"

There were perhaps a dozen people backed up behind me. Faces glistened in the stale air. Outside the Jetway was floodlit tarmac and a black sky with tropical fever. Given our destination, I was surprised there was anyone here at all. This was the last flight south tonight, possibly the last flight south for a very long time. Everyone else was going in the opposite direction: you could see them on the airport's flat-screen TVs, thousands of them, millions.

"HURRICANE KATRINA DEVASTATES SOUTH," read the scrolling caption. "NEW ORLEANS UNDERWATER . . . ONE MILLION WITHOUT POWER . . . FIRES BLAZING THROUGH RUINS . . . MORE AMERICANS TRANSPLANTED THAN DURING DUST BOWL . . ."

There was a man standing next to me. His face said: I saw you drinking, buddy. I saw khakis, polo shirt, belt-mounted cell phone. I wasn't sure if he was an insurance adjuster or a federal agent. Now the floor was vibrating as a mechanical arm carrying chemical breakfasts docked at the other side of the plane. It was imperative that I board this flight. The Beast had demanded it. Admittedly, the two beers in the airport bar had been a mistake. I should have guessed that the alcohol would interact so violently with Lucie's sleeping pills.

"Sir, are you okay?"

"Ambien," I explained. "Took two."

I steadied myself again, a final attempt to prove my fitness for travel. I imagined seeing what the pilot saw: a pale Brit, just turned thirty, thickening around the gut, hair shaved close to disguise baldness. Hanging on my shoulder was a blue messenger bag, in which was a notebook, pens, six pairs of underwear, four T-shirts, a laptop, and a printout of directions from Atlanta to Biloxi. The map was already out of date; from what I could gather Biloxi no longer existed.

"Okay," he said. "You're good."

"Last call for Delta Airlines flight fourteen seventy-five to Atlanta," said a voice on the PA system. "Again, last call for Atlanta."

"Thank you," I managed and waded slowly toward the glowing hatch.

Then black.

I regained consciousness under the yellow glare of the Hertz car rental facility in Atlanta International Airport. Christ knows how I got off the plane. In the glass that separated the parking lot park from the rental counter, I caught my reflection: still no evidence of the caviar glow. On the contrary, I looked like I'd been recently exhumed. On a brighter note, the Ambien had done its job perfectly: my four-hour blackout in the upper troposphere had left me feeling ready for business, even though my stomach was now a landfill of airport hamburger and stress chemicals.

It was six a.m. and still dark.

On the TV above me there was a view of Hurricane Katrina from space. It looked like a wormhole from out in the galaxy, a deep space anomaly that had somehow ended up here on earth. There it was, right over the cupped hand of the Gulf of Mexico, sucking up the matter below and transporting it to another, more violent dimension. The news said that after its first landfall as a category one in Florida, Hurricane Katrina had gone back out to sea for three days, done some thinking about its career, its life goals, its prospects, and come back three days later as a category five. Having reached the ultimate peak of any hurricane's career, Katrina was now winding down, semiretiring to tropical depression status before demoting itself again to an extratropical low. A roll call was now scrolling of all the name-worthy storms of the summer: Arlene, Bret, Cindy, Dennis, Emily, Franklin, Gert, Harvey, Irene, Jose, and now Katrina. And Katrina wasn't even the last of them. Apparently we still had Lee, Maria, Nate, Ophelia, Philppe, and Rita to come. And after them a whole new cast of meteorological villains. This was more than just a storm-season record, said the man on the TV.

This was something else.

Atlanta was as far south as I had been able to fly. Any farther toward the Gulf and the weather was still too bad. Besides, there was nowhere to land: the surviving airports were all being used for evacuations.

So now I had to drive, which meant seven hours and four hundred miles before I reached Biloxi, or what was left of it. This was my assignment: to see Biloxi firsthand, while another of the Beast's correspondents, Jacqui Goddard, reported from what remained of New

Orleans. The last anyone in London had heard from Jacqui was that she was stranded in a flooded hotel with a shark circling outside, and that she might have to claim her rental car on expenses because the black water that had seeped in through the doors had risen to the steering wheel.

I considered my own transportation options.

In the Hertz parking lot I could see a white Hummer with chrome rims, a black town car with tinted windows, and a silver Mustang with a three-foot tail wing. The cost was irrelevant, as this qualified as an emergency, and the Beast was paying. But I controlled the urge to rent the Hummer.

"I'll take the Ford," I said, after rejecting several other models of SUV, most of them named after mountains.

My rental agent was black, female, with beaded hair and an expression that suggested an internal struggle with profound boredom. I wondered if she'd been up all night. We were alone except for the buzz of the fluorescent lights and a mop standing upright in a bucket in the corner.

"Liability insurance supplement?" she asked.

"I'll take it."

"Loss damage waiver?"

"I'll take it."

"Personal liabil—"

"I'll take everything," I interrupted. There was a good chance this Ford wouldn't be coming back in one piece.

"And how long will you be needing the vehicle?"

"That depends."

"Depends on what?"

"Good question."

An hour or so later the freeway heading south was empty. The sun might have been up somewhere but you couldn't see it for the clouds. I began to shut down the nondriving part of my brain, eventually falling into a semitrance. I kept all the windows open to make sure I stayed awake. When the heat finally turned unbearable I sealed the cabin, recalibrated the climate control to "max air," then watched the fuel gauge turn counterclockwise as if in fast forward.

An hour passed.

I braked hard for a roadside stop near Opelika, Alabama. Facing bulletproof plastic, I paid for gas, gum, coffee, and cigarettes. Jesus, it was *hot*. In a diesel fog I ate and enjoyed an egg McMuffin and a solitary hash brown. Tired, sweating, my skin raw from the red-eye, I took a key attached to a concrete block to the bathroom. I emerged a few minutes later, my face a mask of hand soap residue and feeling even dirtier than before. The place was deserted.

Where the hell *was* everyone?

Back on the empty road I kept the radio away from the news channels (plenty of that later) and listened to country rock at high volume. Neil Young was asking an old man to take a look at his life. Johnny Cash was complaining that he had fallen into a burning ring of fire. I knew how he felt. Montgomery came and went. At another roadside stop I fought the urge to pass out. Instead, I dialed up a tub of coffee from a vending machine and downed it in two gulps.

Back in the car my phone buzzed with two voice-mails.

The first was from the publicist for *War Reporting for Cowards*, saying that perhaps we should rethink the timing of the book tour, especially now that Letterman and CNN had canceled because of what appeared to be the imminent end of the world. The second message was from the Beast, informing me that our Baghdad correspondent was now on his way to New Orleans.

When war correspondents start covering the weather, I thought, you know there's a problem.

Biloxi was still two hours away.

I knew the fear would come eventually; it was just a question of when. The answer turned out to be about thirty minutes outside of Mobile, which I approached at eighty-five miles per hour, wrestling with the gale for control of the wheel. That was when I became aware of the skeletons lining the freeway: metal skeletons, with ripped vinyl hanging from them. Before the storm they had been billboards. Some of them had been pulled clean out of the ground and lay in nearby fields, their legs buckled and twisted, like giant robot casualties of some futuristic war. Still alone on the freeway, I ignored the road signs and pushed the Ford up to ninety. The police surely had better things to do today than hand out speeding tickets—besides, I hadn't seen a single state trooper so far. Now it was raining so hard it felt like a million tiny fists trying to smash through the windscreen. The wipers were putting up a fight, but they were losing. I passed a car on its roof, wheels spinning helplessly. This made me slow down. The car was empty; it had been carried there by the wind.

The fields to either side of the road were oceans now, their riptides taking houses, barns, and animals with them. I saw a cow, alone and confused, on what appeared to be a piece of flotsam drifting toward the Gulf. Farther on, trees blocked my lane, so I crashed over the median and drove on the left, pretending to be in England. Nothing was coming in the other direction. Eventually, three hundred miles from Atlanta, the I-65 came to an end and the I-10 began.

Amid the wreckage, a signpost.

WELCOME TO MISSISSIPPI: IT'S LIKE COMING HOME

That was when the real insanity began.

I brought the Ford to a halt and got out with the engine still grinding and the AC blowing. The heat. Christ, the heat. I walked around to the front of the car, shielding my face from the assault of the rain. "You've got to be *kidding,*" I said. And there it was, moored on the hard shoulder of the I-10: a forty-foot yacht, balanced on its hull like a giant bathtub. *There was a yacht on the freeway.* How far was the nearest marina? Two miles, three? I reached for my phone to call London. They were expecting a story by the end of the day. But when I started to dial I saw the message flashing in the upper left corner of the screen: "NO NETWORK."

Shit, I hadn't thought about that. The hurricane had probably taken out all the towers. In fact I remembered seeing one, embedded in the roof of someone's garage. I got back in the Ford and switched on the radio, changing bands until I found the local news. That was when I realized there were a few other things I hadn't thought about, either. For example, the radio station was begging its listeners for diesel so it could keep its generators running and the show on the air. It would be weeks or months before the power grid could be repaired, it said. I wondered why they didn't just go out and *buy* some diesel. That was when the announcer explained that the Gulf of Mexico provides America with a third of its domestic oil, and that Katrina had taken out everything: platforms, refineries, pipelines, you name it. Oil traders on Wall Street were panicking, as was everyone in the South. Hours after the storm, every last drop of oil in the system had been pumped dry. There was no diesel left to buy. There was no gas left to buy, either. The tankers couldn't replace it fast enough and, besides, hundreds of gas stations were destroyed. Production in the Gulf was starting up again, but at a fraction of capacity. It was chaos. It was the oil apocalypse. There were riots at gas stations, with people stockpiling whatever they could find.

I looked up at the dash.

"Oh *no,*" I said.

I knew exactly what the fuel gauge was going to say before my eyes reached the needle. I had just driven three hundred miles in a three-ton vehicle at eighty miles per hour. Of course I knew what it was going to say. And there it was: a diving board over a red precipice marked "empty." The readout underneath guessed my range at twenty miles. I punched the wheel. "Why didn't I *think* of that?" I shouted. In the panic to get to Biloxi I had failed to make the most basic of preparations. I should have known. Of course I should have *known*.

But in my thirty years of life, of first world experience, the oil had never run out overnight.

So here I am, I thought, on an empty freeway, with no phone, no fuel, perhaps half a day's drive from the nearest working pump, with only a beached yacht on the shoulder of the I-10 for company. I admired the hull of the vessel in front of me. Was it a fishing boat? Someone's retirement gift? I couldn't see a name so I decided to Christen it myself.

Lady of Leisure is what I settled on in the end.

Eventually I clunked the Ford back into gear and started to drive again, calculating that I had perhaps thirty minutes until I was stranded in the dead zone of the hurricane. If that happened, I would have to forget about filing a story for the Beast and hitchhike north, in the hope of eventually finding a hotel with a room and working telephone. But I didn't want to think about that. Under normal circumstances, of course, thirty minutes would have been more than enough time to find an exit and refuel. But if there was one thing that could be said about the circumstances it was that they were not normal. I wondered how far back in the opposite direction I would have to drive before I reached the old America, the functioning America, the America with an oil economy. Montgomery, probably. Three hours.

Fuck.

I resumed my journey south, turning off the air-conditioning and opening the windows. The rain had now called off its hostilities, leaving me with only the wind to fight. I couldn't remember what speed you were supposed to drive to save fuel. Was it fifty-five, sixty? I stuck to fifty-five and took the first exit I saw. That was when I realized that the freeway had handled the storm relatively well compared with the towns on either side of it. I could hardly believe what I was seeing. Everything was broken. The cars, the street signs, the traffic lights, the shops, the houses . . . everything. The world looked like it had been picked up twenty feet off the ground, dipped in mud, then dropped back to earth. All the gas stations were out. The branded canopies had been ripped clean off their frames and were probably out in the Gulf of Mexico somewhere, along with the signs advertising unleaded for two dollars and ninety-nine cents a gallon. Finally, I saw a place that looked almost intact. Beside one of the pumps was a man standing next to an eighties-vintage Cadillac. I swung the Ford over the curb and came to a jerky halt behind him. I was in a panic now, being clumsy, doing things too quickly. There was a hotel behind me. It was fine, the hotel—fine apart from the roof, which was in the trees across the street.

I kept the engine running and got out of the car, walking behind it to get to the pump. I noticed a light on inside the attendant's booth. A good sign. But what the hell was that *noise*? A rhythmic mumbling: broken, imploring. I ignored it and lifted the nozzle. The pump looked okay. Please. *Please*. I pulled on the trigger and it clicked uselessly in my hand. I tried again. Again, it clicked uselessly. *Shit*. Now I could see that the LED readout was blank. The glass had a crack in it, too, and there was a panel missing below the credit card reader. A full panic now. I would rather have been stranded on the freeway than stranded *here*.

Fuck.

And then a number of things happened very quickly. First, the mumbling noise stopped and, at the same time, the man with the Cadillac began to assault his pump, using the dead nozzle as a weapon. The mumbling must have been *him*. He must have been talking or weeping to himself. I got a good look at him now. He was white, but so destroyed by the sun you could hardly tell. His shirt was missing and on his arms and back were the kind of tattoos they give you in prison with a wire hanger and a cigarette lighter. He was wearing a bandanna. As I watched him beat up the pump, a terrible, paranoid thought came to me: if you were stranded in your Cadillac at the end of the world with no food and no water and no electricity and no phone and no anything at all, and if there was no law and no society, only wreckage and death, you might consider stealing a car. You might even consider stealing the brand-new SUV right next to you, the one with the driver's-side door open and the engine running, with the laptop on the passenger seat and the iPod charging.

I decided to leave, and quickly.

That was when the man with the Cadillac stopped beating the pump and turned to me, his face wet and filthy.

"Hey *buddy,*" he said, as he began to move toward me, at speed.

20

The White Room

The doctors have been friendly enough, I suppose. They're busy but they still take the time to listen, to reassure. And the food is nowhere near as bad as it's cracked up to be. On the contrary, I've actually taken quite a liking to hospital food. I think it's the lack of choice I enjoy, the inability to pay more, even if I wanted to (and God knows I've tried). They only take cash, too, down in the canteen. I suppose it's fitting that in a place of human inevitability you can get by only with the hard stuff—the *real* stuff. American Express doesn't exist as far as these people are concerned.

I've been doing a lot of thinking since I was brought in here. I've even come up with a new plan, a new mission, to replace the old one—the one about cars and gadgets and clifftop bachelor palaces, the one that ended up working out a bit too well for me in the end. I told one of the nurses about it when she came over to check on me a few minutes ago, but I'm not sure she was listening—she was too busy taking down the details from my insurance card.

Anyhow, so this is it, the new outline, the new strategy: *I'm going to live frugally from now on*. At the very least, I'm going to live within my means. They say an addict is never fully recovered, but I can't see myself making these mistakes again. Christ, no. Not after *this*.

The change will take time, of course. They say it can be hard at first: the adjustment, the recalibration . . . the downgrading. They say it can be a long and bumpy flight back from the never-never.

*   *   *

There are so many other things to update you on that I don't even know where to begin—although I hardly need to fill you in on the headlines. The property market, for example; it crashed. It more than crashed. I remember once hearing Warren Buffett talk about a nuclear terror attack on New York being a "one-trillion-dollar event." Well, the property crash was a *four*-trillion-dollar event. And that's not counting the money that was lost as a *result* of the property crash.

All those dollar bills: Just gone, disappeared, erased.

It all happened a lot faster than anyone thought it would, too. The small-time mortgage lenders went down first. *Temporary correction,* people said. Then two Bear Stearns hedge funds imploded, a result of overenthusiastic investments in the "subprime" sector. In other words, loans given to people with bad credit, people like me. By then no one could stop the inevitable. I knew it was over when Countrywide Financial simply ran out of money. Yes, America's largest mortgage lender —my *own* mortgage company—just ran clean out of cash. That wasn't the official explanation from Calabasas, of course. The official explanation was that the company needed to "supplement its funding liquidity position" with a $11.5 billion loan.

Whatever the case, I don't think many more Ferraris will be sold at that glass-walled dealership across the street.

Come to think of it, I doubt anyone's going to be selling much of anything for a while, not now that there's talk of the Great Depression II.

As for my own little contribution to the destruction—that adjustable rate, negative-amortization time bomb of a home loan—it kept on ticking for eighteen months after we refinanced it. Every month, the balance went up as the value of the house finally went into reverse, having risen by about sixteen grand a month during the last two years of the bubble. And now the house is gone. The keys have been handed in. The mail is being forwarded to a new address.

All of which helps explain how I ended up here, in this mopped and bleached corridor, outside this white room, in this hospital, with my order from the nurses not to disappear again to the canteen.

The man with the Cadillac never got the chance to do whatever it was he was going to do. At the exact moment he began to move toward me, a police car squawked into the gas station. Relieved? I almost wept. Although to be honest with you the officer looked about as crazed and angry as the man who had just been vandalizing the pump. I was probably looking a bit crazed and angry myself. An oil apocalypse can do that to you, especially when you're not expecting one so soon.

"Why do you people *come* here?" yelled the officer from his car. "It's all gone. The pumps are dry."

I asked him if there was anywhere else to refuel.

"*Don't you understand?*" he shouted. "We're out of gas. We're out of gas and there ain't nothin' you or any one of the other one and a half million people down here who are out of gas can do about it."

This wasn't how the End of Oil was supposed to happen. The End of Oil was supposed to take place gradually, over a number of decades: the "peak oil" scenario. All of which was supposed to give us time to buy electric cars made by Americans, who had once sent a man to the moon.

It wasn't supposed to happen like *this*.

I contained the panic and got back on the I-10, now heading northwest, away from my destination. There was no bloody way I was going to run out of fuel in Biloxi, where I could get stuck for weeks. Besides, I had heard on the radio that the looting down on the coast was so bad they were about to declare martial law. People were breaking open ATM machines, stealing plasma TVs from hotel rooms. And what could the police do? They barely had any fuel for their squad cars, and even if they did many of the roads were still impassable. Besides, some of the police stations, not to mention the police officers' homes, had been turned to mud and rubble like everything else. The situation over in New Orleans was even worse: twenty-eight thousand people, most of them black, were now stranded and dying in a wrecked sports stadium called the Superdome—while *dogs* were being airlifted to shelters. The levees had broken, the floodwater had risen so high that the city had merged with Lake Pontchartrain, and there was no power, food, telephones, or medical attention. In the one-fifth of the city not underwater, fires were burning and gangs were looting—even some police officers were looting. People were begging the TV newscopters for help as corpses floated by them in water turned black by every horror imaginable. New Orleans was destroyed. It was gone. The largest city in the state of Louisiana was now officially Baton Rouge. Meanwhile, the president had been seen circling overhead in Air Force One.

He hadn't landed.

Again I passed the yacht on the freeway—*Lady of Leisure*—and kept driving for as far as I dared, eventually taking an exit with a blue pump sign. The service stations at the northbound and southbound ramps were dead. My range was five miles now, and dropping fast.

Defeated and furious with myself, I didn't even bother to get back on the freeway, where it would at least have been easier to hitchhike. Instead I followed the eastbound exit into trees and farmland. I can't remember how far I went before I passed the barn, thinking nothing of it. It was only when I looked in the mirror that I saw the sign.

I smoked the tires to a standstill, fumbled for reverse, then whined backward to get a better look.

"You've got to be *kidding*," I said, for the second time that day.

The barn was in fact a shop. A dog lay asleep by the door amid a brood of restless hens. On a piece of wood was painted FRESH EGGS. But it was the antique pump in the middle of the yard that had my full attention. *The pump can't be real,* I thought. For a start, it had one of those old scrolling-number displays and a nozzle that was bleeding rust. I pulled up beside it regardless, aware of how ridiculous I must have looked. I twisted open the filler cap on the Ford and unhooked the nozzle. I could smell vapor now from the tank of the big SUV—the same vapor that had probably been keeping me going for the past few miles.

In went the nozzle. I kept waiting for someone to come outside and give me the police officer's speech all over again.

No one did.

Taking great care I squeezed the trigger. *Nothing*. I tried again. *Nothing*. And then, with a clunk and a hum, the numbers on the pump jerked slowly upward. It was an almost religious moment. It must have taken twenty minutes to fill up the tank, the pump was so old. Inside the barn, I practically French-kissed the old-timer at the counter. I asked if he had any petrol canisters, so I could take some extra fuel with me.

"*Petrol* canisters?" he asked, baffled.

"Gas canisters," I translated.

"Oh, *gas* canisters," he said.

"Do you have any?"

"Gettin' some next week."

I told him not to worry about it.

He said God bless you.

I said no, no, God bless *you*.

With a full tank I resumed my journey to the scene of the apocalypse, exiting the I-10, which took me over the Back Bay and into the ruins of Biloxi. I remembered once reading a travel article about Biloxi. "good times on the gulf", the headline had read, "here's a town that knows how to have fun." At every exit now there was a milelong line of cars waiting for gas that wouldn't arrive for days, perhaps weeks. The cars looked so useless, so lifeless, without their fuel. People had switched off their engines and were either camped out on the shoulder or just walking around in circles. If the line moved an inch, they pushed. The sight of it was enough to make me panic about the next fill up. I guessed I would just have to drive the three or four hours back to Montgomery. It was going to be a long day.

As Biloxi approached, the road dipped and flooded, and for a moment I worried about stalling. But the engine kept running and the water fell away as the freeway dropped me into the purgatory below.

The cruelest sight was right there in front of me: a giant red electric guitar, at least ten stories high, which marked the entrance of the Hard Rock hotel and casino, the grand opening of which had been scheduled for today, or so the radio told me. The guitar had been built to survive 180 miles per hour winds. Just as well, because that's pretty much the speed at which Katrina made landfall. But while the guitar remained standing nothing else did. To conform with Mississippi law, the floor of the Hard Rock had been constructed to actually *float* in the Gulf of Mexico, so that it was technically offshore. This had allowed the storm to pick it up and throw it like a giant piece of flotsam into the part of the development on dry land. It had cost half a billion dollars to build that casino. It would probably cost as much to repair it.

Down there on the Biloxi waterfront, it was as if matter itself had been dismantled and then put back together in the wrong order—as if an experiment with teleportation had gone horribly awry. The news on the radio reported that just about all the floating casinos in Biloxi had been obliterated. One of them, the Grand Casino, had been tossed over a four-lane highway, sending it crashing into the Ohr O'Keefe Museum, half a mile away. The Grand Casino was twice as long as football field, with almost a thousand rooms on board.

Biloxi was destroyed. It was gone.

For as far as I could see in any direction there was only a junkyard tide line of wreckage. The smell was the worst: death and sewage. In a mound of rubble by the Hard Rock (graffiti: "You Loot, We Shoot") I found a fortyish woman in a ragged dress with blonde hair and a sunburn. Her name was Ida Punzo. She was sitting on a salvaged chair under a ruined tree, which had been decorated with women's underwear, as if it were part of some unfunny student prank. Behind the tree was Ida's rented attic apartment, still standing on two antebellum columns, even though the two floors below it were gone. Nearby, emergency workers were busy pulling thirty bodies from the inappropriately named Quiet Water Apartments.

I asked Ida what it had been like to experience Katrina. She smiled at me and said, "You can't imagine the terror."

I sat down beside her on the vandalized shore and looked out at the Gulf—still restless, still brooding—and for the first time began to understand the physics of what had happened. The storm had blown up a three-story surge of water that had arrived with all the speed and force of a tsunami and then retreated just as suddenly, the violence of its withdrawal almost as bad as its advance. The surge had turned the twenty-first century itself into a weapon—a cluster bomb of refrigerators, cars, power lines, furniture, traffic lights, telephone poles, computers, espresso machines. Every piece of human technology imaginable suddenly possessed by the murderous force of the warmed ocean and the malfunctioning weather system above.

Ida Punzo was right. I couldn't imagine the terror.

I miss Flip Jackman. I really do.

Sometimes I think about calling him, just to remember what it was like when the banks would give you a million dollars for two grand a month, with no money down. But things are so different now. Money is still cheap but the banks won't lend it to anyone. They're too busy borrowing money themselves just to stay in business.

Besides, it would be weird talking to Flip after everything that happened. It would be like calling Courage Macleod. It would be like calling Lara to reminisce about Neverland.

Not that I hold anything against him. He was just doing his job—and he did it well. He never lied to me or sold me anything I didn't want to buy. I knew the risks and I chose to ignore them. Being allowed to know the risks and yet still choose to ignore them is one of the great things about America. And it works out well for everyone, generally. But it doesn't work when half the country starts trying to cheat the system. It turns out that Flip Jackman's less scrupulous counterparts were selling these time bomb mortgages to people who were practically on minimum wage, people whose incomes had zero chance of rising after the expiration of their teaser rates.

And how did they qualify? By lying, of course. No one checked the application forms. No one *wanted* to check the application forms. The banks did the same thing on a bigger scale. After selling these mortgages they divided them up into tiny pieces and passed them on, scattering them over the economy like confetti, without ever really questioning the risk. But every little piece of confetti had its own little detonation pin and its own little explosive charge. And when Greenspan panicked about the bubble and began to raise interest rates—he did it *seventeen times,* in the end—out came the pins, one by one.

Bang.

Greenspan now says he didn't know what was going on until it was too late. He should have called me. I could have told him exactly what was going on. Every time he raised interest rates everyone's mortgage payments went up. And up. In the end, some home owners just hunkered down and waited for the police to evict them; others stole what they could from their properties and vandalized what remained. I've even read about people not making their payments out of *choice,* because their house is no longer worth what they paid for it, so why bother? Now there's talk of the government just bailing everyone out and adding the tab to the national debt, which is going to hit ten trillion dollars pretty soon, thanks in part to the presently estimated three-trillion-dollar cost of the wars in Iraq and Afghanistan. Which means that the National Debt Clock in New York—the one they had to move to make way for the headquarters of a mortgage company—will run out of digits.

Yes, America will soon be so deep in the hole that not even the National Debt Clock will be able to keep up.

Greenspan is long gone, of course. He retired six months before the asteroid landed. He must switch on the news every morning and go red in the face. It turns out that while the Americans were busy financing Chinese-made TVs with the Fed's cheap money, everyone else was staying at home and paying off their debts. Take the Russians. They're completely in the black now. They just wrote the banks a check and that was the end of it. The Indians are doing pretty well for themselves too. They're about to buy Range Rover from Ford because Ford somehow managed to lose thirteen billion dollars last year. And the Chinese? The Chinese have a one-trillion-dollar surplus. The Chinese are having the time of their lives. Every day, they take our money and lend it back to us. In fact, if you do the math, it turns out that over the past ten years every single person in America has in effect borrowed four thousand dollars from every single person in China. The Americans are supposed to be rich, and the Chinese are supposed to be poor. How does this work, exactly?

I have no idea.

I really have no idea.

So the Fed is now lowering interest rates again, as if more cheap money will fix everything. But it's too late. The economy is in such bad shape, no one even cares about inflation any more. It's *de*flation they're worried about. Which of course is much, much worse than inflation. Why? Because at least inflation ultimately shrinks your debts. Thanks to inflation, a million-dollar loan today will seem like a back-of-the-napkin I.O.U. in thirty years' time. Deflation does the opposite. It takes your debts and makes them bigger. It makes a $1-million loan seem like a $1-*billion* loan in thirty years' time. Just what we need.

It's hard not to wonder where it will all end.

I hope not with the Chinese.

If an official in Beijing picks up the phone and says "sell the dollar," the property crash will be the least of anyone's worries. Then again, if the Chinese sell the dollar, they'll nuke their own economy in the process—or so the conventional wisdom goes. It's like mutually assured destruction from the old cold war days: a concept designed to reassure the public, even though it assumes that the apocalypse is not only possible but a worst-case strategic option.

Which isn't very reassuring at all.

Yet everything is mutually assured these days; everything is interconnected. A cow farts in Iowa and a village floods in Dorset. A fifty-inch TV leaves a factory in Beijing and a three-hundred-mile-wide cloud of smog arrives in LA. A man sells his grandmother's sofa bed on Craigslist and . . . Yes, everything is interconnected now, for better and for worse. Which leaves the obvious question: Did we *really* do it? Did we *really* break the weather, just like we broke the economy?

A few weeks after the Gulf coast was destroyed, scientists at Dome Charlie—a base down on the Antarctic Plateau, eight thousand miles south of Biloxi—published the results of an ice-drilling experiment, which gave them samples of the earth's atmosphere dating back more than half a million years. It turns out that the carbon dioxide in the air today is thirty percent more concentrated than at any other point during that period. *Thirty percent.* Soon after came another report, from the Intergovernmental Panel on Climate Change, which stated that human beings had "more likely than not" contributed to the intensification of hurricanes, and that future Katrinas would have higher wind speeds and heavier rain than ever before.

All told, there were twenty-eight tropical storms during the summer of Katrina, including three category-five hurricanes—three of the most powerful hurricanes ever recorded in the Atlantic basin. There had never even *been* three category-five Atlantic hurricanes one year before.

Did we do it? Did we break the weather?

Probably. Christ, yes, probably.

*   *   *

Any minute now they'll let me into the white room where the nurses will be going about their work in their face masks and their uniforms. I'm nervous, and I have a strange pressure behind my eyes, but I'm trying not to show it. When I push through that door, your mother will be there in front of me, lying on the raised and illuminated table, the doctors and anesthetists gathered around the hole in her stomach. And from that hole you will soon emerge, like a long-haul traveler from an aircraft hatch: hungry, spooked, tired, aching . . . desperate to pee. Your teleportation will be complete. You will have switched dimensions, you will have traveled through time and space and you will be here, here in America—here in Beverly Hills.

I should probably tell you right now that your mother has given up pole dancing. It came as a relief to everyone, to be honest. As for your father, he has stopped driving around in a three-ton SUV—it's all part of his new plan to stop borrowing from the future. I have a Vespa now. I wanted something bigger, of course—something with a bit more kick—but your mother preempted me by giving me the Vespa for Christmas. And now I'm stuck with it.

Meanwhile, the Range Rover is in semiretirement, pending the expiration of its lease and its return to the dealership—in return for which I will get nothing but the satisfaction of knowing that I paid for its depreciation, plus interest. I'm going to miss the Range Rover. I'm going to miss the *respect*. Take the other day. I was riding east on Sunset and stopped at a light next to an LAPD officer on a Harley-Davidson. He took one look at the Vespa and revved his engine, making me flinch. This really cracked him up. And it wasn't enough for the bastard, either. After revving his engine two or three more times, he leaned over and said, "Born to be *mild*, huh?"

But that's the price of doing seventy miles per gallon, I suppose. That's the price of being able to buzz up alongside a hybrid in rush-hour traffic and shout *"Polluter!"* at the conscientious celebrity inside.

Give it time, of course, and the LAPD will be riding Vespas too. LA is changing. The world is changing. By the time you read this, you probably won't even recognize the city I describe. You can't impress girls with *consumption* anymore, for starters. Conservation is the new luxury. Saving is the new borrowing. Pretty soon, evolution will take care of the rest. Pretty soon, human beings will be no more likely to burn oil than they will to set fire to their own heads.

If you listen to the neo-Malthusians, of course, it's reproduction that's the problem. I disagree. Reproduction is the *solution*. Evolution—the self-interest of the species—always gets it right in the end.

I am the last of a generation, a relic of a bygone oil age. The programming of my twentieth-century boyhood is as obsolete as the VHS or the Concorde. And now I must download the new code. I must upgrade, shut down, restart.

The infrastructure is already on its way (or so we're told): the solar panels, the wind turbines, the tidal generators. Soon they'll even have electric cars that don't run on coal. In every industry now there are new inventions. On the front page of this morning's *Wall Street Journal* I read a story about cargo ships being fitted with computer-controlled "kites" to assist their engines.

Yes, ships are going back to *sails*.

I wish we had done all this sooner, of course. I wish we had listened to the warnings and avoided having to live out this cautionary tale. And I worry. I worry that it's already too late. A cautionary tale isn't supposed to come *true*, after all. It's supposed to be a warning, told out of love. That's why the violence of the punishment is always so disproportionate, so implausible . . . so entertaining. Take that poem by Hilaire Belloc: Jim lets go of his nurse's hand and within seconds he is dismembered by a lion that *just so happens* to be roaming in the area.

Would this happen in real life?

Not unless Jim was having a very unlucky day.

So far, at least, things haven't turned out so bad. Take the house, the one we bought with that ridiculous mortgage. When your mother found out she was pregnant, we sold it and paid off the loan. The deal closed seven days before the crash. *Seven days*. Not bad, eh? We even made a profit in the end. But then we invested all the money in an even bigger house, with an even bigger mortgage. Still, we have a more sensible loan these days: we pay *all* of the interest, and the rate is fixed for the next seven years. Before the crash, of course, seven years sounded like a long time. It doesn't sound quite so long anymore. But then you can't worry too much, can you? As I've always told myself, in the long term there *is* no long term.

As for the weather—the weather is a problem, I agree. In a few weeks' time, the Santa Ana winds will be here again. And then will come the fires, again, and the floods, and the falling mountains . . . and then it'll be spring, when we get to see what new apocalypse the storm season brings.

But life is good; life is beautiful.

Ah, here comes the nurse. She's telling me that we're ready now, that I should pull my mask up over my face. I do as she says. As the pressure builds behind my eyes, I think about all the things I need to tell you, all the things I need to write down for you to read. All those mistakes—in a way, I suppose, I'm glad I made them. I wouldn't be here otherwise. Neither would you.

I'm pushing through the door now. As it swings shut behind me, an unfamiliar force takes hold. For a moment I feel nothing. Then it comes: a charge of love so absolute, so unconditional, it almost knocks me to the floor. And in that moment of paralysis, I can think of only one thing to say.

I'm just sorry about the weather.

We're all very sorry about the weather.

Acknowledgments and Notes

I would like to thank Roland Philipps and Morgan Entrekin, my publishers at John Murray in London and Grove/Atlantic in New York, respectively, for agreeing to buy this book when it was still just a few pages of notes, and for not asking for their money back when the manuscript failed to show up until fourteen months after the deadline. My only explanation for the delay is that I was busy trying to get myself out of all the trouble that I had managed to get myself into as part of the "research," which turned out to include being complicit in a four-trillion-dollar mortgage crisis, among other things. The upside—if it can be called that—is that the second half of the book is a damn sight more exciting than it was in the proposal.

Thanks also to my editors Rowan Yapp and Jofie Ferrari-Adler, my literary agents Mark Lucas and George Lucas, and my screen agent Nick Harris. I would also like to thank the *Times* of London for being the most supportive employer any reporter could ever hope to have. In particular I would like to thank Robert Thomson, David Chappell, Ben Preston, Martin Fletcher, Martin Barrow, Daniel Finkelstein, Tim Rice, and Robbie Millen. Thanks also to Tom Post at *Forbes* and to Cherry Gee and Nicholas Goldberg in the op-ed department of the *Los Angeles Times,* both of whom have kindly published my freelance columns over recent years.

Writing a book is a solitary business, and it would impossible without the support of friends, family, and readers. Thanks therefore to the

Ayres family (in particular my sister, Catherine, for giving me that copy of *Money* by Martin Amis when I was fifteen years old), the Kotyza family, the Wiesenmaier family, Jeff Rayner, Catherine Elsworth, Jade Chang, Victoria Campbell, Marcus Spiegel, and Erica Rothschild. And thanks to the literally tens of people who e-mailed me after reading my previous book, *War Reporting for Cowards,* in particular Jake Lentz and Jimmy Kimmel. Thanks also to Ken and Teri Hertz for letting me use their pool for the cover shoot. Most of all, however, I would like to thank my wife—the beautiful and mysterious "L"—who put up with me working nights and weekends for two years as I wrote the story of how we met. Every day I spent with the book I was reminded of how lucky—and in love—I am. Thanks also to our son, Milo, (or Milos to the Czechs in our family) who showed his approval of the manuscript by repeatedly vomiting over it.

Finally, a few notes about the text. As mentioned in the preface, the names and biographical details of several people (and associated business names, in some cases) have been changed, either because I thought it would be unfair to identify them or because they requested anonymity. Those people are Lara, Sally Worthington-Haynes, Courage Macleod, Dickie, Bianca Sweetingham, Tony (of Tony's Tuxedos), Bob Jones (of the Twilight Kitty Lounge), Boot Camp Bertha, Bernard Paxman, Flip Jackman, and Brett Minsky. In spite of the name changes, I have tried to remain faithful to what happened and keep embellishments to a minimum. I should also mention that most of the TV news broadcasts cited in the text are not *actual* broadcasts: they are based on my memory of what was going on at the time.

I used many sources for the factual material. Two books were very helpful: *The Great Deluge* by Douglas Brinkley and *Michael Jackson: The Magic and the Madness* by J. Randy Taraborrelli. A full explanation of the phenomenon of LA smog being imported from China can be found in a *Wall Street Journal* article by Robert Lee Hotz, published on July 20, 2007, and entitled "Huge Dust Plumes from China Cause Changes in Climate." The phenomenon of suicidal squid, meanwhile, was reported by Stefan Lovgren in a *National Geographic News* article,

"Jumbo Squid Mass 'Suicide' Stumps California Scientists," dated February 23, 2005. A comprehensive list of the potential "solutions" to global warming can be found in an (unbylined) Associated Press report, "Using Smoke, Mirrors and Faux Trees to Tackle Global Warming, Geoengineers Offer Far-Out Ideas," dated March 17, 2007.

The best sources I found for the drought in the American Southwest were a October 21, 2007, article by Jon Gertiner in the *New York Times,* "The Future Is Drying Up", and another article, "Worst Drought in 500 Years," by Luis Monteagudo Jr., which appeared in the *San Diego Union-Tribune* on June 30, 2004. My data on Las Vegas real estate came from an article entitled "Real Estate: Down, Down, Down" by Hubble Smith, which appeared on February 24, 2008, in the *Las Vegas Review Journal,* and an Associated Press report by Brendan Riley, "Nevada Lawmakers Focus on Property Tax Relief," published on February 8, 2005. As for the economic data in the final two chapters, I consulted an Associated Press report by Tom Raum from December 3, 2007, "National Debt Grows $1 Million a Minute," as well as a brilliant James Fallows piece in the January 2008 issue of the *Atlantic* entitled "The $1.4 Trillion Question." My reference to the estimated cost of the wars in Iraq and Afghanistan came from data compiled by Joseph E. Stiglitz and Linda J. Bilmes in their book, *The Three Trillion Dollar War: The True Cost of the Iraqi Conflict.* My global warming data, meanwhile, was supplied partly from the Pew Center on Global Climate Change and my estimated cost of the housing crash was based on a report entitled "Reports Suggest Broader Losses from Mortgages" by Vikas Bajaj and Edmund L. Andrews, published in the *New York Times* on October 25, 2007.